NAMED &

CHRISTOPHER TOOKEY

NAMED &

THE WORLD'S **WORST**
AND **WITTIEST**
MOVIE REVIEWS
FROM AFFLECK TO ZETA-JONES

Matador
5 Weir Road
Kibworth Beauchamp
Leicester LE8 0LQ, UK
Tel: (+44) 116 279 2299
Fax: (+44) 116 279 2277
Email: books@troubador.co.uk
Web: www.troubador.co.uk/matador

ISBN 978 1848765 603

British Library Cataloguing in Publication Data.
A catalogue record for this book is available from the British Library.

Typeset in 11pt Garamond by Troubador Publishing Ltd, Leicester, UK
Printed in the UK by TJ International, Padstow, Cornwall

Matador is an imprint of Troubador Publishing Ltd

To all honest and fearless critics

PREFACE

"The critic is the only independent source of information. The rest is advertising."

(Pauline Kael)

"Every actor in his heart believes everything bad that's printed about him."

(Orson Welles)

"It's wonderful when it isn't you."

(John Gielgud)

My mother used to tell me that if you can't speak well of someone, you shouldn't speak of him at all. This was exceptionally bad advice for a critic, and I have disregarded it ever since.

This is not just intended to be a slap in the face of celebrity culture – though that would be no bad thing.

I have compiled this book over more than 25 years, and it has confirmed me in the belief that some of the best, funniest and most astute criticism has been hostile, if not downright cruel.

There is a place for encouragement and celebration, of course, but only the worst reviewers speak well of everything and everyone.

Some of the judgments in this volume may seem harsh, but they are all, to some degree, perceptive and, I hope, entertaining. In an age of spin, hype and celebrity puffery, the critics here have tried to tell it like it is.

If you like movies, enjoy witty writing or simply fancy a good laugh, this book is for you.

Christopher Tookey,
London,
England

BEN AFFLECK

Actor, Forces of Nature (1999)

Affleck's character has all the personality of a medicated sloth.

> (Mr Cranky, Mr Cranky Rates the Movies)

Alongside Sandra Bullock, he looks bemused and depressed, like a sane man finding himself on a blind date with Julie Burchill.

> (Christopher Tookey, Daily Mail)

Actor, Pearl Harbor (2001)

Ben Affleck is like a larch in uniform.

> (Christopher Tookey, Daily Mail)

Actor, Paycheck (2003)

The first hurdle is the hardest: accepting Ben Affleck in the role of possibly the most intelligent man on the planet.

> (Matt Brunson, Creative Loafing)

Affleck is just fine when he plays a regular guy, but whenever he tries to, like, act, he ends up looking like a perplexed and mildly retarded simian.

> (Jon Popick, Planet Sick-Boy)

Actor, Jersey Girl (2004)

The good news is that Jennifer Lopez's character dies in the first 20 minutes. The bad news is that Ben Affleck lives.

> (Thomas Delapa, Boulder Weekly)

Actor, Surviving Christmas (2004)

If Hans Blix is still searching for bombs, he should check out Surviving Christmas, a crass, shrill and laughless disaster of a holiday comedy with a desperately mugging Ben Affleck that should be banned under the Geneva Convention.

(Lou Lumenick, New York Post)

Ben Affleck trying to raise a laugh is about as funny and futile as Ben Affleck trying to raise the dead.

(Catherine Shoard, Sunday Telegraph)

JESSICA ALBA

Actress, Honey (2003)

The biggest problem by far is Honey herself - a sort of cheapo Britney Spears by way of Mother Teresa who's just so damn helpful ("I didn't need that money for me, I needed it for the children") that by the end you're almost praying for her to slip a disc.

(Catherine Shoard, Sunday Telegraph)

Actress, Fantastic Four (2005)

The Invisible Woman (Jessica Alba) is, paradoxically, good only to look at: when she opens her mouth to speak, it's clear that she should have been called The Woman With No Visible Charisma.

(Christopher Tookey, Daily Mail)

Actress, Fantastic Four: Rise of the Silver Surfer (2007)

It's a good thing Jessica Alba is easy on the eyes because she belly flops on to the craft of acting like a big black anvil.

(Mark Ramsey, Moviejuice)

Actress, Good Luck Chuck (2007)

Alba performs with all the giddiness of a seventh-grader trying out, badly, for the school play.

(Andrea Chase, Killer Movie Reviews)

Actress, Awake (2007)

The most vapid stars of our age, Hayden Christensen and Jessica Alba, achieve total vapidosity in this jaw-dropping exercise in preposterosity.

(Ken Hanke, Mountain Express, North Carolina)

Awake is Lena Olin's movie. Her Lilith dominates every scene, and watching her eat up Jessica Alba before spitting out the bones is a delight to relish.

(Cole Smithey, colesmithey.com)

JOAN ALLEN

Actress, Death Race (2008)

Into the prison yard strolls the one and only Joan Allen. Yes, Oscar-nominated Joan Allen. Into this mess. To say Joan is slumming is an insult to a slum. Picture Bette Davis in Norbit or Judi Dench in Daddy Day Camp.

(Mark Ramsey, Moviejuice)

KEITH ALLEN

Actor, Beyond Bedlam (1994)

Keith Allen is remarkably unfrightening as the Hannibal Lecter figure; he is not helped by the fact that the hero looks at least six inches taller and five stone heavier than he. Poor little Keith hangs on gamely, but looks like a chihuahua trying to maul a Rottweiler.

(Christopher Tookey, Daily Mail)

Any possible interest the film may hold depends on your view of Keith Allen's slightly over-ripe acting style. If you like it, there might be something to gain from Beyond Bedlam (so that's an audience of one, then – eh, Keith?). And at least with Allen on the team, Craig Fairbrass can breathe a sigh of relief, because unlike Darklands, he's not the worst thing in the picture.

(Chris Wood, British Horror Films)

Actor, Ma Femme Est Une Actrice (2001)

Just as you think this film can't get any worse, Keith Allen strips off and shows us his singularly unappealing bottom.

(Christopher Tookey, Daily Mail)

WOODY ALLEN

Writer, Director, Actor, Annie Hall (1977)

Painful in three separate ways: as unfunny comedy, poor moviemaking, and embarrassing self-revelation. It is everything we never wanted to

4

88

know about Woody's sex life and were afraid he'd tell us anyway. The jokes are tired and can often be seen dragging their feet toward us a mile off; when they finally arrive, we are more apt to commiserate than laugh.

(John Simon, National Review)

Writer, Director, Actor, Stardust Memories (1980)

A dishonest social commentator, metaphysical seeker, and existential sniveler.

(John Simon, National Review)

Actor, Scenes From A Mall (1991)

Woody Allen, supposedly playing a complacent, surfing, 40 year-old LA lawyer with a pony-tail, instead gives us a portrait of a twitchy, 55 year-old, miscast New York actor.

(Christopher Tookey, Sunday Telegraph)

Actor, Writer, Director, Manhattan Murder Mystery (1994)

The picture's one big drawback, which keeps it from being completely amusing, is Allen's performance. He cannot act. He never could act. There's no sign, at this late date, that he ever will be able to act.

(Stanley Kauffmann, New Republic)

PEDRO ALMODOVAR

Writer, Director, Matador (1993)

A dreary piece of camp by one of Europe's most overrated directors. Picador, and leave.

(Christopher Tookey, Sunday Telegraph)

A mess of ludicrously contrived eroticism, pretentious dialogue, and reprehensibly voyeuristic sensationalism. Almodovar's silly, cod-philosophical whodunit impresses only for its bravado.

(Geoff Andrew, Time Out)

Writer, Director, Broken Embraces (2009)

Pedro Almodovar's longest film is also among his least memorable. It marks a continuation of his infatuation with (a) bold primary colours and (b) Penelope Cruz. He is never happier than when dressing (b) in (a). Not for the first time, I found myself wondering whether Pedro might not be happier working in the wardrobe department.

(Christopher Tookey, Daily Mail)

ROBERT ALTMAN

Director, Thieves Like Us (1974)

Altman has most of the qualifications for a major director except the supreme one of having something significant to say.

(John Simon, National Review)

Director, Quintet (1979)

Robert Altman is becoming a public embarrassment.

(Stanley Kauffmann, New Republic)

ANTHONY ANDERSON

Actor, King's Ransom (2005)

If Hell does exist, I'm sure the only movie theatre in town will be playing nothing but Anthony Anderson movies.

(Nick Schager, Slant Magazine)

Watching Anderson try to be funny is like getting a tooth pulled, or sitting through a Tim Burton DVD audio commentary.

(Kevin Carr, 7M Pictures)

GILLIAN ANDERSON

Actress

Gillian Anderson looks like a supply teacher.

(David Baddiel)

MICHAEL ANDERSON

Director, Logan's Run (1976)

It puts the future back two thousand years.

(Benny Green, Punch)

WES ANDERSON

Writer, Director, The Darjeeling Limited (2007)

Writer-director Wes Anderson goes for the same kind of laid-back, would-be cool comedy that won him rave reviews (though not from me) for Rushmore and The Royal Tenenbaums. As usual, he thinks his characters are endearingly quirky, when in fact they are tiresomely juvenile and self-obsessed.

(Christopher Tookey, Daily Mail)

PAMELA ANDERSON LEE

Los Angeles is full of pale imitations of Pamela Anderson and, worse still, Pamela Anderson herself.

(Lisa Marchant)

Actress, Barb Wire (1996)

There's something sad about Lee purposely sculpting her breasts to resemble basketballs, then parading around topless or nearly topless for most of the film, while her character is supposed to comically strike a blow for feminism when she kills bad guys who call her "Babe." Perhaps she would prefer, "Bimbo."

(Chris Hicks, Deseret News)

The plot is a futuristic sci-fi rip-off of Casablanca, with added brutality and torture. Mrs Lee is adventurously cast in the hard-drinking, romantically disillusioned, Humphrey Bogart role.

(Christopher Tookey, Daily Mail)

PAUL W.S. ANDERSON

Director, Mortal Kombat (1995)

This inspiration-free film is directed by a Briton, Paul Anderson, whose first film Shopping was a sad enough piece of exploitation. This one can be recommended only to those who love to watch backbones being crunched and heads exploding, to an ear-splitting heavy-metal soundtrack. One of the most contemptible, repulsive films of the year, if you like that kind of thing.

(Christopher Tookey, Daily Mail)

Writer, Director, Alien Vs Predator (2004)

The biggest problems with AvP are the humans. The blame lies mostly with the writer (Paul W.S. Anderson), but also with the director (Paul W.S. Anderson). Therefore, we can conclude that the primary problem with this movie is Paul W.S. Anderson.

(Sarah Chauncey, Reel.com)

Producer, Pandorum (2009)

As the credit "Produced by Paul W.S. Anderson" attests, this is hackwork of the highest order, lacking in all poetry and barely comprehensible aurally or visually.

(Keith Uhlich, Time Out New York)

JENNIFER ANISTON

Actress, Picture Perfect (1997)

Rock Hudson and Doris Day used to do this kind of fluffy romantic comedy fluff in their sleep. Aniston and [Jay] Mohr do it badly, in other people's sleep.

(Alan Frank, Video Home Entertainment)

Actress, Derailed (2005)

The semi-alert [Clive] Owen and the leaden Aniston go together like sausages and syrup.

(Lawrence Toppman, Charlotte Observer)

Actress, The Bounty Hunter (2010)

Aniston's comedic gift has gone, and all that's left is the hair, the tight skirts and hints of cleavage to keep audiences watching.

(Cosmo Landesman, Sunday Times)

Anyone looking for evidence of the alleged romance between Jennifer Aniston and Gerard Butler will find little here to support it. The much vaunted chemistry between them is about as effective as my pre-teen experiments in alchemy.

(Henry Fitzherbert, Sunday Express)

Whatever they've been up to offscreen, onscreen Gerard and Jen have less sexual chemistry than Ant and Dec.

(Christopher Tookey, Daily Mail)

JUDD APATOW

Producer, Pineapple Express (2008)

Apatow is at great pains to point out that this combination of big-budget violence and low-key buddy comedy has never been done before. And he's right. It hasn't. And guess why? Because they go together as well as chalk and Chewits.

(Robbie Collin, News of the World)

Writer, Director, Funny People (2009)

Judd Apatow, the most tasteless no-talent "director" since John Waters and the Farrelly brothers, follows the abominable Knocked Up with a 146-minute mental lapse that should have been dipped in hydrochloric acid in the editing lab. For anyone with an IQ above 40, there's no relief in sight. If you object to public offenses of decency, smut that reduces the oxygen in the brain or just plain lousy, amateurish filmmaking, it's easy enough to avoid Funny People like the swine flu. Unfortunately, if you're a movie critic, the luxury of self-protection is not an option.

(Rex Reed, New York Observer)

ROSANNA ARQUETTE

Actress, New York Stories (1989)

A whiny, irritating actress of extremely limited range.

(Bruce Bawer, American Spectator)

HAL ASHBY

Director, Harold and Maude (1971)

It has all the fun and gaiety of a burning orphanage... One thing that can be said about Ashby - he begins the film in a gross and macabre manner, and never once deviates from the concept. That's style for you.

(Variety)

ROWAN ATKINSON

Actor, Bean (1997)

Bean uses every washed-up comedy routine made popular by such true comedy greats as Laurel and Hardy, Harpo Marx, and Charlie Chaplin well over half-a-century ago. And yet, millions of people on this planet find Atkinson insanely hilarious. Hitler? We could use your tactics again, guy... These people HAVE to be wiped off the face of the Earth.

(Chris Bjuland, Bad Movie Night)

Actor, Rat Race (2000)

Eyeballs strain, faces contort, voices bellow, legs flail: I've never seen so much anatomy deputising for humour... Worst offender of all, I am not surprised to say, is Rowan Atkinson, who does the coarsest caricature possible of Roberto Benigni's twittering Italian stereotype, and does it in every scene save the ones in which his character, a narcoleptic, closes his eyes and goes to sleep. (At those moments, he's bearable).

(Alexander Walker, Evening Standard)

Actor, Mr. Bean's Holiday (2007)

The older Atkinson gets, the creepier Bean seems. He lacks the guileless charm of Hulot, the quicksilver timing of Chaplin's Little Tramp, and the elegance of either. Petulant and self-centred, with that indistinct, echoing, disembodied voice, Bean may be tolerable in short sketches or as ubiquitous in-flight entertainment, but overstays his welcome at this length.

(David Gritten, Daily Telegraph)

RICHARD ATTENBOROUGH

Actor, Brighton Rock (1947)

Mr Attenborough's Pinkie is about as close to the real thing as Donald Duck is to Greta Garbo.

(Leonard Mosley, Daily Express)

Director, Oh, What a Lovely War! (1969)

Sir Richard ("I'm-going-to-attack-the-Establishment-fifty-years-after-it's-dead") Attenborough is guilty of caricature, a sense of righteous self-satisfaction, and repetition which all undermine the impact of the film.

(Ken Russell, 1993)

Director, A Bridge Too Far (1977)

The director lacks even such small but essential gifts for a war film as being able to make clear where the shooting comes from; instead, people in an attic, say, suddenly keel over without our comprehending whence and how the bullets came.

(John Simon, National Review)

CHRISTIAN BALE

Actor, Terminator: Salvation (2009)

Bale outdoes himself here with a performance of near-epic humourlessness. If his expression became any more intense you'd probably hear his jaw go crack.

(Anthony Quinn, Independent)

The year is 2018, machines rule the world and everyone has had a humour bypass.

(Nigel Andrews, Financial Times)

Hasta la vista, credibility.

(Robbie Collin, News of the World)

ANTONIO BANDERAS

Actor, Assassins (1995)

A performance of such awe-inspiring awfulness from Banderas that he makes Stallone resemble Olivier at his peak.

(Alan Frank, Frank's 500)

Sylvester Stallone is so inert that he seems to have been replaced by his Madam Tussaud's replica, while Antonio Banderas is so hyper-active that a waxwork replacement would be vastly preferable.

(Christopher Tookey, Daily Mail)

Actor, Two Much (1996)

Offscreen rapport notwithstanding, Banderas and Griffith display little chemistry. He has a comic touch so heavy it suggests a cow trying to tap-dance.

(Ralph Novak, People Weekly)

Actor, Ballistic: Ecks vs. Sever (2002)

Banderas mopes through this hideous and unintelligible enterprise like a bloodhound with a hangover

(Keith Lofthouse, Urban Cinefile, Australia)

SACHA BARON COHEN

Actor, Writer, Borat (2006)

Baron Cohen is just another English public school boy who hates Americans. It is fine to hate Americans; it is one of Europe's oldest traditions. But the men who flew the bombing raids over Berlin and the men who died at Omaha Beach and the women who built the Flying Fortresses and Sherman tanks that helped defeat Hitler are the very same people that Baron Cohen pisses all over in Borat. A lot of folks named Cohen would not even be here making anti-American movies if it were not for the hayseeds he despises.

(Joe Queenan)

Actor, Writer, Bruno (2009)

The fallacy that Baron Cohen's comedy is politically pertinent derives from its pandering to Lefty biases.

(Armond White, New York Press)

The final scene in Bruno consists of him singing a Live Aid-style anthem with Sting, Bono and Elton John. We are supposed to admire these pop stars for allowing the comedian to send them up, but, in fact, they're not risking anything. The truth is that Bruno isn't real satire. Rather, it is a huge wet kiss to Hollywood's elitist snobs, reassuring them that their PC values are right and that ordinary people, who don't share their 'enlightened' attitude, deserve nothing but contempt.

(Toby Young, Daily Mail)

CHUCK BARRIS

Actor, Director, The Gong Show Movie (1980)

Life is cruel enough without Chuck Barris around.

(Albuquerque Tribune)

DREW BARRYMORE

Actress, Everyone Says I Love You (1996)

Drew Barrymore sings so badly, deaf people refuse to watch her lips move.

(Woody Allen)

Actress, Charlie's Angels (2000)

Alone of the trio, Drew Barrymore (who also co-produces) makes an attempt to act - a mistake in the context, since she has no character. She also seems to have been eating Ms Diaz's leftovers, with the result that her fight scenes have all the grace and athleticism of John Prescott attempting the title role in Billy Elliot.

(Christopher Tookey, Daily Mail)

KIM BASINGER

Kim Basinger is a blown-up doll come to life: leggy legs, stick-on breasts, pumped-up lips – like a custom-built woman who's been ordered a la carte.

(Mark Steyn)

Actress, Too Hot to Handle (1991)

Alec Baldwin and Kim Basinger are about as sexy a screen partnership as Yogi Bear and Boo-Boo.

(Christopher Tookey, Sunday Telegraph)

Actress, Bless the Child (2000)

Basinger appears to be gaily waltzing through a soap opera while the other cast members are screeching their way through a horror film.

(Paul Gessell, Ottawa Citizen)

Basinger is almost totally planklike, registering little more than mild surprise as she is threatened by rubber rats, or has her life saved from over-elaborate execution by odd angels turning up in the nick of time.

(Christopher Tookey, Daily Mail)

ALAN BATES

Actor, Zorba The Greek (1964)

He stands around dumbly, like a prop mistakenly left over from another movie.

(Elizabeth Hardwick, Vogue)

Actor, An Unmarried Woman (1978)

Alan Bates is between planes.

(Stanley Kauffmann, New Republic)

MICHAEL BAY

Director, Bad Boys (1995)

Michael Bay directs in precisely the way you might expect of a 30 year-old commercials director with more ambition than taste.

(Christopher Tookey, Daily Mail)

Director, Armageddon (1998)

Armageddon, as directed by Michael Bay, doesn't give a hoot about making a deep, humanistic impact on us. Or even a shallow one.

(Richard Schickel, Time)

Insolently bombastic... Watching the movie, you get the feeling that the director, Michael Bay, wants to drill the audience.

(Entertainment Weekly)

Here it is at last, the first 150-minute trailer. Armageddon is cut together like its own highlights. Take almost any 30 seconds at random and you'd have a TV ad. The movie is an assault on the eyes, the ears, the brain, common sense, and the human desire to be entertained. No matter what they're charging to get in, it's worth more to get out.

(Roger Ebert, Chicago Sun-Times)

Director, Pearl Harbor (2001)

Director Michael Bay and producer Jerry Bruckheimer's World War II behemoth has only three operating modes: sub-Titanic romantic mush, jingoistic hokum and lovingly rendered carnage... Bay and Bruckheimer's most impressive technical achievement is retrofitting WWII for the PlayStation 2.

(Jason Anderson)

The effect of watching a Michael Bay film is indistinguishable from having a large, pointy lump of rock drop on your head. I guess we should thank Michael Bay for so bold a revisionist take on the Second World War: no longer the clash of virtuous freedom and a malevolent tyranny but a terrible bummer when a girl is trying to get her dates straight.

(Anthony Lane, New Yorker)

Director, Bad Boys II (2003)

The latest collaboration between director Michael Bay and producer Jerry Bruckheimer, two filmmakers who bring out the worst in each other, is just as bloated and fatuous as their previous efforts.

(Rene Rodriguez, Miami Herald)

Film's bombastic bad-boy Michael Bay mixes idiocy and pretension in a grotesque wreck of epic proportions.

(James Rocchi, Netflix)

Bruckheimer/Bay creed: If your stars are not killing people or destroying other people's stuff, you are boring the audience!

(Victoria Alexander, Filmsinreview.com)

I simply will not, and could not, see a worse film this year than Bad Boys II. Michael Bay and Jerry Bruckheimer are bloodsucking ticks sucking the life out of us all.

(James E. Laczkowski, Hollywood Bitchslap)

Michael Bay, as critics long have suspected, is the devil - and the overblown orgy of gunfire and crumpled cars called Bad Boys II is the spawn of Satan.

(Sean Means, Salt Lake Tribune)

From the team that brought you Pearl Harbor, a Martin Lawrence film. Anyone still not screaming should proceed directly to Bad Boys II... Bad Boys II is the kind of film in which people don't just get shot, they get blown 10 ft. in the air, land on a mine, then have their decapitated heads fly towards camera. And there's scant relief in the romance. Will Smith gets jiggy with a dull lady cop, and Lawrence drools over a busty beauty who just happens to be, er, dead.

(Catherine Shoard, Sunday Telegraph)

Director, Transformers (2007)

With Transformers, director Michael Bay has once again claimed the year's top honors for loud, stupid filmmaking.

(Rex Reed, New York Observer)

In many ways, this is the ultimate Michael Bay movie – full of punishing sound and fury, and indicative of nothing except overweening corporate greed. Compared with this, some of Bay's earlier lamebrain blockbusters were sensitive think-pieces.

(Christopher Tookey, Daily Mail)

In previous movies, Michael Bay dabbled wearily in Homo sapiens. At last he has summoned the courage to admit that he has an exclusive crush on machines, and I congratulate him on creating, in Transformers, his first truly honest work of art.

(Anthony Lane, New Yorker)

Director, Transformers: Revenge of the Fallen (2009)

If you want to save yourself the ticket price, go into the kitchen, cue up a male choir singing the music of hell, and get a kid to start banging pots and pans together. Then close your eyes and use your imagination.

(Roger Ebert, Chicago Sun-Times)

When it comes to artistic aspirations, Bay has never exactly been up there with Bergman, but he did show a kind of ambition in Pearl Harbor and a certain elan in Armageddon, so can he really be happy churning out this inhuman rubbish?

(Edward Porter, Sunday Times)

Bay is at his most obnoxious when he shows gigantic machines casually destroying icons of Ancient Egyptian civilisation. Some may find this a depressingly accurate metaphor for what people like him are doing to our own culture.

(Christopher Tookey, Daily Mail)

SEAN BEAN

Actor, Anna Karenina (1997)

Bean has two facial expressions - perplexed and constipated - and his impersonation of a Russian count is so stolidly proletarian it makes Michael Caine's toff in Zulu look like model casting.

(James Delingpole, Sunday Telegraph)

Marceau and Bean have all the on-screen sexual chemistry of Michael Howard and Ann Widdecombe. Bean has a cruel, predatory smile, and anyone coming to the film with no knowledge of the novel might assume initially that he is the villain, or later on (when his smile has turned to an anguished stare and he keeps groaning "This is intolerable!") that he is a martyr to haemorrhoids.

(Christopher Tookey, Daily Mail)

Bean is so far out of his depth you feel a certain pathos; he delivers his lines like a man who's suddenly been asked to translate them from the Russian on an autocue.

(Anthony Quinn, Mail on Sunday)

WARREN BEATTY

Actor, Splendor in the Grass (1961)

The handsome young man is played by a newcomer named Warren Beatty, who looks very surprised to discover himself in pictures.

(New Yorker)

Actor, McCabe and Mrs Miller (1971)

As usual, Beatty plays a cocky schmuck; and, whenever called upon to register much in the way of emotion, he simply turns his back to camera.

(Christopher Tookey, Sunday Telegraph)

TONY BENNETT

Actor, The Oscar (1966)

Tony looks like a sad, abandoned bullfrog.

(Cue)

ROBERTO BENIGNI

Actor, Director, Writer, Life Is Beautiful (1998)

Benigni's self-love, if not his comic skills, could charitably be described as Chaplinesque, or perhaps more accurately as Robin Williamsish... Sentimentality is a kind of fascism too, robbing us of judgment and moral acuity, and it needs to be resisted. Life Is Beautiful is a good place to start.

(Richard Schickel, Time)

Actor, Director, Writer, Pinocchio (2002)

As the wooden puppet who yearns to be human, Benigni... is steadfastly insufferable, from his naughty, naïve stage through a transformation to a state of virtue that is steeped in a self-congratulatory martyrdom and nobility.

(Kevin Thomas, Los Angeles Times)

No matter how much he runs around and acts like a doofus, accepting a 50-year-old in the role is creepy in a Michael Jackson sort of way.

(Sean Means, Salt Lake Tribune)

Benigni's Pinocchio is meant to be adorable, but he comes off as less an enchanted puppet than as a harmlessly deranged middle-aged man prancing about in the kind of froufrou cream-colored pantsuit that Dinah Shore retired to her back closet in 1977.

(Owen Gleiberman, Entertainment Weekly)

By film's end I was fantasizing that Peter Stormare would drop by with his Fargo wood-chipper in tow, but it was not to be. Appalling.

(Marc Savlov, Austin Chronicle)

PATRICK BERGIN

Actor, Adventures of Robin Hood (1991)

The most wooden thing in Sherwood Forest.

(Christopher Tookey, Sunday Telegraph)

Actor, Merlin: The Return (2000)

Patrick Bergin (King Arthur) looks like an embarrassing dad (complete with silly wig and glitzy, disco-friendly pullover).

(Michael Thomson, BBC i)

As King Arthur, Patrick Bergin looks as glassy-eyed and lumpish as an indifferently stuffed yak.

(Christopher Tookey, Daily Mail)

ELIZABETH BERKLEY

Actress, Showgirls (1995)

Berkley alternates between shrieking her lines and pouting, neither being dramatically effective choices.

(Leah Rozen, People Weekly)

That Berkley cannot act is indisputable. But her dancing looks like a seizure.

(Barbara Shulgasser, San Francisco Examiner)

Elizabeth Berkley is a supple rather than subtle actress, with a maximum of two expressions: hostile and loopy.

(Christopher Tookey, Daily Mail)

STEVEN BERKOFF

Actor, Writer, Director, Decadence (1993)

Steven Berkoff writes, directs and overacts in such a way as to render the last three letters of his name superfluous.

(Christopher Tookey, Daily Mail)

SANDRA BERNHARD

Actress, Without You I'm Nothing (1990)

Anyone who goes to see Sandra Bernhard's Without You I'm Nothing under the delusion that it's going to be funny will probably want to strangle the projectionist within 20 minutes. On the other hand, if you feel like witnessing a rare spectacle of American show-biz narcissism gone psychotic, there is much to savor here.

(Owen Gleiberman, Entertainment Weekly)

Sandra Bernhard's one-woman revue Without You I'm Nothing shows that she has considerable bravado, but then the Gulf War demonstrated the same about Saddam Hussein. The film is an interminable in-joke about her above Edna Everage ego, her bisexuality (which appears aggressive to the point of psychosis), and her compulsive need to fraternize with the great (the gods of her universe being Madonna and Warren Beatty). The entire masturbatory act is delivered deadpan to an elaborately, and understandably, uninterested audience. The film, miserably scripted as a series of poorly differentiated character studies and acted with monotonous and groundless self-confidence, should interest anyone researching how psychological disorders drive certain unfortunate and unsuitable people into torturing themselves and others by going into show business.

(Christopher Tookey, Sunday Telegraph)

HALLE BERRY

Actress, Gothika (2003)

The film seems chiefly to have been an excuse to give another of those anguished, tear-stained performances to which she is regularly drawn. At one point her distraught ramblings are interrupted by a concerned friend (Robert Downey Jr). "You have to stop doing this," he says, and that sounds like good career advice.

(Edward Porter, Sunday Times)

Actress, Catwoman (2004)

Halle Berry has by now thrown away all of the goodwill she gained from appearing in Monsters Ball. One is tempted to say that ritual disembowelment is too good for those who have perpetrated this abomination on the comic book-loving movie-going public. But that would be hyperbole, if only barely.

(James Berardinelli, Reelviews)

In one amazingly embarrassing scene, Catwoman enters a nightclub and starts swinging her whip around in the middle of the dance floor before attacking one of Laurel's goons. It's moments like these that make me long for the quiet dignity of Arnold Schwarzenegger's performance in Batman and Robin.

(Jeffrey Lyles, Gazette)

So amateurish is her acting, so dreadful her comic timing, and so desperate her attempts to appeal to males of a neanderthal persuasion (odd this, since she is supposed to be some kind of model of liberated female self-empowerment) that she must be a shoo-in for every Worst Actress award this year. What Gigli did for Jennifer Lopez, and Swept Away did for Madonna, Catwoman is about to do for Ms Berry. For reasons that are as abstruse as anything else in the picture, an Egyptian cat endows her with feline powers. Some of these genuinely are catlike – the ability to leap around, see in the dark and scratch people, for instance. And there's a scene where she rubs catnip rapturously over her face that is destined to be some kind of camp classic. But is she endlessly fascinated by wool or easily sidetracked by crumpled-up balls of paper? Not a bit of it. Her other powers seem to have more to do with certain Hollywood executives' taste in sex kittens: the dressing up in form-fitting leather and spiky stilettos, cracking of whips, eagerness to let us look down her cleavage at every opportunity, and her decision to indulge a taste for very red lipstick. Presumably in order to impress male sports fans, she even develops an astonishing talent for basketball. By all means write in if you've ever seen a cat doing any of these things.

(Christopher Tookey, Daily Mail)

BERNARDO BERTOLUCCI

Writer, Director, 1900 (1976)

Scales new heights of dreadfulness in film. When the film was over, I felt that we ought to be shown the menu on the back of which the script was outlined at the very first lunch of director and producer.

(Stanley Kauffmann, New Republic)

Director, The Dreamers (2003)

Bernardo Bertolucci's latest, and arguably worst, film (it's even more inert and tedious than Besieged) celebrates everything that's loathsome about so many film buffs: especially their emotional immaturity, isolation from the real world and mostly unfounded delusions of intellectual superiority. Poor old Bertolucci used to call himself a revolutionary Communist. Now he doesn't even have the courage of his convictions, and simply looks pathetic. In his prime, he'd have

communicated the virtues of activism and commitment. His ending here strikes a "cool", ambiguous, open-ended note as the young American turns away from his sexy friends when they throw bombs and become full-blown urban terrorists. I emerged from this picture with a new respect and sympathy for riot police.

(Christopher Tookey, Daily Mail)

LUC BESSON

Director, Writer, Joan of Arc (1999)

I've never left a Luc Besson movie not thinking that the guy has Froot Loops for brains.

(Charles Taylor, Salon)

Director Luc Besson's films are famously long on style and short on intellect. Joan of Arc, clocking in at 167 interminable minutes, is his most spectacularly stupid film yet... Besson's attention to detail is so perfunctory that within a few frames of the opening, he has called Scotland part of England. His kitsch rendition of Joan's childhood, with much running through flowery fields, suggests prolonged study of the opening scene of The Sound of Music. Someone should have told him that Joan came from Domremy, not that she sang Do Re Mi.

(Christopher Tookey, Daily Mail)

Writer, Taken (2008)

Taken is the kind of exploitative junk everyone expects from no-talent French hack Luc Besson.

(Rex Reed, New York Observer)

PAUL BETTANY

Actor, Dead Babies (2000)

Ghastly characters with whom no one would wish to be for one minute, let alone 105 of them, are made even more unbearable by atrocious over-acting (even by Paul Bettany, who thinks that being a toff involves sneering out of both sides of his mouth at once).

(Christopher Tookey, Daily Mail)

JESSICA BIEL

Actress, Stealth (2005)

A concession to the feminist lobby makes Biel's fly-girl the rugged equal of her two male colleagues, yet it is she who develops a girly crush on the whiter of her two chums, and frolics around in waterfalls wearing only a thong bikini (which may be going out of fashion, but never will in this kind of guy flick). And by the end she's the damsel in distress who must, of course, be saved by White Dude. Jessica Biel is like no woman I have ever met, and – despite her undoubted physical charms - I don't mean that as a compliment. The way she flaunts her body in front of her overwhelmingly male crew is tantamount to sexual harassment, and her idea of sexily flirtatious dialogue – my favourites were "Pardon my C-cup" and "Just tell me you love me, you pussy!"- didn't strike me as terribly plausible.

(Christopher Tookey, Daily Mail)

Sadly, no one told poor Biel that acting was not required for this project. In fact, it would simply slow things up. Hence everyone else in the film, instead of emoting, is doing his best GI Joe impression. That

would be the action figure, not the character from the animated series. She's left out there actually trying to find an emotional center for her character and the people behind the cameras let her. Shame on them.

(Andrea Chase, Killer Movie Reviews)

Actress, I Now Pronounce You Chuck and Larry (2007)

If there were Oscars for stripping to your bra and panties, Biel would be Meryl Streep. Jessica has no boyfriend in this movie. The odds of that happening in real life are roughly on par with the odds of Earth being decimated by an interstellar asteroid between now and the time Lindsay Lohan next enters rehab.

(Mark Ramsey, Moviejuice)

JANE BIRKIN

Actress, Monsieur Docteur Rey (2002)

As for Jane Birkin's performance as a burbling neurotic, there is so great a gap between willingness to go over the top and the feebleness of her lines that you feel impelled to look away, as from a disastrous speech at a wedding.

(Edward Porter, Sunday Times)

BJORK

Actress, Dancer in The Dark (2000)

The scenes at the jail, when Björk sings a ditty to bring comfort to her condemned cellmates, only confirms there should be a Death Row specially reserved for pop singers.

(Alexander Walker, Evening Standard)

This controversially won the Palme d'Or at Cannes, along with Best Actress for its leading lady, the pop singer Bjork. Bjork inhabits the part with amazing self-belief and intensity, but a total lack of discipline, leaving her fellow actors in a state of visible confusion. It looks less like a performance than a mental breakdown on film.

(Christopher Tookey, Daily Mail)

JACK BLACK

Black – the classic example of the raffish outsider who initially spits on the entertainment industry, then is seduced by it, and then comes to epitomise everything that is wrong with it... He sucked in Shallow Hal, he sucked in Orange County, he sucked in The Holiday, and he sucked in Tenacious D in the Pick of Destiny. He also sucked in King Kong, Saving Silverman, Year One and yes, Kung Fu Panda. It is almost impossible to suck in a film in which only your voice is used, but Black sucked anyway.

(Joe Queenan)

Actor, Year One (2009)

Black was fresh and funny once... but here he forgets to act and simply announces his lines.

(Roger Ebert, Chicago Sun-Times)

Black behaves like a coke-crazed parody of himself, and thinks it's funny to eat excrement. I too was left with a nasty taste in my mouth.

(Christopher Tookey, Daily Mail)

ORLANDO BLOOM

Actor, Troy (2004)

As for Orlando Bloom - Orlando Wilt more like. Judging by this performance, Bloom's is a career which will persist a little longer in Hello and Company Magazine but nowhere else.

(Antonia Quirke, Islington Tribune)

Actor, Kingdom of Heaven (2005)

Orlando Bloom doesn't have that 'It" factor to carry a film like this. Yes he's pretty to look at, but he comes across as a vapid California surfer boy trying to be a serious "artist."

(Michelle Alexandria, Eclipse Magazine)

As heroes go, Balian is ahead of his time - about eight centuries ahead. He basically just wants everyone to get along, so perhaps it's fitting that Bloom plays this boy like a painfully earnest sociology student on his gap year. Rich tan, wuffy hair, beard manicured to look not manicured - you only miss the travel beads.

(Tim Robey, Daily Telegraph)

Surrounding Orlando Bloom with heavyweight actors serves only to show up how callow and lightweight he is, how desperately lacking in life behind those photogenic eyes. It's like watching David Beckham essay the role of Hamlet, alongside Dame Judi Dench as Gertrude and Sir Derek Jacobi as Claudius.

(Christopher Tookey, Daily Mail)

Actor, Elizabethtown (2005)

Bloom's inability to convey convincing emotion is manifest; if he has any allure in this movie, it's got to be the hair gel.

(Desson Thomson, Washington Post)

Orlando Bloom was a late substitute for Hollywood's goofy dude of the moment, Ashton Kutcher, who left the leading role during rehearsals when Crowe expressed dissatisfaction with his acting skills and suggested he take lessons. Why Kutcher's ineptitude came as a surprise to Crowe, I don't know. Perhaps he'd never seen any of his films. But replacing Kutcher with the equally callow, just as achingly superficial Bloom is like curing yourself of typhoid and then succumbing to the common cold.

(Christopher Tookey, Daily Mail)

PETER BOGDANOVICH

Writer, Director, What's Up, Doc? (1972)

A comedy made by a man who has seen a lot of movies, knows all the mechanics, and has absolutely no sense of humour. Seeing it is like shaking hands with a joker holding a joy buzzer: the effect is both presumptuous and unpleasant.

(Jay Cocks)

Director, At Long Last Love (1975)

Sitting through this movie is like having someone at a fancy Parisian restaurant who neither speaks nor reads French read out stentoriously the entire long menu in his best Arkansas accent, and occasionally interrupt himself to chortle at his cleverness.

(John Simon, National Review)

This is failure so dismal that it goes beyond failure. The musical is not trash, exactly. Its rottenness lies in the pretension and inflated ego behind its conception, in its pandering to film-buff nostalgia, and in some of the sorriest casting ever to sink a production.

(Hollis Alpert, Saturday Review)

UWE BOLL

The Jonas Brothers of movie directors.

(Jim Craddock, VideoHound's Golden Movie Retriever)

Director, Alone in the Dark (2005)

If anyone were pondering what Ed Wood would be like today if he were armed with foreign financing and computer effects, look no further than Uwe Boll.

(Brian Orndorf, Film Jerk)

Saying Uwe Boll's Alone in the Dark is better than his 2003 American debut House of the Dead is akin to praising syphilis for not being HIV.

(Nick Schager, Slant Magazine)

Never trust a movie that opens with a written introduction scrolling by that's longer than the collected works of Tom Clancy.

(David Hiltbrand, Philadelphia Inquirer)

Director, Bloodrayne (2005)

Who is Uwe Boll and why does he hate moviegoers so? The German hack, the one-man Blitzkrieg of Bad, is the worst filmmaker in the movies today.

(Roger Moore, Orlando Sentinel)

How fitting that director Uwe Boll (House of the Dead) would choose a vampire flick as his latest project - the man has a career that, despite the horror he continually inflicts on innocent moviegoers, simply will not die.

(Elizabeth Weitzman, New York Daily News)

Writer, Director, Postal (2007)

With Postal, Boll clearly set out to make history's most offensive, hateful movie. As is his custom, he failed spectacularly.

(Nathan Rabin, The Onion)

Imagine what Catch-22 might have been like if it had been written by that creepy grade-school classmate of yours who was always talking about how cool it would be to stick a cherry bomb under that dead squirrel he found on the side of the road.

(Peter Sobczynski, eFilmCritic.com)

Director, In The Name of the King: A Dungeon Siege Tale (2008)

Mention the name Uwe Boll to any film reviewer whose beat includes genre movies, and you'll probably detect immediate signs of post-traumatic stress disorder.

(Frank Scheck, Hollywood Reporter)

Only Uwe Boll would assume that the moviegoing public craved a trashy Lord of the Rings rip-off starring Burt Reynolds and Matthew Lillard, and only he could then manage to make such a potentially riotous endeavor so humorless.

(Nick Schager, Slant Magazine)

Worse than a high school production of Lord of the Rings and as incoherent as a Miss Teen USA contestant.

(Matt Pais, Metromix.com)

ZACH BRAFF

Actor, The Last Kiss (2006)

Braff plays another Everyman confused and at a crossroads, one sadly unfrequented by speeding haulage vehicles.

(Tim Robey, Daily Telegraph)

KENNETH BRANAGH

Actor, Director, Writer, Much Ado About Nothing (1993)

Such is the lack of crackle between Ken and Em [his then wife, Emma Thompson] that they might as well be tucked up in separate beds drinking a cup of cocoa. In terms of sexual electricity, these two are the filmic equivalents of John and Norma Major.

(Anne Billson, Sunday Telegraph)

Actor, Director, Writer, Hamlet (1996)

Throughout its hubristic length, Hamlet kept reminding me of some other, pointlessly star-studded film. It wasn't Olivier's Hamlet. Only later did the title come back to me: Around the World in Eighty Days. There is something funny, but also tragic, about a genuinely promising young talent - once hailed as the new Laurence Olivier - turning out instead to be the new Mike Todd.

(Christopher Tookey, Daily Mail)

With bleached blond hair and a moustache shaped like a stealth bomber, he looks less like Olivier than a denizen of one of Old Compton Street's gay bars. Ignoring his own advice to the Players, he saws the air, splits the ears of the groundlings and generally tears passion to tatters; if this were a live performance, the front rows of the auditorium would be drenched in spittle. It's not so much a great film performance as an uncanny impersonation of an old-style actor-manager at full-throttle rant.

(Anne Billson, Sunday Telegraph)

Branagh is most at ease when among the Players, telling them how they all ought to act. Mind you, he would be more impressive if he weren't guilty of overacting himself - his "What is a man?" speech before the intermission is a hilariously misconceived piece of declamatory self-indulgence, not helped by awful back projection. It has all the restraint of P.J. Proby performing I Believe... Among the many moments of awesome vulgarity is the ending, where Branagh insists on getting himself carried off with his arms out, as though crucified. Not many Hamlets overact even after they are dead.

(Christopher Tookey, Daily Mail)

Actor, Wild Wild West (1997)

What can one say about Kenneth Branagh's performance? No one could complain that it lacks airy self-confidence. However, it sails far beyond the bounds of the merely excruciating, and comes to rest in the wildest, darkest realms of the inexplicable.

(Christopher Tookey, Daily Mail)

Director, Sleuth (2007)

What's clear from the opening shot of Branagh's version is that he desperately wants this Sleuth to be not the record of a play but a real, filmy film. Unfortunately, his notion of film is a combination of bizarre camera angles and an alternation of baffling long shots and punishing closeups. Once upon a time, Branagh directed some agreeable movies: the burly Henry V, the inventive Much Ado About Nothing. So

I can't say his visual choices here are made from ignorance. They have to be called willfully stupid.

(Richard Corliss, Time)

A classic two-hander, directed by a proper one-hander.

(Robbie Collin, News of the World)

Perhaps the most charitable view is to suspect that the whole film is some kind of sadistic mind-game, in which Branagh and Pinter are hell-bent on humiliating their actors. If that's the case, they've succeeded magnificently.

(Christopher Tookey, Daily Mail)

RUSSELL BRAND

Actor, St Trinian's (2007)

Where the fifties films had the splendidly furtive George Cole as the girls' underworld mentor Flash Harry, the new Flash is the puzzlingly ubiquitous Russell Brand, looking as usual like the bastard offspring of Captain Jack Sparrow and Amy Winehouse, and mugging to camera as though he's in a panto matinee. I'm not convinced that the arrival of Mr Brand on our cinema screens constitutes progress.

(Christopher Tookey, Daily Mail)

Actor, Forgetting Sarah Marshall (2008)

As for Mr Brand, shorn of the flamboyant, cod-period verbiage that he passes off as wit, he reveals all the allure of a funnel-web spider on heat. I would have thought his character loses any vestige of attractiveness when he casually reveals that he has a sexually transmitted disease he might easily have passed on to all the other leading characters. Publicists keep telling me that Mr Brand radiates sex appeal – but to what species, it is difficult to say.

(Christopher Tookey, Daily Mail)

MARLON BRANDO

Actor, The Chase (1966)

Brando, who gave up acting shortly after On the Waterfront, is now simply a balding, middle-aged, pot-bellied man driven to undisciplined excesses that are clearly inexcusable on the screen. In one scene, he becomes so enraptured in a love affair with his own thumb that he actually appears to forget his own lines. The embarrassment on his face when he is forced to say Miss Hellman's lines is understandable, but most of the time he sounds like he has a mouth full of wet toilet paper.

(Rex Reed)

Actor, The Missouri Breaks (1976)

Marlon Brando at 52 has the sloppy belly of a 62 year-old, the white hair of a 72 year-old, and the total lack of discipline of a precocious 12 year-old. His acting is full of fussy, pointless business. It's pure corn.

(Sun)

If Brando hates acting, why doesn't he quit?

(Stanley Kauffmann, New Republic)

Actor, Apocalypse Now (1979)

Brando has become an obscene, secular Buddha with shaven head and ballooning midriff, whose voice emerges like the squeal of a mouse from a ridiculous mountain.

(John Simon, National Review)

Actor, Christopher Columbus: The Discovery (1992)

As Torquemada, the inquisitor, Brando sulks about the set looking moody and delivering his lines with the absolute minimum of energy necessary to be audible to the camera. He's phoned in roles before, but this was the first time I wanted to hang up.

(Roger Ebert, Chicago Sun-Times)

BENJAMIN BRATT

Actor, Catwoman (2004)

Benjamin 'Box Office Ebola' Bratt is in this movie. The last time Ben was in a star vehicle it was Julia Roberts' Cadillac Escalade.

(Mark Ramsey, Moviejuice)

LESLIE BRICUSSE

Composer, Lyricist, Goodbye Mr Chips (1969)

An overblown version with songs where they are not needed (and Leslie Bricusse's songs are never needed).

(Pauline Kael, New Yorker)

A lot of sentimental, dewy-eyed old muck. I guess you could call it a musical, although to insinuate that Leslie Bricusse's plodding score is merely dreadful would be an act of charity.

(Rex Reed)

CHARLES BRONSON

Actor, Death Wish (1974)

The central credibility problem in Death Wish is the casting of Charles Bronson in anything but a primitive form of life on this planet.

(Molly Haskell, Village Voice)

KELLY BROOK

Actress, Three (2006)

Kelly Brook, the curvaceous model-turned-Big Breakfast-presenter-turned-actress-turned-atomic-physicist (okay, I made that last bit up), spends much of the movie in a white bikini, which for some will be recommendation enough. To say that she acts would be to overstretch the truth. It would be fairer to say that she registers emotions, some of them appropriate.

(Christopher Tookey, Daily Mail)

Actress, Piranha 3D (2010)

Kelly plays a simpering, can't-act, cantaloupe-jugged dimwit. You'll be amazed by how convincing she is.

(Robbie Collin, News of the World)

ALBERT BROOKS

Writer, Director, Actor, Defending Your Life (1991)

The film seems to have been written by someone who has had his sense of humour removed by excessive therapy. The screenplay is full of what may pass on America's west coast for life-enhancing profundity, but will look to most people like terminal self-indulgence.

(Christopher Tookey, Sunday Telegraph)

PIERCE BROSNAN

Pierce Brosnan is an exceptionally handsome man, but he always reminds me of the models in men's knitwear catalogues.

(Paul Hoggart)

Actor, Mamma Mia: The Movie (2008)

The man's got a voice like an outboard motor chewing through seaweed... He bellows his way through S.O.S. like a harpooned wildebeest.

(Robbie Collin, News of the World)

It contains a bunch of middle-aged actors who can't really sing or dance, and look vaguely uneasy about it. "What am I doing here?" asks Pierce Brosnan plaintively, and I could see his point.

(Christopher Tookey, Daily Mail)

Actor, Percy Jackson and the Lightning Thief (2010)

It's nice to see Pierce Brosnan playing a centaur, a man with the body of a horse. Mainly because it's a step up from Mamma Mia, in which he played a man with the voice of a horse.

(Robbie Collin, News of the World)

JERRY BRUCKHEIMER

Producer, Coyote Ugly (2000)

For hyper-successful producer Jerry Bruckheimer (the force behind 2000's Gone In 60 Seconds and about a dozen major hits over the last 20 years), Coyote Ugly represents a new low - a creative pit so deep that he has never seen its like. However, that's what happens when a testosterone magician attempts a crowd-pleasing drama with a female protagonist. Coyote Ugly is loud, gaudy, underacted, and completely without a soul. By comparison, Flashdance (Coyote Ugly's closest relative on the producer's resume) is a marvel of subtlety and character development.

(James Berardinelli, Reelviews)

Our heroine cures her stage fright the way any sensible girl might do. She gets a job at a sleazy drinking club called Coyote Ugly, puts on skintight pants and a skimpy halter-top and shakes her diminutive protuberances at men on top of the bar, pausing only to pour water invitingly over her tee-shirt, or hurl ice at the customers whenever they attempt rape. Yes, I know that becoming a sex object is an unconventional way of overcoming stage fright; but then producer Jerry Bruckheimer has always had a problem distinguishing between female self-fulfilment and female degradation.

(Christopher Tookey, Daily Mail)

Producer, Pearl Harbor (2001)

Without contest, the most extravagantly bloated summer blockbuster in several years. The most expensive movie ever greenlit for release, it comes from director Michael 'I Like Mindless Destruction' Bay and producer Jerry 'No I Like it More' Bruckheimer (who collaborated on the dumbbell asteroid-hurtling-through-the-stratosphere flick Armageddon).

(Jamey Hughton)

Producer, Kangaroo Jack (2003)

Are there three words more calculated to strike apprehension in a critic's heart than "Jerry Bruckheimer presents"? The producer who brought us such stinkers as Bad Company and Gone in 60 Seconds now serves up a crass adventure-comedy starring a rapping, computer-generated kangaroo and three flatulent camels.

(Christopher Tookey, Daily Mail)

SANDRA BULLOCK

Actress, Speed 2 – Cruise Control (1997)

That perky playfulness which some found so fresh in her early films has swiftly begun to grate, coming over now as inane self-satisfaction.

(Quentin Curtis, Daily Telegraph)

In the original Speed, Sandra Bullock was gutsy and cute. In Speed 2, she's gut-heavingly cutesy.

(Christopher Tookey, Daily Mail)

Actress, Forces of Nature (1999)

It's official: Sandra Bullock is no longer the girl next door - unless, maybe, you're living next door to an anorexia treatment centre. When at one point in Forces of Nature, Bullock stripped down to her underwear, variations of "yuk" and "ugh" was heard from the preview audience with whom I watched this dull amalgam of Planes, Trains and Automobiles and Something Wild. Gone is the pleasant-looking girl of Speed and While You Were Sleeping - replaced by about 85 pounds of skin, bones and nervous energy.

(Malene Arpe, eye-onscreen)

Actress, Miss Congeniality (2000)

If there were lingering doubts that the time has come to write an obituary for Sandra Bullock's days as a leading lady, Miss Congeniality should dispel them.

(James Berardinelli, Reelviews)

Actress, The Lake House (2006)

At certain angles, she is starting to resemble a young Joan Rivers.

(Peter Whittle, Sunday Times)

Actress, The Proposal (2009)

The sight of Bullock doing a rap dance with granny in the woods is a traumatising experience.

(Cosmo Landesman, Sunday Times)

Actress, All About Steve (2009)

Acting like a 12-year-old following the Jonas brothers, Bullock runs around this 98-minute film in a pair of red boots and a short skirt giggling and bouncing as if she was having a mental breakdown. Personally I thought the now 45-year-old Bullock looked downright ridiculous chasing around Ryan Reynolds in The Proposal, but at least in that movie she was acting her age. Here, she is chasing the 34-year-old Bradley Cooper and to estimate the mental capacity of her character would be a complete shot in the dark, but to describe her as a thinking adult would not be the first thing that comes to mind.

(Brad Brevet, Rope of Silicon)

Actress, The Blind Side (2009)

Sandra invites a young, disadvantaged lad to live in her house. She may

very well be happy about this, although it's hard to tell, given that her face is drawn tighter than a bongo skin.

(Robbie Collin, News of the World)

EDWARD BURNS

Writer, Director, Actor, She's The One (1997)

Burns's methodology is to place himself and geeky-looking co-star Mike McGlone at the centre of a film so they can talk about their problems with girls.   Hence we're asked to believe scenes in which superbabes Jennifer Aniston and Cameron Diaz plead to have sex with these boring, ugly guys who have the most tragic hairdos in the history of coiffing. As if.

(Anne Billson, Sunday Telegraph)

Actor, Writer, Director, Ash Wednesday (2002)

There ought to be a directing license, so that Ed Burns can have his revoked.

(Mark Olsen, LA Weekly)

If Burns wants to give up something for Lent, directing mightn't be a bad place to start.

(Jason Solomons, Mail on Sunday)

Cinema has given us many epic love affairs: Bogey and Bacall, Hepburn and Tracey, Ed Burns and Ed Burns. Yes, the hunky Irish-American's self-infatuation shows little sign of cooling off, and this latest love-letter has the usual signatures: pouty close-ups, tight T-shirts, women who reach for the razor the moment he leaves the room.

(Catherine Shoard, Sunday Telegraph)

Actor, Confidence (2003)

As for Ed Burns, I used to hope he'd concentrate on acting because then he'd direct fewer movies. But I can avoid the movies he directs, whereas he shows up as an actor in movies I want to see. What a hard call.

(David Edelstein, Slant)

Any film that begins with Edward Burns dead has got off to a pretty good start, but the prospect of being spared the actor's vain whining for a couple of hours, like everything else in this snappy, perfectly watchable, irritatingly self-satisfied scam flick, proves illusory.

(Tim Robey, Daily Telegraph)

RICHARD BURTON

Actor: The Exorcist II- The Heretic (1977)

Richard Burton is attacked by a swarm of locusts. He deserves all he gets, believe me.

(Ian Christie, Daily Express)

GERARD BUTLER

Actor, PS I Love You (2007)

Gerard Butler is Scottish, not Irish, and his attempt to twinkle from beyond the grave are more than a little forced. It's like watching Gordon Brown attempting to impersonate Terry Wogan.

(Christopher Tookey, Daily Mail)

Gerard Butler dies at the beginning of this film. Disappointingly, it's not the last we see of him.

(Robbie Collin, News of the World)

Actor, The Bounty Hunter (2010)

Imagine, if you can, a remake of Midnight Run in which the deader-than-deadpan Robert De Niro and Charles Grodin are replaced by the smirking, shrieking Gerard Butler and Jennifer Aniston. Then imagine every inch of sardonic humour being sucked out of the script like fat through a liposuction tube, the movie being directed by a team of advertising agents with a megaphone in one hand and an audience demographic in the other, and the resultant farrago being marketed on the basis of an utterly nonexistent sexual chemistry between the leads for whom sparks singularly fail to fly. Got it? Right, well the film you are currently picturing is still infinitely more entertaining than The Bounty Hunter, which really is quite indescribably inferior fare in every possible way... Butler simply dusts off his lovably gruff shtick and parades around looking pleased with himself for cracking the lucrative comic beefcake market. Fair play to him – it's just a shame the rest of us have to watch.

(Mark Kermode, Observer)

The trouble is not so much that Butler isn't funny - he isn't, even slightly - but that he sucks the merest hint of humour from the entire enterprise.

(Tom Huddleston, Time Out)

Death, taxes, Gerard Butler. Wish them away all you like: still they befall us. Actually, Butler, like a mutant virus that neither modern medicine nor fervent prayer can eradicate, is worse than taxation; I'd happily pay an annual tithe banning him from being allowed anywhere near a cinema.

(Sukhdev Sandhu, Daily Telegraph)

ED BYE

Director, Fat Slags (2004)

Then there's director Ed Bye. Ed, you directed Red Dwarf, man! How can YOU not know that this stuff is as funny as eating heaped spoonfuls of broken glass?

(Gary Panton, Movie Gazette)

An insult to the eye and the intelligence. It's directed by Ed Bye (alias Mr Ruby Wax) with all the savoir-faire of David Beckham trying to convince us he isn't dim. It's hard to believe that this is the director who brought us the relatively nuanced Kevin and Perry Go Large.

(Christopher Tookey, Daily Mail)

JAMES CAAN

Actor, The Gambler (1974)

James Caan is like the first laboratory-made film star, the outside fabricated acceptably but the insides omitted.

(Stanley Kauffmann, New Republic)

Actor, Flesh and Bone (1993)

Poor old James Caan looks as if he has been semi-embalmed by an absent-minded mortician.

(Christopher Tookey, Daily Mail)

NICOLAS CAGE

Actor, Leaving Las Vegas (1995)

Loathsome. I have seen more charisma in Bowery bums, and better acting (not to mention looks) in a chimpanzee.

(John Simon, National Review)

Actor, Next (2007)

Nicolas Cage, looking more than ever like a waxwork dipped in butterscotch, delivers his particular brand of single-expression robotics.

(Andrew Pulver, Guardian)

Actor, Bangkok Dangerous (2008)

Nicolas Cage plays a hired assassin. May I kindly suggest his next target should be whoever sold him that wig, because - Lord almighty - it's like a squashed chinchilla fell on his head, then almost fell off again.

(Robbie Collin, News of the World)

Actor, Knowing (2009)

The mentalist's mentalist is back, with his trademark hair-don't and a face like a disappointed elk, once again on a mission to save humanity while dressed like a hungover supply teacher.

(Robbie Collin, News of the World)

MICHAEL CAINE

Michael Caine is an over-fat, flatulent 62 year-old windbag, a master of inconsequence, now masquerading as a guru, passing off his vast limitations as pious virtues.

(Richard Harris)

Michael Caine can out-act any, well nearly any, telephone kiosk you care to mention.

(Hugh Leonard)

Actor, Alfie (1966)

Caine did not manage to convey Alfie's supposedly irresistible charm.

(Richard Roud, Guardian)

Women in the audience may feel the excitement, but it seemed to me that Caine lacked the charm of subtlety and was sweating rather freely.

(Robert Hatch, Nation)

Actor, Bullseye! (1990)

There is not a single passable performance. Few leading actors as feeble, lazy and self-indulgent as Michael Caine and Roger Moore in this could reasonably expect to work again.

(Christopher Tookey, Sunday Telegraph)

SIMON CALLOW

Actor, Merci Docteur Rey (2004)

The youth accepts payment to act as a voyeur by a middle-aged gay (Simon

Callow) who wants him to witness him having rough sex with a young man. The good news is that, though Callow strips naked in Merchant Ivory movies at the drop of a towel, his piece of rough trade stabs him in the back before he can unleash his privates on us again. Seldom have I been so grateful for the premature death of a leading character.

(Christopher Tookey, Daily Mail)

That the film's cameo from Simon Callow is not the most irritating part of the proceedings should give you an idea of just how extraordinarily hammy and irritating this film is.

(Edward Porter, Sunday Times)

Actor, Chemical Wedding (2008)

Most of the cast underact. The one, big – and I do mean big – exception is Simon Callow, who appears to have been taking acting lessons from Brian Blessed and, possibly as a result, gone stark staring bonkers. Callow is at his exuberant worst as a stuttering Cambridge academic who – because of some incomprehensible scientific experiment that goes wrong – is taken over by the spirit of Aleister Crowley. Mr Crowley was known to his early 20th century contemporaries as "the wickedest man in the world" – which strikes me as a little unfair to Hitler, Stalin and Mao. In real life, Crowley was a relatively harmless old bore with a sleazy interest in deviant sex and an unpleasant tendency to relieve himself on the carpet and, occasionally, other people. In this film, however, he enlarges upon these experiments in self-expression and becomes a sweaty serial killer with a hideous taste in purple suits and a tendency to shout obscenities Occasionally, various nubile young ladies disrobe on his command ("You must free yourself of your restrictive knickers!"), in order to cavort before his lubricious gaze. They then meet an untimely end, usually without their knickers. I have a horrible feeling that we're meant to find this erotic, but Crowley doesn't come across as even slightly heterosexual. Callow is camper than the late Frankie Howerd, and about as dangerous.

(Christopher Tookey, Daily Mail)

JAMES CAMERON

The High Priest of Hollywood bloat.

(Richard Corliss, Time)

On set, Cameron behaves like a Renaissance Pope.

(David Gritten, Daily Telegraph)

Writer-director, Titanic (1997)

It's like an episode of The Love Boat, directed by Cecil B. De Mille.

(Christopher Tookey, Daily Mail)

According to Hollywood logic, none of the actual Titanic passengers was interesting enough, so the writer-director had to invent a Romeo and Juliet-style fictional couple to heat up the catastrophe. This seems a tiny bit like giving Anne Frank a wacky best friend, to perk up that attic.

(Paul Rudnick, aka Libby Gelman-Waxner, Premiere)

JANE CAMPION

Director, In The Cut (2003)

The overall effect is of a particularly sordid episode of Sex in the City, made by the confused offspring of Andrea Dworkin and the Marquis de Sade... These are clearly the last, incoherent ramblings of an exhausted minor talent, stuck in the humourless-to-the-point-of-hysterical feminism of the early 1970s.

(Christopher Tookey, Daily Mail)

FRANK CAPRA

Director, It's a Wonderful Life (1946)

Christmas movies come in four basic varieties: the cuddly, the cloying, the cretinous and the cute. It's a Wonderful Life, a putatively heartwarming story about a small-time banker with a heart of gold, manages to combine all four elements, as it inexplicably lionises a lunkheaded ninny who risks the financial health of his community by making a series of bad loans to people who are in no position to repay them. Particularly unsuitable for holiday viewing this year, the 1947 Frank Capra classic should really be called It's a Wonderful Subprime Life.

(Joe Queenan, 2008)

Director, Pocketful of Miracles (1961)

The effect is less one of whimsy than of being beaten to death with a toffee apple.

(Peter John Dyer)

MARIAH CAREY

Actress, Glitter (2001)

Ms. Carey sure can sing but she sure can't act.

(Tom Maurstad, Dallas Morning News)

Carey seems most concerned about keeping her lips tightly sealed like a kid with braces, and when she tries for an emotion — any emotion — she looks as if she's lost her car keys.

(Michael Atkinson, Village Voice)

Mariah shows that she is to acting what Dame Maggie Smith is to welterweight boxing. Whenever Mariah tries to register an emotion, it's with a fixed smile and an ingratiating, little-girl simper as though her mind is really set on a My Little Pony as a Christmas present.

(Christopher Tookey, Daily Mail)

Actress, You Don't Mess With The Zohan (2008)

Mariah Carey sets a terrifying new low for cameo roles by struggling to act as herself.

(Robbie Collin, News of the World)

ROBERT CARLYLE

Actor, Eragon (2006)

Winner of the acting wooden spoon, however, must be Robert Carlyle who overacts hilariously with some of the worst and most variable make-up ever, the black nail varnish that Kelly Osbourne rejected, and a scraggy wig that looks as if it was thrown out by the late, great Max Wall as simply too laughable.

(Christopher Tookey, Daily Mail)

Jeremy Irons hams it up badly, but he's a piker compared to Carlyle (who, with his long stringy hair looks a bit like Bette Davis in Whatever Happened to Baby Jane - and masticates the scenery as much as she did, too).

(Frank Swietek, One Guy's Opinion)

JIM CARREY

Actor, Ace Ventura, Pet Detective (1994)

If you thought movie comedy had scraped bottom with the Ernest series, check out Jim Carrey as Ace Ventura, pet detective and postmodern doofus. His "characterization" consists of strutting around in a Hawaiian shirt and Li'l Abner pompadour, flashing his big, creepy-preppy grin like a junior Richard Nixon on Jolt cola, and punching home every last one of his so-stupid-they-really-are-stupid lines. Carrey suggests an escaped mental patient impersonating a game-show host - and, what's worse, his hyperbolically obnoxious shtick is the whole damned show.

(Owen Gleiberman, Entertainment Weekly)

Actor, Ace Ventura 2: When Nature Calls (1995)

Wearying, stupefying, dumber than dumb, When Nature Calls would be a career ender for Carrey - except that a zillion people have seen it. Stop this, folks. It'll only encourage him.

(Richard Corliss, Time)

This is aimed squarely at the Beavis and Butthead market, the dumb (and increasingly dumber) teenagers who may still find Carrey's antic amusing. Someone, somewhere, put him out of his misery.

(Alexander Walker, Evening Standard)

Actor, The Number 23 (2007)

Jim Carrey gives the worst performance of his, or indeed any other actor's, career.

(Christopher Tookey, Daily Mail)

Contrived, incomprehensible gibberish that exists for the sole purpose of exposing a miscast star in a career stretch for which he is pathetically unprepared.

(Rex Reed, New York Observer)

Actor, Yes Man (2008)

Carrey flails about trying to recapture the zaniness of his early years. It's a sad spectacle, rather like watching Jerry Lewis playing the shrieking adolescent well into his forties.

(Frank Swietek, One Guy's Opinion)

Carrey's repetitive gurning is extremely tired. Behaviour that seemed merely weird when he was in his twenties now looks sinister.

(Christopher Tookey, Daily Mail)

DANA CARVEY

Actor, Trapped in Paradise (1994)

Imagine an addled Mickey Rourke on helium, if you dare.

(Steve Davis, Austin Chronicle)

Actor, The Master of Disguise (2002)

The only camouflage Carvey should now be considering is a paper bag to wear over his head when he goes out into public, to avoid being recognized as the man who bilked unsuspecting moviegoers.

(Peter Howell, Toronto Star)

The film's star and co-writer Dana Carvey has been away from the screen for 6 years, during which he has been hospitalised repeatedly after botched heart by-pass surgery. I don't wish to be unkind but, to judge by this dreck, he was more in need of a brain transplant. You may remember Carvey as Garth on Wayne's World, a role in which he occasionally made people laugh. Here, he plays Pistachio Disguisey, a nutty Italian waiter. You can tell the film is in deep trouble when he upsets plates of spaghetti over a table of innocuous customers and doesn't apologise but merely tries to scrape parmesan cheese over them. This may sound a passable sight gag, except that it's so comprehensively bungled that you just feel sorry for the extras who must have been sitting there for the best part of a day with sauce all over them, and a bad actor pulling unfunny faces.

(Christopher Tookey, Daily Mail)

CEDRIC THE ENTERTAINER

Actor, Man of the House (2005)

Every so often, an already slow film grinds to a halt in order to accommodate the dubious talents of Cedric the Entertainer, as a convict turned preacher. He can't be on the screen for more than ten minutes in total, but they seem an eternity. He was merely rotten in last week's Be Cool. Here, he's so embarrassingly, toe-curlingly unwatchable that henceforth he should be known only as Cedric.

(Christopher Tookey, Daily Mail)

JOHN CENA

Actor, 12 Rounds (2009)

John Cena is so wooden that one worries about his being in scenes with fire for fear that he'll catch a spark and burst into flame.

(James Berardinelli, Reelviews)

Cena is a no-hoper. A wrestling star on American television - imagine

Matt Damon with gigantism - but when it comes to charisma, he barely deserves to be playing a background thug, let alone the main man.

(Edward Porter, Sunday Times)

Mr Cena is a bulked-up, charisma-free ex-wrestler whose only previous film was The Marine (2006), in which he had to rescue his kidnapped wife. Here, he has to rescue his kidnapped girlfriend. If ever he's allowed to make a third movie, he'll probably have to rescue his kidnapped gerbil. It is all too evident that he finds acting a strain. His attempts to look anguished when his vapid girlfriend Molly (Ashley Scott) is threatened with death make Steven Seagal look like Daniel Day Lewis.

(Christopher Tookey, Daily Mail)

JACKIE CHAN

Actor, The Medallion (2003)

Jackie Chan will be back in a good movie soon, and then we can forget about this misstep once and for all. Oh wait, I've forgotten it already.

(Mike McGranaghan, Aisle Seat)

JAY CHANDRASEKHAR

Director, The Dukes of Hazzard (2005)

Jay Chandrasekhar (of the unfunny comedy troupe Broken Lizard) directs without wit or style.

(Jim Lane, Sacramento News Review)

Chandrasekhar isn't much of an action director - he constantly keeps the camera too close and edits the action sequences like a hyperkinetic junior Michael Bay … Several times the movie stops a la the TV show so that the narrator (known as "The Balladeer") can comment on the action. In the show, these narrative freezes had a purpose because they led to the commercial breaks. Here, they have no purpose other than frustrating the audience by teasing us with the tantalizing idea that maybe this immediately forgettable waste of a movie has ended prematurely.

(Jay Kendrick, Qnetwork.com)

The clue to the thinking behind its revival lies in an early slapstick sequence. In it, the two heroes, southern cousins and good ol' boys Bo Duke (Seann William Scott from Dude, Where's My Car?) and Luke Duke (Johnny Knoxville from Jackass!) take turns to hit each other hard around the head with the Atlanta telephone directory, a bulky publication that has clearly caused extreme and irremediable brain damage to both of them. This is reflected in their severely diminished vocabulary (which consists principally of shrieking "Yee haw!" and "Whoo-hoo!") and their inability to keep their car on the road for long before sending it airborne or crashing it into someone else. It soon becomes worryingly apparent that in the new American South Bible-punching is out, and braincell-battering with the Atlanta telephone directory is in. Everyone involved in the production, in front of and behind the camera, shows evidence of serial brain-abuse. The most obvious victim is director Jay Chandrasekhar, whose previous two films were Super Troupers (2001), a repellent glorification of police brutality, and Club Dread (2004), a puerile spoof of slasher movies. Both are masterpieces compared with The Dukes of Hazzard, which is infinitely more infantile, stupid and depressing. It wouldn't surprise me if Mr Chandrasekhar is a ten telephone directories a day man.

(Christopher Tookey, Daily Mail)

HAYDEN CHRISTENSEN

Actor, Star Wars III: Revenge of the Sith (2005)

Christensen is less Anakin, more mannequin.

(Tim Robey, Daily Telegraph)

Actor, Awake (2007)

Awake features what is perhaps cinema's most punchable screen couple in Alba and Christensen. Outacted by his egregious sideparting, it's not so much a heart transplant Christensen needs as a talent transplant. The man can't even shave convincingly.

(Matt Glasby, Film 4)

This film's about a mega-rich property heir who stays awake, but fully paralysed, during heart surgery. And what do you do when you need an actor who can struggle through the worst physical and emotional trauma while displaying all the emotion of a Primark window dummy? You send for Hayden Christensen.

(Robbie Collin, News of the World)

ROGER CHRISTIAN

Director, Battlefield Earth (2000)

Battlefield Earth is directed by Roger Christian, also responsible for the involuntarily hilarious Nostradamus, and every creative decision he makes is a dud. He uses irritating wipes and slo-mo when they aren't needed, cuts frenetically just when it would be nice to see what is going on, and tilts the camera for no reason other than he thinks it looks cool. It doesn't.

(Christopher Tookey, Daily Mail)

MICHAEL CIMINO

Director, The Deer Hunter (1978)

Try to imagine a big, boneless elephant sitting in your lap for three hours while you're trying to think. It's flabby beyond belief, convinced not only of its importance but of its relevance to Americans (i.e. human beings) everywhere... If only we could get this heavy gray lump off to school or at least get it a respectable job in the circus.

(Jonathan Rosenbaum, Take One)

Writer, Director, Heaven's Gate (1980)

You might suspect Mr Cimino sold his soul to the devil to obtain the success of The Deer Hunter and the devil has just come round to collect. Mr Cimino has written his own screenplay, whose awfulness has been considerably inflated by the director's wholly unwarranted respect for it.

(Vincent Canby, New York Times)

Director, The Desperate Hours (1987)

Cimino's direction is innocently unfettered by notions of taste, proportion or suspense.

(Christopher Tookey, Sunday Telegraph)

Director, Sunchaser (1996)

Cimino's most excruciating film yet. It's a grotesquely long, shapeless road movie. The director's obvious taste for Native American mysticism, New Age mumbo-jumbo, foul language and unconscious misogyny raises the interesting possibility that Michael Cimino may, after his initial success, have looked at the face of some latter-day Gorgon and gradually be turning into Oliver Stone.

(Christopher Tookey, Daily Mail)

NOEL CLARKE

Writer, Director, 4.3.2.1 (2010)

Showy-off posturing without any direction or point. It brings me no joy to say it, but Clarke's filmmaking is like a narcissistic strut from someone who needs to brush up on his walking.

(Tim Robey, Daily Telegraph)

Dude, don't try and claim that this is some unique insight into the female psyche. Don't try and argue that these women are real. And, if you will insist on appearing in the film yourself, here's a tip — don't write a line that has one of the stars say of your character: "He's hot, brooding, arrogant — and he probably has a really big dick!" That's just sad.

(Wendy Ide, Times)

Only a year ago, Mr Clarke won the Orange Rising Star Award at the BAFTAs. One clue that this may, just conceivably, have gone to his head is that in this movie he gets his leading actress to commend the size of his manhood. He has also taken the unusual step of boasting that he wrote the script in a month. On the evidence of the finished movie, it's a marvel that it took him that long.

(Christopher Tookey, Daily Mail)

JOHN CLEESE

Actor, The Secret Policeman's Ball (1979)

There is something peculiar about Mr Cleese. He emits an air of overwhelming vanity combined with some unspecific nastiness, like a black widow spider on heat.

(Roger Gellert, New Statesman)

GEORGE CLOONEY

Actor, One Fine Day (1996)

Clooney is one of those people who look like Identikit composites of a man you might suspect of being a star. But I can't warm to him. He's all surface, which is characteristic of TV-serial performers who suddenly get enlarged to cinema-screen size.

(Alexander Walker, Evening Standard)

Actor, Batman and Robin (1997)

George Clooney is the big zero of the film, and should go down in history as the George Lazenby of the series.

(Mick LaSalle, San Francisco Chronicle)

Actor, Ocean's Twelve (2004)

George Clooney is all by himself among living leading men in making smarm pass triumphantly for charm.

(David Edelstein, Slate)

Actor, The Good German (2006)

I could have managed to bear all the film's shortcomings if it weren't for Clooney. Where was he during the making of this film? His face is there, he knows his lines, he moves as needed, but any traces of the intelligence and rapport, the subtlety and understanding, that have marked his best work are excruciatingly missing. Clooney behaves as if he discovered after he had committed to the film that he really didn't like the script as much as he thought he did but would go through with it anyway. The result is puppetry.

(Stanley Kauffmann, New Republic)

GLENN CLOSE

Actress, The House of the Spirits (1994)

Glenn Close, as Irons's repressed, lesbian, moustachioed sister, gives us a cross between Mrs Danvers from Rebecca and the late Sir Gerald Nabarro. I remain uncertain as to whether she's funniest when she's spelling out her carnal longings in the confessional to a badly dubbed priest, or when she's playing a ghost like a Victorian commode on castors.

(Christopher Tookey, Daily Mail)

ROB COHEN

Director, Stealth (2005)

Cohen (The Fast and the Furious, xXx) is no stranger to cornball excess but Stealth is his chef-d'oeuvre, a movie so audaciously preposterous and jingoistic it plays like a parody of the genre.

(Liam Lacey, Globe and Mail)

I submit that when your movie is about a magical talking airplane, and yet the magical talking airplane is NOT the silliest thing about the movie, then you should not make any more movies.

(Eric D. Snider, Land of Eric)

Stealth is an offense against taste, intelligence and the noise pollution code.

(Roger Ebert, Chicago Sun-Times)

The dialogue is atrocious in three different ways. There is pseudo-scientific mumbo-jumbo, as when Sam Shepard (himself a playwright –

how he must have cringed to deliver this) says of the new robo-fighter "it's got a brain like a quantum sponge". Quantum sponge??? Then there is the pseudo-philosophical, as when principal fly-boy Lucas muses "I don't think war should be some kind of video game" – a thought which seems to have passed right through director Rob Cohen's head and out the other side, without leaving even the faintest residue of guilt... The most worrying aspect of Stealth isn't just that it's dumb, Many films are dumb. But this one is dangerously, even apocalyptically, dumb.

(Christopher Tookey, Daily Mail)

Director, The Mummy: Tomb of the Dragon Emperor (2008)

Takes the franchise to a stunning new low. Director Rob Cohen (you know, the visionary who made Stealth, Fast and the Furious, and xXx) replaces Stephen Sommers here, and if there's one guy who could make Sommers appear as cinematically resonate as Spielberg, it's Cohen. As lead-footed a filmmaker as the factory churns out, Cohen picks up on the same beat of noise pollution that was left hanging in 2001, only he manages to craft a sequel more obnoxious and defeating than previously anticipated.

(Brian Orndorf, Film Jerk)

JOAN COLLINS

To the unwashed public, Joan Collins is a star. But to those who know her, she's a commodity who would sell her own bowel movement.

(Anthony Newley, her former husband)

Actress, The Bitch (1979)

A tasteless farrago in which Collins treats every line, even "Hello", as an innuendo and stares at every available male with an unbridled lust

Mae West would have deemed excessive. Only for campaholics who delight in the misfortunes of aging actresses.

(Steven H. Scheuer)

Actress, The Clandestine Marriage (1999)

Miss Collins used to be a national institution. Here, she looks as if she may need locking up in one.

(Christopher Tookey, Daily Mail)

Actress, The Flintstones in Viva Rock Vegas (2000)

It's an especially bad sign that, as Wilma's ghastly mother, Joan Collins deputises for Elizabeth Taylor. In a variety of pantomime dame costumes, Collins delivers her lines with perfect clarity and consummate distaste, like Margaret, Duchess of Argyll depositing remnants of ill-smelling haddock in a dustbin.

(Christopher Tookey, Daily Mail)

CHRIS COLUMBUS

Director, Nine Months (1995)

Columbus directs with all the light-fingered precision of a drugged elephant attempting microsurgery.

(Christopher Tookey, Daily Mail)

Director, Bicentennial Man (1999)

Bicentennial Man is a film about artificial intelligence, so it's a pity it doesn't show any intelligence, artificial or otherwise. It's a wildly misjudged attempt by director Chris Columbus to turn the ideas of sci-

fi novelist Isaac Asimov into two hours ten minutes of shallow philosophising and toe-curling schmaltz.

(Christopher Tookey, Daily Mail)

Director, I Love You, Beth Cooper (2009)

Perhaps Columbus was involved in a hideous car accident recently that left him partially brain damaged, or maybe tragic senility is creeping up on the 51-year-old filmmaker. I simply refuse to believe Columbus willingly created something as monstrously unfunny and schizophrenic as Cooper. Yes, it's worse than Bicentennial Man.

(Brian Orndorf, Film Jerk)

SEAN CONNERY

Actor, Diamonds Are Forever (1971)

Revealed a Connery who was now packing flab as well as a Walther PPK. His style resembled an elder statesman of espionage with an implanted pace-maker.

(Alexander Walker)

Actor, Never Say Never Again (1983)

Well into his fifties, the thrill was indubitably gone - and so, sadly, was a great deal of Mr Connery's hair.

(Julie Burchill, Girls on Film)

Actor, The Avengers (1998)

Sean Connery puts the cause of Scottish nationalism back a hundred years with hamming that would have got him booed out of the White Heather Club.

(Christopher Tookey, Daily Mail)

DANE COOK

Actor, Employee of the Month (2006)

Dane Cook, the worst movie leading man since - Pauly Shore? No? Toby Keith! - makes his starring debut in Employee of the Month... Whatever that "it" is that comic screen stars have, Cook doesn't have it.

(Roger Moore, Orlando Sentinel)

Have you studied Cook's horrifically unsettling smile lately? It's like William Castle's Mr. Sardonicus crossbred with Conrad Veidt in The Man Who Laughs... Cook's creepy smirk is downright hypnotic. You keep staring at it, seeking to find the gears and flywheels beneath the flesh, but the harder you look, the less you see. It's an unnerving expression, devoid of anything other than reptile calculation and something approaching disdain. It'd look great on the wall of the MoMA, or even the Smithsonian, but in a movie? Not so good.

(Mark Savlov, Austin Chronicle)

American stand-up comic Dane Cook is unknown in Britain and, on this evidence, will remain so.

(Christopher Tookey, Daily Mail)

Actor, Good Luck Chuck (2007)

Cook is a cut-price, desperately hyperactive clone of Will Ferrell.

(Christopher Tookey, Daily Mail)

The ultimate low point comes during the closing credits, when Dane Cook's Charlie performs bestial acts with a stuffed toy penguin.

(Louise Keller, Urban Cinefile, Australia)

FRANCIS FORD COPPOLA

Director, Jack (1996)

Coppola proves once again (as in New York Stories) that he is to light comedy what Hulk Hogan is to ballet. It is a painful experience to see him labouring a schmaltzy metaphor here (a dying butterfly, a shooting star), bungling an attempt at slapstick there (he even fails to extract a laugh from that old standby, a collapsing treehouse). He alternates between farce and melodrama, realism and expressionism, tweeness and filthy-mindedness, with no apparent awareness that there is any difference between them.

(Christopher Tookey, Daily Mail)

Suggests that Coppola's brains have finally turned to linguine. It is one of the worst films I have ever seen.

(Neil Norman, Evening Standard)

SOFIA COPPOLA

Actress, The Godfather, Part 3 (1990)

Sofia Coppola's painfully inadequate and embarrassing acting is a deadly warning against nepotism.

(Alan Frank, Frank's 500)

KEVIN COSTNER

Actor, Director, Dances With Wolves (1991)

This is a nature-boy movie, a kid's daydream of being an Indian.

When Dunbar has become a Sioux named Dances with Wolves, he writes in his journal that he knows for the first time who he really is. Costner has feathers in his hair and feathers in his head. The movie – Costner's debut as a director – is childishly naive. There isn't even anything with narrative power or bite to it. This Western is like a New Age social-studies lesson. This epic was made by a bland megalomaniac. (The Indians should have named him Plays with Camera.) You look at that untroubled face and know he can might everything lightweight. How is he as a director? Well, he has moments of competence.

(Pauline Kael, New Yorker)

Actor, Robin Hood: Prince of Thieves (1991)

That Costner wasn't able to nail an authentic English accent would only be a minor quibble if one weren't so distracted by the variety of accents his Robin Hood mouths.

(Marjorie Baumgarten, Austin Chronicle)

Costner suggests Dan Quayle with a sword.

(Mike Clark, USA Today)

Actor, Dragonfly (2002)

The undisputed king of the cornball concept, Kevin Costner has an uncanny aptitude for gravitating toward the dopiest projects in sight, but this time he's outdone himself.

(Jonathan Rosenbaum, Chicago Reader)

It is most of the things Costner movies are known for; it's sanctimonious, self-righteous and so eager to earn our love that you want to slap it.

(Chris Hewitt, St. Paul Pioneer Press)

Actor, The Guardian (2006)

Kevin Costner – with that hangdog expression and bland delivery that used to represent quiet masculinity and now just means deficient in haemoglobin.

(Mark Ramsey, Moviejuice)

NOEL COWARD

Actor, Boom! (1968)

The once delightful Coward is now a mincing senior citizen of Leprechaunia, still aiming for rapid-fire repartee with one foot in his mausoleum and the other in his overdentured mouth.

(John Simon, National Review)

CINDY CRAWFORD

Actress, Fair Game (1995)

Cindy Crawford is not the worst thing about Fair Game. Her fully poseable action-figure performance is about what you'd expect: studied and empty at the same time. Far worse is Fair Game's script.

(Gary Dauphin, Village Voice)

In her movie debut, supermodel Cindy Crawford makes a sporting attempt to act. She plays the kind of high-powered lawyer who goes to work in a very short miniskirt, just prior to mislaying her bra and putting on a series of rapidly diminishing T-shirts. Anyone curious about the extent of Miss Crawford's thespian abilities may rest assured that yes, one of her T-shirts does get wet, and yes, she does take it off before the end.

(Christopher Tookey, Daily Mail)

JOAN CRAWFORD

A cheap flapper who liked to get laid.

(Louis B. Mayer)

She should have had puppies, not children.

(Oscar Levant)

Joan Crawford would have made an exemplary prison matron, possibly at Buchenwald.

(Harriet van Horne)

Actress, Mildred Pierce (1945)

So they gave Joan Crawford an Academy Award for her performance in Mildred Pierce... Myself, I found the range of expression with which she greeted divorce, death, remarriage, financial ruin and murder so delicate as to approximate to indifference.

(Dilys Powell, Sunday Times)

MACKENZIE CROOK

Actor, Sex Lives of the Potato Men (2004)

Sex Lives of the Potato Men is being billed as an "erotic, testosterone-charged comedy" about a pair of Brummie yobs called Dave and Ferris, who are according to the publicity notes "two good-looking young blokes living by their own rules". The truth is that they live by no rules discernible to the naked eye, and one of these "good-looking blokes" is played by arguably the ugliest, most obese, least sexy comedian in Britain, Johnny Vegas. Vegas's equally unfunny sidekick is Mackenzie Crook from The Office, who is meant to be

God's gift to women, but exhibits slightly less erotic appeal than road kill.

(Christopher Tookey, Daily Mail)

LINDSAY CROUSE

Actress, The Desperate Hours (1987)

As a hyper-aggressive female FBI agent, Lindsay Crouse gives a ludicrous performance, behaving irrationally at the top of her voice, like Hitler addressing the Nuremburg rally on acid. Towards the end, when someone tries to slow her down by shooting her in the leg, she abandons all restraint and gives us her Long John Silver.

(Christopher Tookey, Sunday Telegraph)

RUSSELL CROWE

Actor, A Good Year (2006)

Russell Crowe and comedy. There's a partnership that works about as well as the Arabs and Israelis.

(James King, Kingy's World of Film)

Crowe has some formidable qualities as an actor – among them rugged virility, a magnificent speaking voice and more than a hint of belligerence; but charm and underlying sweetness do not come easily to him.

(Christopher Tookey, Daily Mail)

TOM CRUISE

Actor, Top Gun (1986)

Cruise strikes designer-jeans poses, and his blank, fixated stare and teeth-baring smile make him seem as flat and despiritualized as a Sunset Strip billboard portrait.

(Peter Rainer, Los Angeles Herald Examiner)

The weakest link in the chain is without question the vaingloriously vapid Tom Cruise. His performance as Maverick is downright ludicrous. He stalks through the movie with a board up his back and a macho snarl frozen on his face. The point of the snarl, apparently, is to make him look more like a man than a boy, but it backfires: He looks more than ever like an adolescent playing a grownup in a junior high school show — an adolescent, I might add, who has absolutely no star quality, no charisma, no presence whatsoever, but whose every move demonstrates that he himself believes quite the opposite to be the case.

(Bruce Bawer, American Spectator)

Actor, Rain Man (1988)

Cruise is an actor in the same sense that Robert Taylor was an actor. He's patented: his knowing that a camera is on him produces nothing but fraudulence.

(Pauline Kael, New Yorker)

Actor, Cocktail (1988)

The star's narcissism rapidly becomes insufferable.

(Christopher Tookey, Sunday Telegraph)

Cruise is walking in the footsteps of Troy Donahue and John Travolta

here. He does what comes easy. He bumps and grinds and grins till his lips ache. It's a performance with all the integrity of wax fruit.

(Rita Kempley, Washington Post)

Actor, Vanilla Sky (2001)

A good example of what self-destructive cinematic havoc can be wrought by handing over millions of dollars to movie stars to produce their own ego trips.

(Rex Reed, New York Observer)

At the end, the audience feels uncomfortably aware that Vanilla Sky is a monument to Cruise's awe at his own beauty, wealth and magnetism. This near-unwatchable folly leaves Cruise with ego all over his face.

(Christopher Tookey, Daily Mail)

Actor, The Last Samurai (2003)

For some reason, Cruise seems to have confused the art of acting with the act of looking at something really hard.

(Aaron Lazenby, filmcritic.com)

Actor, Knight And Day (2010)

If you are a fan of either Tom Cruise or Cameron Diaz, I would highly suggest taking a trip to Madame Tussauds and staring at their wax likenesses because they will offer more skilled performances cast in wax than they did on screen. If Cruise's performance were any more phoned in, AT&T would've sponsored the film... I'm sorry, Tom, but even you have to exert yourself just an iota to be charming.

(Brian Salisbury, Hollywood.com)

All I can say about Cruise is that he seems to have lost what's left of his mind. He emanates a terrifying vacuity, and thinks that flashing his teeth a lot is the same thing as charm and sex appeal. Maybe this will persuade some people, but Gordon Brown made the same assumption during the last General Election, and look what happened to him.

(Christopher Tookey, Daily Mail)

ICE CUBE

Actor, Dangerous Ground (1997)

The rapper-turned-actor Ice Cube has lived up to his name in past movies, by exhibiting slightly less warmth and acting range than a refrigerator.

(Christopher Tookey, Daily Mail)

Actor, xXx: State of the Union (2005)

The man plays on two levels: angry and angrier.

(Berge Garabedian, JoBlo's Movie Emporium)

For any of you who have not witnessed Ice Cube in action, he's a former rapper whose best-loved compositions include the sensitive Gangsta Gangsta and the even more spiritually intense Fuck Tha Police. Ice is, sadly, quite a bit less cool than his name. A more honest name for him would be Lead Weight. He's a black Steven Seagal, minus the acting talent - and the physique. There's no getting away from the fact that nowadays Mr Cube verges on the spherical. When we see him leaping fences and easily outrunning federal agents, it's slightly less plausible than Johnny Vegas winning the London Marathon.

(Christopher Tookey, Daily Mail)

ALAN CUMMING

Actor, Son of the Mask (2005)

Further embarrassments include the now dependably atrocious Alan Cumming as Loki, Norse God of mischief. He's clearly confused Norse with nauseating, and capers about like the attention-seeking, hyperactive love-child of Graham Norton and Julian Clary.

(Christopher Tookey, Daily Mail)

MILEY CYRUS

Actress, Hannah Montana: The Movie (2009)

"You know what I've learned over the last 20 years?" asks Miley Cyrus at the end of Hannah Montana: The Movie. "Life's a climb, but the view's great." Aye. And unless you're a girl between six and 14, her movie's like a climb too. Breathing apparatus is recommended to maintain consciousness, and you may feel the need to reach for an ice axe.

(Robbie Collin, News of the World)

Creepy child-woman Miley Cyrus plays Miley Stewart, an ordinary teenager who becomes singing superstar Hannah Montana, simply by putting on a blonde wig. This makes her utterly unrecognizable to anyone not in the know. The plot premise is that 16 year old Miley Stewart has fallen too much in love with her own celebrity, which any of you who caught Miss Cyrus's toe-curling bumptiousness on Jonathan Ross's TV show may suspect is not too far from the truth.

(Christopher Tookey, Daily Mail)

MILEY CYRUS

Actress, The Last Song (2010)

Cyrus plays an angry, heartbroken girl in a way that, sad to say, shows off her 'Hannah Montana'-drilled tricks and tics and air of entitlement more than her dramatic range.

(Michael Phillips, Chicago Tribune)

Acting, for the moment at least, seems almost entirely beyond her. In The Last Song she pouts, slouches, storms in and out of rooms and occasionally cracks a snaggle-toothed smile, but most of the time she seems to be mugging for the camera, play-acting rather than exploring the motives and feelings of her character.

(A. O. Scott, New York Times)

Cyrus is ghastly in The Last Song, bad not just in one or two ways, but in all kinds of ways. It was a disservice to the audience, to the material and to Cyrus herself that she was put in this position. Cyrus can't think onscreen, which means she really can't act. All she can do is play an attitude. Cast as a teenage girl in pain over her parents' divorce, Cyrus plays one note - rage - in scene after scene. There's no motivating anguish underneath the anger. It's all surface snarling and sneering, and within minutes, she alienates the audience. She makes herself repellent and doesn't seem to know it... Though Cyrus moves well enough within the controlled atmosphere of her music videos, The Last Song reveals her as an ungainly presence, galumphing from scene to scene. Her face, which turns down when it should turn up, is without wit, and her smile is not warming or convincing. She has the look and aura of a character actress, minus the acting and the character. Then again, charm can go a long way onscreen toward covering up performance flaws. Alas, Cyrus either has no cinematic charm or does one of the best jobs of suppressing it in living memory.

(Mick LaSalle, San Francisco Chronicle)

The Last Song, from Miley Cyrus. If only we lived in a world where movie titles were legally binding.

(Robbie Collin, News of the World)

BILLY RAY CYRUS

Actor, Hannah Montana: The Movie (2009)

I don't buy Billy Ray Cyrus as Miley's dad.

(Fred Topel, Can Magazine)

WILLEM DAFOE

Actor, Speed 2 – Cruise Control (1997)

Like Dennis Hopper in the first movie, Willem Dafoe is harbouring a grudge - not against the Los Angeles Police Department this time, but against the cruise line that used to employ him as a computer genius. Long exposure to electromagnetic fields has, we are told, given him copper poisoning. We're not told if this is fatal or not, but it causes Dafoe to open his eyes very wide and cackle maniacally, so it evidently has disastrous effects on your inhibitions.

(Christopher Tookey, Daily Mail)

Actor, The Reckoning (2004)

Whole new scenes seem to have been added simply to show Dafoe's talent for contortion. It's grotesquely impressive, but you can't help but wonder whether his time might have been better spent working on his accent, or at least deciding on one.

(Catherine Shoard, Sunday Telegraph)

MARION DAVIES

Marion Davies has two expressions: joy and indigestion.

(Dorothy Parker)

TERENCE DAVIES

Writer, Director, Distant Voices, Still Lives (1988)

For much of the film Davies' camera is locked off, as in the very early days of the Biograph, where the camera stays clamped to its tripod on the station platform, filming miles of empty track before the train finally comes into shot. I believe Mr Davies went to film school - presumably not for long.

(Ken Russell, 1993)

Writer, Director, The House of Mirth (2000)

Terence Davies is a British director much loved by a few critics but largely ignored by the public. One reason is that he is to pace what Eric "the Eel" Moussambani is to Olympic swimming.

(Christopher Tookey, Daily Mail)

Writer, Director, Of Time and the City (2008)

Rarely have I had to sit through such a relentlessly maudlin drool of cliches and sentiment.

(Sukhdev Sandhu, Daily Telegraph)

Davies' sadly minor talent is for being uniquely dismal, which means that this film is unlikely to appeal to many non-critics, inside or outside Liverpool. Ken Dodd might have done this a whole lot better. He would certainly have kept more people awake.

(Christopher Tookey, Daily Mail)

BETTE DAVIS

Surely no one but a mother could have loved Bette Davis at the height of her career.

(Brian Aherne)

Take away the pop eyes, the cigarette, and those funny clipped words and what have you got?

(Joan Crawford)

GEENA DAVIS

Actress, Cutthroat Island (1995)

The best that can be said of Mr Harlin's lover, Geena Davis, in the kind of part which used to be played by Errol Flynn or Burt Lancaster, is that she is tall. But she looks about as vicious as Gabriela Sabatini, and the only interesting aspect of Miss Davis's performance is the way her chest has of appearing then disappearing, like an ocean swell.

(Christopher Tookey, Daily Mail)

DORIS DAY

As wholesome as a bowl of cornflakes and at least as sexy.

(Dwight MacDonald, Esquire)

Actress, Romance on the High Seas (1948)

This was Doris Day's first picture; before she became a virgin.

(Oscar Levant)

CECIL B. DEMILLE

Director, The Ten Commandments (1956)

The whole experience (with an interval) lasts roughly four hours. I am afraid that long before the time was up I was silently imploring Mr DeMille (for a critic, too, can misquote Scripture for his purpose) to let his people go.

(Dilys Powell, Sunday Times)

ROBERT DE NIRO

Actor, Greetings (1968)

Of Robert De Niro and Jonathan Warden, the latter gives at least some evidence of a little talent.

(Howard Thompson, New York Times)

Actor, Raging Bull (1980)

What De Niro does in this picture isn't acting, exactly. I'm not sure what it is. Though it may at some level be awesome, it definitely isn't pleasurable.

(Pauline Kael, New Yorker)

Actor, We're No Angels (1989)

De Niro gives the most wretched performance of his career. He is about as convincing a priest as Rin Tin Tin would be, impersonating a cat, and tries to raise laughs by pulling faces like Phil Cool. If he hadn't been Executive Producer, perhaps someone might have dared to tell him he was overacting a little.

(Christopher Tookey, Sunday Telegraph)

VITTORIO DE SICA

Director, A Place For Lovers (1969)

Looks not so much directed as whittled to death.

(Rex Reed)

The only smidgen of plot is that Dunaway makes a late abortive attempt at suicide, something the film successfully achieves after about ten minutes.

(Time)

The most God-awful piece of pseudo-romantic slop I've ever seen.

(Roger Ebert, Chicago Sun-Times)

The worst movie I have seen all year round and possibly since 1926.

(Charles Champlin, Los Angeles Times)

JEFFREY DEAN MORGAN

Actor, The Losers (2010)

He's going for George Clooney. He gets George At Asda.

(Robbie Collin, News of the World)

JAMES DEAN

Mr. Dean appears to be wearing my last year's wardrobe and using my last year's talent.

(Marlon Brando)

JAMES DEARDEN

Writer, Director, A Kiss Before Dying (1990)

The quality of his direction rarely rises high enough to merit the description "dull".

(Christopher Tookey, Sunday Telegraph)

It's as exciting as watching someone go bald.

(Anthony Lane, Independent on Sunday)

DUILIO DEL PRETE

Actor, At Long Last Love (1975)

Duilio Del Prete, as a merry Italian lothario, might conceivably play a street arab, but in a sophisticated role, with his thick accent and thin talent, he has as much charm as a broomstick with a smile painted on it, and turns every Porter lyric into a verbal jigsaw puzzle we are supposed to piece together on the wing.

(John Simon, National Review)

Duilio Del Prete, an Italian discovery, sings as if he came to paint the mansion and stayed on to regale the company with wobbly impersonations of Louis Jourdan and Maurice Chevalier.

(Bruce Williamson, Playboy)

CATHERINE DENEUVE

Actress, April Fools (1969)

The waxen animation of Catherine Deneuve, who should never ever appear in anything without subtitles, reminds me of a shiny new refrigerator that has just come unplugged from the wall.

(Rex Reed)

IAN DENYER

Director, Rabbit Fever (2006)

The clod-hopping, ham-fisted direction is by one Ian Denyer, whose previous work for television includes Inside The Mind of Paul Gascoigne, so he is obviously up for a challenge. Sadly, this one is completely beyond him.

(Christopher Tookey, Daily Mail)

GERARD DEPARDIEU

Actor, 102 Dalmatians (2000)

Adults should be aware that the increasingly bulky Depardieu is first seen in leopardskin shorts, not a sight for those of a nervous disposition.

(Christopher Tookey, Daily Mail)

BO DEREK

She turned down the role of Helen Keller because she couldn't remember the lines.

(Joan Rivers)

Actress, Tarzan, The Ape Man (1981)

To walk around naked and yet be uninteresting is a curious achievement, but one Bo achieves with charmlessness to spare.

(David Quinlan)

PABLO DI PACE

Actor, Three (2006)

The third party on the island, a dishy deckhand played by newcomer Juan Pablo Di Pace, looks like someone who has won third place in an Antonio Banderas lookalike competition, and can't believe that he's getting paid for gazing at Ms [Kelly] Brook's extremely nice body and occasionally fondling it. I couldn't believe he got paid for it either.

(Christopher Tookey, Daily Mail)

CAMERON DIAZ

Actress, Charlie's Angels (2000)

Someone close to Diaz really should warn her that excessive dieting is not making her any more beautiful. It's merely emphasising the size of her nose and mouth: she's starting to look like an anorexic duck-billed platypus.

(Christopher Tookey, Daily Mail)

Actress, The Holiday (2006)

"You look like my Barbie doll," a little girl tells Cameron Diaz in The Holiday. Bingo! She may be pretty, but the gal is a mannequin on the screen, a blob of inert plastic who cannot hope to engender our sympathy no matter how desperate she tries… She's just a blob of Barbie plastic who, when you pull her string, brightly spouts, "I can't cry!"

(MaryAnn Johanson, Flick Filosopher)

Cameron Diaz can "do" two things as a movie star: gorgeous airhead and driven neurotic. She tries to combine the two here, with limited success. It's hard to imagine her as the character written, which is an intelligent career-woman with literary leanings. There's a pile of reasonably heavyweight novels she means to read over the holiday, and it's impossible to imagine her taking the time to open them, let alone comprehend anything within them. Trying to look as if she might be romantically interested in an English publisher who speaks in complete sentences and refers to himself as "one", she looks as relaxed as a giraffe trapped in a string quartet.

(Christopher Tookey, Daily Mail)

Actress, What Happens in Vegas (2008)

Ms Diaz, so gorgeous in her debut The Mask (1994), is starting to look much too old to behave like a ditzy teenager, and age has turned her so orange that she's starting to resemble David Dickinson's long-lost sister.

(Christopher Tookey, Daily Mail)

Actress, Knight And Day (2010)

Diaz is a complete doorknob. Her "fish out of water" routine more often than not devolves into completely inauthentic

(Brian Salisbury, Hollywood.com)

Diaz, whose career choices are looking increasingly desperate, struggles – and who wouldn't? - to make a seamless transition from being panic-stricken one moment to an ice-cool assassin the next, and ends up looking like a demented duck.

(Christopher Tookey, Daily Mail)

VIN DIESEL

Actor, The Pacifier (2005)

At one point, Diesel literally wades into a rancid sewer and emerges covered in feces, an image that sadly doubles as a metaphor for his career.

(Nathan Rabin, The Onion)

Try as he might, he simply cannot act. Any household appliance could deliver his lines just as convincingly. So could most recently polyurethaned floors.

(Joe Queenan)

MARLENE DIETRICH

Actress, Blonde Venus (1932)

Dietrich walks through her part with all the warmth and quiet restraint of a poker leaning against the fireplace.

(Cy Caldwell, New Outlook)

MATT DILLON

Actor, You, Me and Dupree (2006)

I doubt I'll win the Pulitzer for revealing that Matt Dillon can't act. Still, I have to write it because it's just not fair to anyone forced to watch. He's a catastrophic choice for the Carl role. He acts with all the subtlety of an incontinent dog. He has so little chemistry with Kate Hudson that I thought it was possible he had been green-screened in next to her. There were certain points in the movie it seemed like he was invisible. That is not what they call in the film business "presence."

(Mr Cranky, Mr Cranky Rates The Movies)

VINCENT D'ONOFRIO

Actor, The Winner (1997)

It doesn't help that D'Onofrio chooses to mumble and stagger through it like Marlon Brando performing a music-hall drunk act.

(Christopher Tookey, Daily Mail)

JASON DONOVAN

Actor, Rough Diamonds (1995)

Mr Donovan no longer looks boyish and - for all but his most ardent admirers - turns out to have the big-screen charisma of a dead wombat.

(Christopher Tookey, Sunday Telegraph)

KIRK DOUGLAS

I suppose Kirk Douglas looks all right if your tastes happen to run to septuagenarians with blow-waves and funny stretch-marks round the ears.

(Lynn Barber)

Actor, Tough Guys (1986)

Kirk Douglas's performance has a self-conscious, noblesse-oblige quality about it; it's the sort of acting job you might imagine him giving in a slapped-together, tongue-in-cheek skit at the Friars Club. He does everything but wink into the camera and say, "Hey, I'm not this pathetic has-been, I'm Kirk Douglas, a big Hollywood wheel, still on the 'A' list after all these years. This is just a picture." Physically, he is in excellent shape, though his face looks a bit strange, as if he's had one too many face-lifts; come to think of it, he looks like somebody wearing a Kirk Douglas mask.

(Bruce Bawer, American Spectator)

ROBERT DOWNEY, JR.

Actor, Home From the Holidays (1995)

Then there is the horrible performance by Robert Downey, Jr, who has been allowed to "improvise", that is, chew the scenery and get on everybody's nerves. (Is he on drugs or something?)

(Anthony Quinn, Mail on Sunday)

Actor, Sherlock Holmes (2009)

Robert Downey Jr's performance suggests he must have misheard the title as Sherlock Hams.

(Christopher Tookey, Daily Mail)

HAILIE DUFF

Actress, Material Girls (2006)

"This thing is screwier than Courtney Love!" whimpers Hilary Duff in her usual chihuahua-on-helium whine. Even she, however, manages to shine next to her aggravating older sister [Hailie Duff], saddled as she is with all the comic timing of a mortally wounded elephant.

(Neil Smith, Total Film)

HILARY DUFF

Actress, The Lizzie McGuire Movie (2003)

Duff (by name...?) must be one of the most maddening leads in recent memory, a narcissistic, lip-chewing retard inside the body of a wealthy West Coast mom. The only moment that rings true is when Lizzie belts out a love song, to herself.

(Catherine Shoard, Sunday Telegraph)

Actress, The Perfect Man (2005)

The Perfect Man brings a new meaning to the word "cheese," but then again, what did you expect from the latest Hilary Duff flick. At least she doesn't sing in this one.

(Kevin Carr, 7M Pictures)

Hilary Duff has a remarkable screen presence, if only because not everyone can convey such effortless artificiality. Without mussing a hair, Duff delivers her lines as if she'd memorized them with the quotation marks intact. She's a performer, not an actor, and she performs as if the successful completion of each scene could earn her a prize. It almost takes talent to do what she does. Almost... Every time

Duff opens her mouth, she confirms that her natural home is in magazines. Or voicing animated squirrels. Either one would work.

(Keith Phipps, The Onion)

DENNIS DUGAN

Director, Grown Ups (2010)

Director Dennis Dugan is to screen comedy what the atomic bomb was to Nagasaki.

(Matt Brunson, Creative Loafing)

FAYE DUNAWAY

Actress, Mommie Dearest (1981)

Dunaway does not chew scenery. Dunaway starts neatly at each corner of the set in every scene and swallows it whole, co-stars and all.

(Variety)

HARVEY DUNN

Actor, Bride of the Monster (1955)

Harvey Dunn was a clown for children's parties, specializing in a bird act. So his police captain has a parakeet with him most of the time, sitting on his shoulder or walking around the desk. To say that this is distracting would imply that there was something to be distracted from. Still, the sight of a pudgy policeman playing with a little birdie in the middle of a movie called Bride of the Monster at least gives one pause.

(Bill Warren, Keep Watching The Skies!)

KIRSTEN DUNST

Actress, Elizabethtown (2005)

Kirsten Dunst, who puts the "oy" in "cloying" is the world's most aggressively adorable flight attendant… She's maybe meant to disarm, but she's scarier than anything in Flightplan.

(Michael Phillips, Chicago Tribune)

I can not recall a more annoying leading lady. Cameron Crowe obviously wishes us to smile delightedly at her endless pulling of faces and her oh-so-adorable habit of taking pretend-pictures with an invisible camera. He really expects us to nod wisely as our cheerily platitudinous heroine reveals that "men see things in a box, women see them in a round room". It just shows that one man's fount of New Age wisdom is another's living nightmare. To me, she's a smug, garrulous, insensitive bore. Whenever this ghastly creature is on screen, and sometimes when she isn't, Crowe's script turns into a preachy, pretentious, relentlessly upbeat homily about how good can come out of evil. Dunst's character is intended to be an encapsulation of the American "can-do" mentality, but serves instead as an awful warning against the way exposure to psychobabble can rot the brain.

(Christopher Tookey, Daily Mail)

DANNY DYER

Actor, City Rats (2009)

Danny Dyer still hasn't washed.

(Tim Robey, Daily Telegraph)

Actor, Pimp (2010)

Danny Dyer attempting to be this mob boss would be funny if it weren't so pathetic and tragic. Even by Danny Dyer's standards, it is rot of the highest order.

(Mark Kermode, Radio 5)

What with his writing, TV presenting and movie acting, one might argue that Danny Dyer has – like Peter Ustinov before him – become the counter-cultural media polymath of the age. He restlessly churns out content, but when it comes to film his name is fast becoming a byword for the unutterably dreadful.

(David Jenkins, Time Out)

Danny Dyer stars as a London porn baron being filmed by a documentary crew. Pimp is the title, although I prefer to think of it as Lock, Stock And One Smirking A***hole.

(Robbie Collin, News of the World)

CLINT EASTWOOD

Actor, Kelly's Heroes (1980)

Eastwood manages not to change expression once during the 149 minutes of this nonsense.

(Judith Crist, New York)

Actor, Director, The Rookie (1990)

The plot makes no sense from start to finish, and is rendered even less plausible by the casting of the patently non-Teutonic Raul Julia and Sonia Braga as German villains. The scene where Miss Braga rapes

Clint while he is tied to a chair is silly, gratuitous, and a rather disgusting display of directorial vanity.

(Christopher Tookey, Sunday Telegraph)

CHRISTOPHER ECCLESTON

Actor, Revengers Tragedy (2003)

The normally introverted Eccleston hams the thing up as though he's in a provincial panto, looking especially uncomfortable when conducting a weird ventriloquist double-act with his dead wife's skull, a sort of Keith Harris and Awful.

(Christopher Tookey, Daily Mail)

AARON ECKHART

Actor, The Core (2003)

Ben Affleck with a bigger dimple.

(Christopher Tookey, Daily Mail)

BLAKE EDWARDS

Writer, Director, Producer

A man of many talents, all of them minor.

(Leslie Halliwell, Halliwell's Film Guide)

BRITT EKLAND

Actress, The Man With The Golden Gun (1974)

Britt Ekland doing her well-known showroom-dummy routine.

(Julie Burchill, Girls on Film)

TED ELLIOTT AND TERRY ROSSIO

Writers, Pirates of the Caribbean: At World's End (2007)

If it's true that if you put 1,000,000 monkeys at 1,000,000 typewriters, one will type out Hamlet, the script for this film is what the other 999,999 will produce.

(Tony Medley, tonymedley.com)

The plot is not only hard to follow, there seems to be nothing real at stake. Half the characters are already dead, and half the movie seems to involve swordfights with dead people who can't be killed with swords.

(David Ansen, Newsweek)

BEN ELTON

Writer, Director, Maybe Baby (2000)

It's inspired by its author/director Ben Elton's own experiences, which makes one dread the day he develops a bowel malfunction.

(Steve Grant, Sunday Times)

ROLAND EMMERICH

Director, The Patriot (2000)

The true reasons for the American War of Independence are fudged, and it is presented as a straightforward struggle between aggrieved nice guys inhabiting a Garden of Eden avenging themselves against murderous Nazis with English accents. British annoyance is likely to be compounded by the fact that the director Roland Emmerich is himself from the nation that really did carry out such outrages. Atrocities committed by the Germans during the twentieth century have cynically been transposed two hundred years earlier to a different continent, and reallocated to the English.

(Christopher Tookey, Daily Mail)

Writer, Director, 10,000 BC (2008)

You may have seen worse movies than 10,000 B.C., but you'll have to work hard to find a dumber one. Even for a Roland Emmerich picture, this sets new standards for stupidity. This is like Uwe Boll with a budget. This is the village idiot of movies.

(Ken Hanke, Mountain Express, North Carolina)

Emmerich and co-writer Harold Kloser are clearly open to capricious historical invention, so it was a bit disappointing not to see a passing Mayan checking his sundial watch, or Noah sailing by waving hello from his arc's upper deck. (If you thought 300 was silly, think of 10,000 BC as 33.333 times sillier.)

(Liam Lacey, Toronto Globe & Mail)

My poor brain hung in there for as long as it could, but it lost its grip during the giant chicken attack and I haven't seen it since.

(Rob Vaux, Movie Flipside Emporium)

Roland Emmerich loves to make big, dumb movies, and though this may not be his biggest, it's certainly his dumbest. Yes, more preposterous than The Patriot. Goofier than Godzilla. Sillier than Stargate. Dopier than The Day After Tomorrow. For a start, it's isn't clever to try and remake the first two-thirds of Mel Gibson's Apocalypto only a couple of years after Mel did it, but without the thrills or half-decent acting. It's not bright to employ a narrator (Omar Sharif) who talks a load of pompous rubbish and whose accent is so thick, it's impossible to understand what he's on about anyway. And it's really bone-headed if you're one of the clumsiest wordsmiths in Hollywood – as Herr Emmerich undoubtedly is - to employ a co-screenwriter with even less imagination, writing ability and knowledge of the paleolithic world.

(Christopher Tookey, Daily Mail)

Writer, Director, 2012 (2009)

Emmerich's vision of global huddling and new-dawn optimism has a harebrained naivety you almost want to treasure, but that's this idiot behemoth of a film all over: dim, dim, dim, and so absurdly overscaled that we're not supposed to mind.

(Tim Robey, Daily Telegraph)

ROBERT ENGLUND

Actor, The Mangler (1995)

Women start dying at the local laundry, crushed and mangled to death by its malevolent, metallic machinery. In case we don't get the general idea, we get to see the whole bloody process in close-up, time after time. No one else in the town seems unduly concerned; but the cop becomes a shade suspicious of the laundry owner (Robert Englund). It's hard to know why. Could it be the way he snarls encouragement to the machine as it mangles his employees? his incestuous passion for his

niece? his black eye-patch? his mechanical legs and crutches? his scar? or his nervous tic?

(Christopher Tookey, Daily Mail)

JOE ESZTERHAS

Writer, Basic Instinct (1992)

The dialogue often resembles a chat between a brain transplant patient and his pet goldfish.

(Sun)

Writer, Showgirls (1995)

A sleazefest like Showgirls promises the inside dope on Las Vegas, stripping, hooking and all that stuff. What Showgirls delivers, however, seems basically to be Joe Eszterhas' masturbatory fantasies. The screenplay is the fevered invention of a very limited imagination, brought to a high gloss in a slick, expensive soap opera.

(Roger Ebert, Chicago Sun-Times)

The script is as hoary as it is whore-y, whipping out every backstage cliché as he recycles his Flashdance plot into Trashdance.

(Susan Wloszczyna, USA Today)

The story is so shabbily built that it can make no valid claim to motives other than the filmmakers' mercenary desires to cash in on the public's prurient interests.

(Marjorie Baumgarten, Austin Chronicle)

Showgirls approximates the feeling of someone sleazy putting the make on you. Its brand of sexual harassment makes you feel dirty and not at all flattered.

(Joe Baltake, Sacramento Bee)

Normally the reasons children are forbidden to see films are explicit sex and spectacular spasms of violence. In the case of Showgirls, though, the list of no-nos might read, "Obscene level of incompetence, excessive inanity in the story line, gross negligence of the viewer's intelligence, a prurient interest in the quick buck." For 2 hrs. 11 min., Showgirls offers a slumming party inside the moviemakers' libidos. Ladies and gents, no matter how curious or horny you think you are, you don't want to be there.

(Richard Corliss, Time)

EMILIO ESTEVEZ

Actor, Writer, Director, Men at Work (1990)

Mr Estevez's screenplay is garbage, his direction trashy, and the end-product the cinematic equivalent of toxic waste. Still, unlike the real thing, it should sink without trace.

(Christopher Tookey, Sunday Telegraph)

LEE EVANS

Actor, The Medallion (2003)

Lee Evans's clowning falls as flat as Norfolk.

(Edward Porter, Sunday Times)

Lee Evans indulges in such horrendous, unfunny, over-the-top gurning that one can only watch with appalled fascination as he systematically destroys his own reputation. Following a disastrous TV sitcom and a hideous attempt at straight-acting in the British film flop The Martins, Evans seems to have lost both his talent and his self-control. This is a "comic" performance so embarrassingly unfunny that it's actually

painful to watch. It's like seeing your favourite granny wandering naked down Oxford Street. You just wish someone would bundle Evans into an ambulance and take him away to sort him out.

(Christopher Tookey, Daily Mail)

CRAIG FAIRBRASS

Actor, Beyond Bedlam (1994)

Ex-bodybuilder Craig Fairbrass, unintentionally hilarious in his first big movie, Cliffhanger, once again speaks his lines with slightly less animation and spontaneity than the average speak-your-weight machine; he is to screen acting what Robert De Niro is to flower-arrangement.

(Christopher Tookey, Daily Mail)

COLIN FARRELL

Actor, Alexander (2004)

We gaze at Colin Farrell, in the leading role, and wonder if Alexander was impelled to reach the limits of the known world purely in order to forget the tragedy of his wig.

(Anthony Lane, New Yorker)

A major part of Anthony Hopkins's role, as the narrator Ptolemy, is to act as Alexander's posthumous PR man and persuade us at every available moment of his greatness. The diminutive Colin Farrell undermines this by portraying Alexander as a snivelling hysteric who doesn't get on with his parents. He's not so much impressively imperial as pointlessly petulant, like Elton John throwing a series of hissy fits. Colin Farrell roaring his head off strikes as ludicrous a figure as Kylie

102

Minogue essaying the role of Margaret Thatcher. Farrell is many things, but a blond he ain't, His eyebrows stand throughout the picture as a mousy rebuke to the series of tousled, golden fright-wigs perched precariously above them.

(Christopher Tookey, Daily Mail)

MIA FARROW

Actress, Secret Ceremony (1969)

Mia Farrow, I am convinced, is incapable of playing anything but demented creeps. The simplest gestures, like opening doors and saying "Dinner is served," defeat her.

(Rex Reed, Holiday)

JON FAVREAU

Director, Iron Man 2 (2010)

The first Iron Man film was hailed as the goose that laid the golden egg. This'll be remembered as the time Jon Favreau not only killed that goose, but plucked it, roasted it, ate it with sprouts and gravy, then burped in fans' faces for two hours straight.

(Robbie Collin, News of the World)

FARRAH FAWCETT-MAJORS

Actress, Myra Breckenridge (1970)

Farrah is uniquely suited to play a woman of limited intelligence, but the subtle sexual tension intended for her role is completely lost on her.

She fits in perfectly with the general texture of this abysmal film and radiates all the intense sensuality of an inflatable sex doll.

(Harry & Michael Medved, The Golden Turkey Awards)

FEDERICO FELLINI

Writer, Director, Satyricon (1969)

Barely satiric and a huge con.

(John Simon, National Review)

SHERILYN FENN

Actress, Three of Hearts (1993)

The film's view of lesbianism is laughably crude. Fenn, fresh from being a love object in Boxing Helena, evidently got confused between latent lesbianism and blatant thespianism.

(Christopher Tookey, Daily Mail)

WILL FERRELL

Writer, Actor, A Night at the Roxbury (1998)

Let's look at the bright side. America is still the land of opportunity if Will Ferrell and Chris Kattan can make a movie. At the very least, A Night at the Roxbury will encourage new talent. Hundreds of thousands will see it this weekend and walk out saying, "I could do better than that". They'll be right.

(Mick LaSalle, San Francisco Chronicle)

Actor, Kicking & Screaming (2005)

Will Ferrell is far from a scream, and I kept wanting to kick him… Ferrell hogs the screen with the least funny gurning since Jim Carrey in Ace Ventura 2. He's a horrific sight – quite, quite dead behind those little, piggy eyes. It's as though someone has Botoxed the upper half of his face, and the lower half is madly over-compensating.

(Christopher Tookey, Daily Mail)

Actor, Land of the Lost (2009)

As for the alarmingly ubiquitous Ferrell (eight films in the last three years), one does feel he has delighted us long enough.

(David Gritten, Daily Telegraph)

JOSEPH FIENNES

Actor, Rancid Aluminium (1999)

The accountant is played by Joseph Fiennes with an Irish accent and a desperate expression reminiscent of a lemming that knows it's going over the edge of a cliff and has lost the phone number of its agent.

(Christopher Tookey, Daily Mail)

Actor, Killing Me Softly (2002)

The story is rendered ludicrous by Fiennes, who can't tell the difference between smouldering and mouldering.

(Christopher Tookey, Daily Mail)

RALPH FIENNES

Actor, The Avengers (1998)

Ralph Fiennes, who plays secret agent John Steed (the role filled by Patrick Macnee in the BBC-TV series), must have grown tired of giving good performances. So he decided to phone in his performance as Steed, reciting his lines in a dull upper-class monotone occasionally punctuated by a smug little smirk. The result is stunning - the worst acting by a great actor since Al Pacino in Revolution, though unlike Al, Ralph doesn't get to deliver a line as fabulously shitheaded as "My mouth belongs anywhere I put it."

(Rob Gonsalves, eFilmCritic.com)

Ralph Fiennes as John Steed meanders through it all, looking mildly bewildered and disdainful, like a Methodist minister at a papal orgy. He betrays no sense of humour, still less any sense of Uma.

(Christopher Tookey, Daily Mail)

COLIN FIRTH

Actor, Hope Springs (2003)

Colin Firth seems initially distraught at his own ineptitude when playing physical slapstick, then appears in a state of deep dejection about the script, and ends up giving a bad imitation of Hugh Grant flailing about in his very own stateside turkey, Nine Months.

(Christopher Tookey, Daily Mail)

Actor, St Trinian's (2007)

Firth looks like he's changing his mind about being in this movie while the cameras are running.

(Michael Phillips, At The Movies)

TARA FITZGERALD

Actress, Rancid Aluminium (1999)

Tara Fitzgerald, as the gangster's daughter, does a career-threatening impersonation of Greta Garbo with lockjaw, except for one bedroom scene, which she plays inexplicably as a sex-crazed schoolgirl from Roedean.
(Christopher Tookey, Daily Mail)

ERROL FLYNN

Actor, Edge of Darkness (1943)

Errol Flynn brings to the part of the revolutionary leader all the authority, passion, and mobility of a starfish.
(Sunday Times)

JANE FONDA

Actress, Any Wednesday (1966)

Jane Fonda is about as funny as a manic-depressive having her first nervous breakdown.
(Rex Reed)

Actress, The Game Is Over (1966)

Miss Fonda is less attractive with her clothes off than with them on, which knocks out the only plus factor that Mr. Vadim might have had going for him.
(Bosley Crowther, New York Times)

Actress, Barbarella (1967)

Fonda's reputation as an air-headed activist is sadly borne out here.

(Robert Asahina, New Leader)

HARRISON FORD

Actor, The Empire Strikes Back (1980)

Harrison Ford offers loutishness for charm.

(John Simon, National Review)

Actor, Random Hearts (1999)

Dour and grouchy, like Edward Heath making a half-hearted attempt to grope Arianna Huffington.

(Christopher Tookey, Daily Mail)

Actor, Hollywood Homicide (2003)

When it comes to hilarity, who doesn't think of the first names in comedy, Harrison Ford and Josh Hartnett?

(Mark Ramsey, Moviejuice)

One source of unintentional comedy is seeing 60-year old Harrison Ford engaging in foot chases and various other physical activities. Ford was getting too old for this kind of stuff 15 years ago when he last played Indiana Jones. Today, it's laughable to see him as a character doing this sort of stuff. (And, on more than one occasion, the stunt man's presence is obvious.) There's no rule that someone into his seventh decade of life has to sit back and relax in a rocking chair, but this is ridiculous.

(James Berardinelli, Reelviews)

In the comedy department actor Harrison Ford comes across being about as funny as President Jerry Ford.

(Gary Brown, Houston Community Newspapers)

Actor, Crossing Over (2009)

Harrison Ford plays a grizzled old immigration cop with a hangdog, defeated expression, as though he's just been taken to see Land of the Lost. It's hard to figure out whether Ford is trying to invest the film with gravitas, or is just terribly depressed.

(Christopher Tookey, Daily Mail)

JOHN FORD

Director, Fort Apache (1948)

There is enough Irish comedy to make me wish Cromwell had done a more through job.

(James Agee, Nation)

WILL FORTE

Actor, Writer, MacGruber (2010)

Will Forte, who hasn't starred in a movie before and looks extremely unlikely to do so again, lacks the slightest vestige of credibility or charm as MacGruber. He also co-wrote the script. Let's just say that comedy is not Forte's forte.

(Christopher Tookey, Daily Mail)

Leading man Will Forte will make you pine for the graceful savoir faire of a Jack Black or an Adam Sandler.

(Catherine Bray, Film 4)

JODIE FOSTER

Actress, Nim's Island (2008)

Jodie Foster, giving an even more excruciatingly hammy performance than she did in Nell... A nervy, agoraphobic authoress who keeps falling over things, under the mistaken impression that she is being funny. That's Ms Foster, in one performance that definitely won't win her an Oscar... Long before the end I was hoping for a public-spirited shark to put Ms Foster and the grownups in the audience out of our collective misery.

(Christopher Tookey, Daily Mail)

EDWARD FOX

Actor, Adventures of Robin Hood (1991)

A kamikaze cameo appearance. Shamelessly ham-acting his way through his one scene as Prince John, he adopts an astonishing vocal delivery which is one-third Edward VIII, one-third Vincent Price, and one-third Mr Spock from Star Trek. It was greeted with appreciative hoots of derision at the national press screening, and I can't recall a barmier performance since Nicol Williamson's Merlin in Excalibur.

(Christopher Tookey, Sunday Telegraph)

Actor, A Month by the Lake (1995)

Redgrave looks handsome in an equine sort of way, but it doesn't help that the object of her affections, over-projecting like mad in a series of bizarre hats and unsuitable suits, looks less like an eligible bachelor than a sozzled TV racing correspondent competing for first prize in a gurning contest.

(Christopher Tookey, Daily Mail)

Actor, Prince Valiant (1997)

It would be kinder not to name anyone involved, but connoisseurs of ham-acting will not wish to miss Edward Fox exercising his eyebrows as King Arthur.

(Christopher Tookey, Daily Mail)

JAMIE FOXX

Actor, Stealth (2005)

As far as I know, this movie was made prior to Ray, but I still think they should take Jamie Foxx's Oscar away just for being in it.

(Mr Cranky, Mr Cranky Rates The Movies)

MICHAEL J. FOX

Actor, Casualties of War (1989)

The credibility of the film suffers further because the devil has all the best actors. Sean Penn and his evil sidekicks are totally convincing. Deep in the jungle with this lot, an amiable light comedian such as Michael J. Fox looks as incongruous as Bambi.

(Christopher Tookey, Sunday Telegraph)

MORGAN FREEMAN

Actor, An Unfinished Life (2005)

Even more trite is Morgan Freeman, playing Redford's only friend in

exactly the same way he plays most roles nowadays: as if he's trying to impersonate Nelson Mandela and hopes shortly to be elected Pope.

(Christopher Tookey, Daily Mail)

JASON FRIEDBERG

See Aaron Seltzer & Jason Friedberg.

SADIE FROST

Actress, Captain Jack (1998)

Sadie Frost, eccentrically cast as a schoolgirl, tries to compensate for her distinctly mature looks with a performance that suggests mental retardation. When she and Peter McDonald finally get spliced by kindly old Captain Jack, your feelings are not so much joy at their good fortune, as fears for the genetic inheritance of their unborn children.

(Christopher Tookey, Daily Mail)

Rancid Aluminium (1999)

Pride of place in this terrible, terrible film must go to Sadie Frost. Being involved with Jude Law has seen her status elevated, yet she delivers here the worst performance I have ever seen committed to celluloid. Wooden doesn't even cover it, plate tectonics have more vitality. Every line she delivers is a struggle, and I started groaning every time she came on screen.

(Punkass, eFilmCritic.com)

Sadie Frost, as Ifans' steady girlfriend, plays her emotional scenes with the groundless self-confidence of Posh Spice attempting Hedda Gabler.

(Christopher Tookey, Daily Mail)

STEPHEN FRY

Actor, Wilde (1997)

Fry often lumbers when he needs to effervesce, and a certain lack of commitment to the actor's craft undermines the otherwise touching scene in prison where he expresses remorse to the wife he has shamed and betrayed (charmingly portrayed by Jennifer Ehle). Not even liberal dollops of make-up can disguise that two years of bread, water and tramping a treadmill leave this particular Wilde looking as though he hopes to reinvigorate his career by becoming a Teletubbie.

(Christopher Tookey, Daily Mail)

Writer, The Magic Flute (2006)

Stephen Fry may be a polymath, but on this evidence he is to lyric-writing what Stephen Sondheim is to quantity surveying. This is a shockingly inept libretto, lacking wit, intelligence or even basic competence. Fry attempts to rhyme girls and world, tease me with easy, and – ghastliest of all - dominion with wisdom.

(Christopher Tookey, Daily Mail)

Actor, Alice In Wonderland (2010)

Stephen Fry plays the Cheshire Cat, the only beast in fiction that's smugger than he is.

(Robbie Collin, News of the World)

CLARK GABLE

His ears make him look like a taxicab with both doors open.

(Howard Hughes)

MICHAEL GAMBON

Actor, Dancing at Lughnasa (1998)

Michael Gambon is dreadful as the women's brother, a defrocked priest with an accent that's as wobbly as his walk. It's hard to know whether he's genuinely drawn to Celtic paganism, prematurely senile or (in his funny plumed hat) suffering from a delusion that he's Governor of the Falkland Islands.

(Christopher Tookey, Daily Mail)

SUSAN GEORGE

Actress, Straw Dogs (1971)

Susan George, pop-eyed starlet acting as the pouting target in Straw Dogs, was the first girl to build a career of sorts out of being a punch-bag.

(Julie Burchill, Girls on Film)

RICHARD GERE

Actor, Worth Winning (1989)

Richard Gere appears to have been novocained shortly before shooting.

(Harlan Kennedy, Film Review)

Actor, Pretty Woman (1990)

Richard Gere has become the Sonny Tufts of his day. His every line is spoken in a flat monotone. He has no timing, and he never, never focuses his beady little eyes on another actor.

(Gary Giddins, Village Voice)

MEL GIBSON

Actor, Lethal Weapon (1987)

Gibson's performance should make him a shoo-in for an honorary degree from the Rodney Dangerfield school of eye-bulging, nose-twitching histrionics. Trouble is, he didn't mean to be funny.

(Johanna Steinmetz, Chicago Tribune)

Actor, Edge of Darkmess (2010)

Mel Gibson seems both over the proverbial hill, and physically smaller than ever before. He looks not so much like a battered but defiant hero bucking the system, as an old gnome who's mislaid his fishing rod. The ravages of time and booze are only too visible, and far from pretty. He's turned into the Wizened of Oz.

(Christopher Tookey, Daily Mail)

TERRY GILLIAM

Director, Twelve Monkeys (1995)

A mess... confused, overwrought, illogical and derivative. Far too much is going on inside Gilliam's head, little of it original.

(Alexander Walker, Evening Standard)

LILLIAN GISH

Actress, Birth of a Nation (1915)

Every inch the smarmy charmer who'd get a monumental kick out of setting up a sub-human ex-slave on a sex assault charge.

(Julie Burchill, Girls on Film)

IAIN GLEN

Actor, Resident Evil: Extinction (2007)

There's the added sadness of seeing that fine actor Iain Glen mutate into a mega-zombie with tentacles, trying to extract some facial reaction from the lovely but perennially useless Milla Jovovich. Clearly, he's the kind of actor who'll do anything for a few squid.

(Christopher Tookey, Daily Mail)

JEAN-LUC GODARD

Director, Breathless (1959)

Godard's directorial abilities seem to me to be rather flash-in-the-pan-ish. He lacks intellectual and artistic integrity. Breathless upholds, and promotes, the idea that theft, murder and amoral nihilism are legitimate reactions in contemporary society. Any society which abets such propaganda is doomed.

(Henry Hart, Films in Review)

WHOOPI GOLDBERG

Actress, Corrina Corrina (1994)

There must be a lot of people out there who find Whoopi Goldberg hilarious; how else could anyone bear to sit through Sister Act 2? It is possibly my loss that I find her vulgar, obnoxious and sanctimonious.

(Christopher Tookey, Daily Mail)

Actress, Moonlight and Valentino (1995)

Are there any three words more likely to strike terror in the heart of a male film viewer than the dread legend: "... and Whoopi Goldberg"? Pity, then, the hapless boyfriends and husbands whose partners drag them to see Moonlight and Valentino. From the opening credits, they'll know exactly what they're in for: a film in which Whoopi will play the warm, down-to-earth yet ever-so-slightly-kookie sidekick to one or more vulnerable females; a three-handkerchief schmaltz-fest from which one half of the audience will emerge smiling thrrough the tears, and the other half gasping for a pint and a restorative video of Euro 96.

(James Delingpole, Daily Telegraph)

AKIVA GOLDSMAN

Writer, Batman and Robin (1997)

Far more scary is screenwriter Akiva Goldsman's idea of family entertainment, which is to have a young woman in stockings and suspender-belt rub her body against Schwarzenegger's and say "Freezy, I'm feeling... hot!" Mr Goldsman is the son of two prominent New York child psychiatrists, so perhaps he has clinical evidence that small children are amused and improved by this kind of material.

(Christopher Tookey, Daily Mail)

Writer, The Da Vinci Code (2006)

Goldsman's determination to cram the entirety of the plot into the constricted frame of a feature film – even one that runs a lengthy 149 minutes - means that he leaves no time for the audience to ponder the significance of anything we are told, let alone work out a possible solution. He is too busy giving the characters long speeches of indigestible exposition. If ever he knew the old movie maxim "Show, don't tell", Mr Goldsman has forgotten it.

(Christopher Tookey, Daily Mail)

Writer, Angels & Demons (2009)

I knew it without even seeing the credits; it was the familiar stench of screenwriter Akiva Goldsman, who wrote the previous film, as well as the awful Batman & Robin (1997). He also inexplicably won an Oscar for A Beautiful Mind (2001), which is, frankly, just as awful as any of them… Goldsman's method is to show a scene, and then have some character describe what is happening in the scene. And then someone repeats everything again later. He seems to think we have an attention span of about six seconds. Also, he has apparently never once heard or experienced a human conversation in real life, because not one written word sounds like it could have been spoken by live people.

(Jeffrey M. Anderson, Combustible Celluloid)

SAMUEL GOLDWYN

Producer

Sam Goldwyn was a sensitive, creative artist with a fine sense of double-entry book-keeping.

(Alexander Woolcott)

The only man who could throw a seven with one dice.

(Harpo Marx)

MATTHEW GOODE

Actor, Brideshead Revisited (2008)

Mr. Goode shows all the charisma of a stalk of boiled asparagus molded into the likeness of Jeremy Irons.

(A.O. Scott, New York Times)

Actor, Leap Year (2010)

His accent is not so much Irish as dirish.

(Christopher Tookey, Daily Mail)

CUBA GOODING, JR.

Actor, Lightning Jack (1993)

As the black mute, Cuba Gooding Jr rolls his eyes and overacts to an extent unseen since the heyday of Al Jolson. He mimes so vigorously that you half-expect him to demonstrate walking into a gale or being trapped behind invisible glass.

(Christopher Tookey, Daily Mail)

Actor, Boat Trip (2002)

Cuba Gooding Jr. is the kind of guy who does ten minutes of shtick every time the little light in the fridge comes on, and for years I've been waiting for him to just go away. If this dud comedy is any indication of the scripts he's getting, I may not have to wait much longer.

(J.R. Jones, Chicago Reader)

Cuba Gooding Jr. achieved fame by shouting "Show me the money". Obviously he was not acting.

(Tom Long, Detroit News)

Only Cuba Gooding Jr., the Olivier of his generation, could pull off such a daring commentary on modern manners. A lesser actor would have alienated the audience by participating in, but not devoting himself to, the ungendered nihilism required by the screenplay. The boat-as-moral universe allegory, intricate as it is robust, will no doubt consume serious students of film for years to come.

(Martin Scribbs, Low IQ Canadian)

Actor, Daddy Day Camp (2007)

All you really need to know about this excruciatingly inane sequel to the surprisingly tolerable family comedy, Daddy Day Care, is that Eddie Murphy refused to be in it. That's right: the same Eddie Murphy who agreed to star in Norbit. His replacement, the hyperactive and unbearable Gooding, manages to surpass even his previous least funny performance, in the abominable Boat Trip.

(Christopher Tookey, Daily Mail)

ELLIOTT GOULD

Actor, The Long Goodbye (1973)

This Marlowe is an untidy, unshaven, semi-literate dimwit slob who could not locate a missing skyscraper and who would be refused service at a hot dog stand.

(Charles Champlin, Los Angeles Times)

HUGH GRANT

Actor, Nine Months (1995)

A star is not so much born as aborted. Neither Grant nor Julianne Moore act as if they have had a relationship for five minutes, let alone five years. And as a child psychologist, Grant makes Bruce Willis's misbegotten analyst in The Color of Night look like Anthony Clare. His struggle to remove his clothes when his wife offers the possibility of sex after a long lay-off is an embarrassingly inept attempt to portray an embarrassingly inept attempt to remove his clothes.

(Neil Norman, Evening Standard)

In the absence of funny lines, Grant crinkles his eyes and grimaces at the camera, as if he is Jim Carrey giving a cruel impersonation of Hugh Grant.

(Christopher Tookey, Daily Mail)

Actor, Extreme Measures (1997)

Accepting Hugh Grant as a doctor in a serious drama takes some getting used to, especially when his character displays not even a hint of sexual impropriety. But accepting Hugh Grant as a doctor in a thriller that has him climbing into an elevator shaft and beating an FBI thug senseless is too much to ask. Extreme Measures was produced by Grant's girlfriend, the tolerant Elizabeth Hurley. Perhaps she sees heroic qualities in him that elude the casual observer.

(Brian D. Johnson, Maclean's)

Actor, Did You Hear About The Morgans? (2009)

The true horror comes from seeing Grant, formerly a shrewd judge of scripts, becoming ever more agonized in his screen persona. His Englishness, always heightened for easy export, now looks as authentic

as some of the Union Jack merchandise sold around Piccadilly Circus; in certain scenes, he can't put one foot in front of the other without appearing to have an umbrella inserted in his behind.

(Mike McCahill, Sunday Telegraph)

He works too hard at being Hugh Grant, and has throughout the film the stiff over-emphaticness of Prince Charles addressing a tribal people. Watching his performance, you realise that Grant has already given up on acting. When, I wonder, will the public give up on him?

(Cosmo Landesman, Sunday Times)

TOM GREEN

Actor, Writer, Director, Freddy Got Fingered (2001)

Green's got no talent to speak of, unless you count the willingness to do almost any sordid, disgusting thing to elicit a reaction from people. Move over, Adam Sandler, there's a new poster child for arrested development in town and his name is Tom Green.

(Brenda Sokolowski, Anchorage Press)

Green surpasses "annoying" in the opening ten minutes when he decides to molest a horse. I felt dirty, and I still do.

(Jamey Hughton, Movie Views)

Green is like that irritating kid in every junior high school who wants desperately to be the class clown.

(Todd Anthony, South Florida Sun-Sentinel)

Green is perhaps the only person on earth who could make a moviegoer actually nostalgic for the subtle intellectual brilliance of Pauly Shore.

(Jim Lane, Sacramento News & Review)

Green plays, in a bold stroke of casting, a self-absorbed moron. He is almost frighteningly persuasive in the role.

> (Joe Leydon, San Francisco Examiner)

Actor, Stealing Harvard (2003)

A film which would have been merely horrible without Green becomes unendurable as soon as he lurches on screen and starts pulling would-be hilarious comic faces. Hardened critics still go a funny colour and cross themselves at the mention of Green's gross-out comedy Freddy Got Fingered, but at least that had the courage to be outrageous.

> (Christopher Tookey, Daily Mail)

Aficionados will be pleased to know that his interest in bestiality remains strong.

> (Catherine Shoard, Sunday Telegraph)

PETER GREENAWAY

Writer, Director, The Draughtsman's Contract (1989)

A load of posturing poo-poo.

> (Alan Parker, director)

Emperors' new clothes have never been worn with more confidence. It is a murder mystery without a solution, an essay in precious pomposity with cardboard characters, abominable dialogue, and the pace of a drugged snail. It is familiarly known among Greenaway's detractors as The Draughtsman's Con-Trick; a more appropriate title, in view of its strenuous attempts to emulate Revenge Drama, might be 'Tis Pity He's a Bore.

> (Christopher Tookey, Daily Mail)

Writer, Director, The Cook, The Thief, His Wife and Her Lover (1989)

I have always considered the interior decorator one of the more sinister influences on modern life, particularly when, like Peter Greenaway, he sets himself up as a social-metaphysical moviemaker. The Cook, the Thief, His Wife & Her Lover is part post-modern vomitorium, part pseudo-Bunuelian existential parable, and altogether undesirable.

(John Simon, National Review)

Clunkingly banal when it is not being ludicrously pretentious. It is a measure of Greenaway's failure that he takes such delight in his anti-hero's monstrosity and shows so little sympathy for the other characters (Greenaway's attitude towards the wife, in particular, is one of the most disgustingly sadistic prurience) that I came away worrying not so much about capitalism, as about Mr Greenaway.

(Christopher Tookey, Sunday Telegraph)

Writer, Director, Drowning by Numbers (1991)

What is it about Greenaway's films that makes the flesh crawl? I think it's his apparent loathing of the human race. Unable to watch the humiliating spectacle of that fine actor, Bryan Pringle, cavorting drunk and naked in a tin bath in what must be the worst performance of his career, I switched channels. An hour or so later I switched back, to see if he'd sobered up, to find a chubby, ten-year-old boy sitting up naked in bed, surrounded by bloodstained sheets. I seem to remember two alarmed women entering the room, and asking what had happened. "I've circumcised myself," replied the boy, "with a pair of scissors." Is this gross, or is this gross? I remember Michael Nyman, who composes most of Greenaway's film scores, telling me that he usually supplies the director with reams of music, not necessarily composed for any particular scene, which Greenaway cuts into arbitrary chunks according to his needs. It seems to me that

Greenaway treats the human race in much the same way. And he is more interested in shit than soul.

(Ken Russell)

Writer, Director, Prospero's Books (1991)

Some directors have interpreted The Tempest as being about colonialism, or mid-life crisis, or the conflict between nature and civilisation: Peter Greenaway's approach in Prospero's Books is simply to emphasise the extraordinary affinity between Prospero, Shakespeare, Sir John Gieigud and himself. Greenaway's determination to leave nothing unillustrated makes Shakespeare's play, already his richest and heaviest in verbal imagery, utterly indigestible. Instead of being a piquant blend of textures, the result when mixed in the Moulinex of Greenaway's psyche is bland and monotonous. The Tempest is brought further down to earth by Greenaway's writing, which is as awful as ever: lame interpolations in Civil Service prose jar with some of the finest verse Shakespeare ever wrote, while the humourlessness of Greenaway's direction destroys even the famous drunk scene between Trinculo, Stephano and Caliban.

(Christopher Tookey, Sunday Telegraph)

Greenaway had no idea what the play was about.

(John Gielgud, 1996)

Writer, Director, The Baby of Macon (1993)

Greenaway tells this story with his usual self-satisfied and gross pomposity, mixing ornately stylised visuals with truly unpleasant moments. Despite the unfiltered gore and cinematic dare, however, the film is stultifyingly boring, as murky and static as a painting badly in need of restoration. Little is said about just how bad Greenaway is at composing dialogue. Give it a miss.

(Stephen Amidon, Financial Times)

Here is one of the worst screenwriters in the world, with a cloth ear for dialogue, utter narrative incompetence, and no interest in character except as melodramatic mouthpieces. And, like the dreariest adolescent, he seems concerned to elicit no reaction from his audience except shock, disgust and admiration for his cleverness. A picture which is intended, if Greenaway's production notes are to be taken seriously, to be some kind of meditation upon the connection between greed and child abuse stands instead as a horrible example of audience abuse: an exercise in film-making decadence, the product of a barbaric, unfeeling aestheticism. Here is a man who delights in talking dirty and rubbing our noses in sexual humiliation. Watching this movie is about as pleasurable, and rewarding, as being subjected to a 120-minute dirty phone call.

(Christopher Tookey, Sunday Telegraph)

SHANI S. GREWAL

Writer, Director, Double X (1992)

The worst British film for decades. A truly dreadful amateurish shambles.

(Alexander Walker, Evening Standard)

Enjoyable only under the influence of a six-pack and a stiff vindaloo.

(Sheila Johnston, Independent)

I suppose the team's next project will star Charlie Drake in a remake of Die Hard set in a bungalow in Clacton.

(Sean French, Observer)

Suggests that the British film industry is bent on ritual suicide.

(Leslie Halliwell, Halliwell's Film Guide)

Double X is unmissably awful, a turkey to savour, the kind of movie which really should be imprisoned rather than released. Even recent abominations such as Tank Malling and Bullseye! had flashes of near-competence. Double X stands head-and-shoulders below all competitors for its kamikaze casting, deplorable direction, preposterous plot, abysmal acting, catatonic cinematography and pathetic production values. I shudder at the thought of what the out-takes must have been like, if indeed there were any out-takes. As the film's executive producer Noel Cronin says, "If you make a film of high quality with a low budget, it will make money". Daringly, however, he has avoided doing anything so obvious: instead, he has made a film of such baroque incompetence that it will make money by attracting the kind of audience which slows down to watch traffic accidents.

(Christopher Tookey, Daily Mail)

MERV GRIFFIN

Actor, Hello Down There (1969)

Co-starring are two dolphins and Merv Griffin, all three of whom act as though they are going to be rewarded any second with a cold sardine.

(Rex Reed)

HUGH GRIFFITH

Actor, Tom Jones (1963)

It is hard to think of a role for which Mr Griffith would not be Too Much, with his piercing glare, his insanely dominant nose, his beetling brows, and cavernous mouth, his overripe diction. Perhaps God.

(Dwight MacDonald, Esquire)

MELANIE GRIFFITH

Melanie Griffith is very sweet but dumb. The lights are on, but the dogs aren't barking.

(Joan Rivers)

Actress, A Stranger Among Us (1992)

Cast as a hard-bitten New York cop, Melanie Griffith looks and behaves more like a fluffy-headed manicurist. Her attempts to portray spiritual awakening are painful to behold; and the hallucination that she could pass without comment as an undercover agent inside New York's ultra-conservative Hassidic community, shows Hollywood film-making at its most bizarre.

(Christopher Tookey, Sunday Telegraph)

Actress, Born Yesterday (1993)

As Griffith appears in one ludicrously low-cut outfit after another, it is hard not to keep thinking of her reconstructive surgery.

(Brian D. Johnson, Maclean's)

RUPERT GRINT

Actor, Driving Lessons (2006)

Grint makes no attempt to raise his accent to the received pronunciation of his parents (Laura Linney and Nicholas Farrell, who struggle with undeveloped roles). This makes him look and sound like a slob. Nothing he says, does or writes suggests that Dame Evie is anything other than deranged when she praises him for having "the soul of a poet". The soul of a motor-bike messenger, possibly.

(Christopher Tookey, Daily Mail)

Actor, Cherrybomb (2009)

I've seen some harrowing images in this job. Lars Von Trier's Antichrist. Michael Haneke's Funny Games. But now I've witnessed hell. And it's Ron Weasley pulling his sex face on widescreen like some massive, randy turnip lantern. Grint has said that filming the scene was "traumatic". Try watching it, son.

(Robbie Collin, News of the World)

CHARLES GRODIN

Actor, Thieves (1977)

Charles Grodin plays Martin as if a sufficiency of slack in the mouth absolved one from all further comedic endeavor.

(John Simon, National Review)

GERI HALLIWELL

Actress, Fat Slags (2004)

Geri Halliwell's face-pulling is the best argument yet for making superannuated pop stars wear burkas.

(Christopher Tookey, Daily Mail)

MARK HAMILL

Actor, The Empire Strikes Back (1980)

Mark Hamill (Luke) is still the talentless Tom Sawyer of outer space — wide-eyed, narrow-minded, strait-laced.

(John Simon, National Review)

TOM HANKS

Actor, The Da Vinci Code (2006)

Sadly, the normally reliable Tom Hanks is at his most reserved, stiff and undignified, thanks to the presence on his head of a mullet hairstyle that resembles something Chris Waddle might have ill-advisedly tried out in his football-playing prime.

(Christopher Tookey, Daily Mail)

Hanks's performance inspires the question 'Who shot this actor with a tranquilizer dart?'

(Andrea Chase, Killer Movie Reviews)

Actor, Angels & Demons (2009)

Tom Hanks' haircut has improved since the first movie, but God only knows why he wished to extend the agony of his dreadful initial performance. The wise decision to leave out Brown's sleazy sexual sub-plot between his hero and a pretty physicist (ineffectively played by Israeli actress Ayelet Zurer) has the undesirable side-effect of leaving Langdon with no personality whatsoever. His fear of enclosed spaces – so laboriously set up in The Da Vinci Code – seems abruptly to have vanished, which is lucky for him but baffling for the rest of us. His one character quirk is his Mickey Mouse watch, which he glances at from time to time, though far less frequently than I looked at mine.

(Christopher Tookey, Daily Mail)

JOHN HANNAH

Actor, Sliding Doors (1998)

What women don't want, I can tell you now, is the sort of man played by Hannah: someone who entertains his friends by reciting Monty Python sketches in cringe-making silly voices, or who leads embarrassing sing-alongs in pubs. I can't think of a single universe in which any sane girl would touch this drongo with a barge-pole.

(Anne Billson, Sunday Telegraph)

Actor, The Mummy (1999)

Whoever asked John Hannah to play a yellow British buffoon. was presumably blind to the fact that he is sly, slender, smart, and extremely Scottish. However much he was paid to shout the words "I say, bloody good show, chaps", it was not enough.

(Anthony Lane, New Yorker)

Actor, The Mummy: Tomb of the Dragon Emperor (2008)

As usual, director Rob Cohen seems principally obsessed with blowing things up, not always underneath the right people. John Hannah survives, for a start.

(Christopher Tookey, Daily Mail)

DAVID HARE

Writer, Director, Paris By Night (1988)

David Hare claims to have written this would-be thriller in six weeks; it shows... Hare's shoddy plotting kills off both plausibility and suspense.

(James Park, Film Review)

The right-wing woman provides an excuse for the insidious misogyny so well practised by members of that protected species - the lefty playwright... (The) appalling dialogue... may well sound meaningful on stage but, as a film script, is awkwardly pretentious.

(Suzanne Moore, New Statesman)

Writer, The Hours (2004)

One of those insufferable, dull, pseudo-literary pieces of sludge that elitists mistake for cinematic genius because of the cultured names involved.

(Jeffrey Westhoff, Northwest Herald)

RENNY HARLIN

Director, Exorcist: The Beginning (2004)

Renny Harlin is kind of a like a poor man's Michael Bay, which is the political equivalent of saying that George W. Bush is the poor man's Dan Quayle. Basically, this means that no matter what he does, no matter what genre he happens to be in, his association with a film is apt to send shivers up and down your spine as though somebody just delivered the bad news that all your living relatives were killed in a plane crash.

(Mr Cranky, Mr Cranky Rates the Movies)

WOODY HARRELSON

Actor, Indecent Proposal (1992)

The whole thing needed a leading man with snap and vim, instead of which it gets Woody Harrelson. Admittedly, it's an awful part, which calls for little more than unfocussed emoting, but then Woody trying to emote looks like anyone else trying to go to sleep.

(Anthony Lane, New Yorker)

Actor, The Walker (2007)

The Walker stars the thuggish Woody Harrelson as a flamboyant, upper-class homosexual, which is about as brilliant a casting idea as hiring Vinnie Jones to play the lead in The John Inman Story. Harrelson lumbers through the movie with the clumsy over-confidence of an actor who thinks he's extending his range, when really he's just showing off his limitations.

(Christopher Tookey, Daily Mail)

NAOMIE HARRIS

Actress, After the Sunset (2004)

Hearing Naomie Harris attempt a Caribbean accent is like eavesdropping on someone's GCSE Welsh oral.

(Tim Robey, Daily Telegraph)

RICHARD HARRIS

Actor, This Sporting Life (1963)

With his mascaraed eyes and charismatic presence, Richard Harris is every inch a cut-price Marlon Brando, whom he appears to be impersonating.

(Ken Russell, 1993)

Actor, The Molly Maguires (1970)

Richard Harris has the attention span of a cocker spaniel and all the emotional depth of a plastic cabbage.

(Rex Reed)

JOSH HARTNETT

Actor, Blow Dry (2001)

Finally, a word about Josh Hartnett: unnnghhhhh! Every time he opens his mouth the picture grinds to a sudden halt, as both he and the audience grapple with a tortuous hybrid of (vague) Yorkshire, Geordie, California, Oxbridge and Irish accents - the latter probably a subconscious mimickry of director Breathnach's own brogue - all delivered in a rumbling slacker mumble. Couldn't they have just made him mute?

(Neil Young, Jigsaw Lounge)

Actor, Wicker Park (2004)

Josh Hartnett, he of the squashed face and burpy voice, attracts unlikely amounts of female attention in this rubbish remake.

(Catherine Shoard, Sunday Telegraph)

Has there ever been a more inadequate leading man than Josh Hartnett? Whenever Josh tries to act, he never can manage to register more than one crude emotion at a time, and with each emotion he seems to be trying so hard to get his face, eyes and body language to say the same thing, he inspires pity more than empathy.

(Christopher Tookey, Daily Mail)

ETHAN HAWKE

Actor, Gattaca (1997)

Hawke's charisma is so negligible it's miraculous he even registers on film.

(Alan Frank, Video Home Entertainment)

GOLDIE HAWN

Actress, Bird on a Wire (1990)

There is something ominous about any film which depends so much on chases - there's a car chase, a motorbike chase and even an air chase. Throughout each, the 46 year-old Goldie Hawn - supposedly depicting a high-powered, successful lawyer - screams and gibbers like a 12 year-old Bonnie Langford with a spider down her back.

(Christopher Tookey, Sunday Telegraph)

Actress, Town & Country (2001)

Eerie, horribly stretched and bizarrely coiffed, like Joan Rivers attempting an impersonation of Britney Spears.

(Christopher Tookey, Daily Mail)

JONATHAN HEAP

Director, Benefit of the Doubt (1993)

It is described in the credits as "A Jonathan Heap Film". It is certainly a heap of something, but film is not the word that immediately sprang to mind.

(Christopher Tookey, Daily Mail)

KATHERINE HEIGL

Actress, The Ugly Truth (2009)

As in Knocked Up, Heigl seems to have palpable contempt for the material (not that she's much better than it).

(Adam Nayman, Eye Weekly)

Katherine Heigl once complained that Judd Apatow's Knocked Up, in which she starred, was way too guy-centric and made the women humorless shrews. Heigl owes Apatow an apology... The Ugly Truth, Heigl's new romcom, is the real sexist swill. There's not a genuine laugh in it, unless you think vibrating underwear is hoot material. As Abby Richter, the producer of a morning TV chatfest in Sacramento, Heigl practically defines humorless shrew.

(Peter Travers, Rolling Stone)

PAUL HEINREID

Actor

Paul Heinreid looks as though his idea of fun would be to find a nice, cold, damp grave and sit in it.

(Richard Winnington, News Chronicle)

DAVID HEMMINGS

Actor, The Charge of the Light Brigade (1968)

David Hemmings, besides being a mediocre actor, looks in long shots like something out of Planet of the Apes.

(John Simon, National Review)

MARTIN HENDERSON

Actor, Bride and Prejudice (2004)

I know Darcy is a pig of a part but honestly, stick Henderson next to one of those still just-about fashionable Indian coffee tables, and it would be hard to know which is the more wooden.

(Matthew Bond, Mail on Sunday)

New Zealander Martin Henderson makes a good-looking but bland Darcy, and he's a bit too much of a stiff, starchy, stuffed shirt. Most young women I know would be hard pressed to know whether to marry him or iron him.

(Christopher Tookey, Daily Mail)

CHARLTON HESTON

Hollywood – that's where they give Oscars to people like Charlton Heston for acting!

(Shirley Knight)

Although we all like to think that cinema is the most important culture on earth, we are fooling ourselves in the same way Charlton Heston is each morning when he sticks a Shredded Wheat on his head.

(Boyd Farrow)

Actor, The Ten Commandments (1956)

Heston throws all his punches in the first ten minutes (three grimaces and two intonations) so that he has nothing left four hours later when he has to react to the Crucifixion. (He does make it clear, I must admit, that he disapproves.)

(Dwight Macdonald, Esquire)

Actor, Ben-Hur (1959)

When I arrived for the filming of Ben-Hur, all the sets had been built, including Charlton Heston.

(Gore Vidal)

ARTHUR HILLER

Director, Love Story (1970)

One of the most ineptly made of all the lump-and- phlegm hits.

(Pauline Kael, New Yorker)

Camille with bullshit.

(Alexander Walker, Evening Standard)

A lying, thoughtless and evasive piece of nonsense... A slum, for the film, is a nice flat you rent at $82.50 a month. Poverty is when you both have to work. A tragedy is a painless disease.

(James Fenton, New Statesman)

PARIS HILTON

Actress, House of Wax (2005)

Paris Hilton is the least of the film's problems, and when Paris Hilton is the least of your problems, you know you're in trouble.

(Eric D. Snider, ericdsnider.com)

Actress, The Hottie and the Nottie (2008)

You've got to admire Hilton's complete conviction in herself as the center of all that is beautiful and good. And maybe such unwavering self-regard is actually kind of hot. Or not.

(Elizabeth Weitzman, New York Daily News)

As Humphrey Bogart remarked with frightening foresight towards the end of Casablanca, "We'll always have Paris". There's only one memorable movie this week, but it sticks in the mind for all the wrong reasons. It's a jaw-droppingly vile, vulgar, vanity production, produced by and starring Paris Hilton, the high priestess of dim... Let's get the obvious over with. Paris is to acting what Dame Judi Dench is to swimsuit-modelling. The hotels heiress is even more laughably inept here than she was in her first starring role, in House of Wax. She delivers lines as if (a) she's heavily sedated, (b) English is not her first language, and (c) she's reading them with difficulty off a distant autocue. There is absolutely nothing going on behind those bright, blue contact lenses.

(Christopher Tookey, Daily Mail)

DUSTIN HOFFMAN

I'd never work again for an Oscar-winner who is shorter than the statue.

(Larry Gelbart)

Actor, Rain Man (1988)

Rain Man is Dustin Hoffman humping one note on a piano for two hours and eleven minutes. It's his dream role. Autistic means self-involved, and Raymond is withdrawn in his world of obsessive rituals. So Hoffman doesn't have to play off anybody; he gets to act all by himself.

(Pauline Kael, New Yorker)

HULK HOGAN

Actor, Suburban Commando (1991)

Hogan's timing makes Arnold Schwarzenegger look like Cary Grant.

(Christopher Tookey, Sunday Telegraph)

ANTHONY HOPKINS

Actor, The Desperate Hours (1987)

Anthony Hopkins, playing the father of the family held prisoner, gives easily the most embarrassing performance of his career. One problem is that Hopkins seems fantastically unaware of what nationality he is: though clearly Welsh, he keeps trying to pretend he is American and served in Vietnam. Another is that, from the first moment we see him, he is quite obviously more psychotic than the character played by Mr Rourke. Even Anthony Perkins in Psycho would think twice about booking this guy into his motel.

(Christopher Tookey, Sunday Telegraph)

Actor, Alexander (2004)

Last but not least reprehensible is Anthony Hopkins, delivering the kind of interminable voice-over narration that suggests severe panic in post-production. Hopkins spends the picture telling us things that we should already know, ordering us to feel emotions that we most certainly don't, and filling us in on important narrative events that Stone has forgotten to shoot. His Ptolemy is inptolerable.

(Christopher Tookey, Daily Mail)

BOB HOSKINS

Actor, Son of the Mask (2005)

Bob Hoskins as Odin wisely attempts to be unrecognizable beneath a long grey beard and latex wrinkles, but still manages to be deeply annoying by shouting at us, when clearly he would be much better employed shouting at his agent.

(Christopher Tookey, Daily Mail)

HUGH HUDSON

Director, Revolution (1985)

Dingily photographed with the compositional eye of an earthworm.

(Toronto Globe and Mail)

KATE HUDSON

Actress, The Four Feathers (2002)

Another standout is Kate Hudson, although for all the wrong reasons. Her performance is awful and her clumsy acting is further damaged by her failed attempts to employ a now-you-hear-it-now-you-don't British accent. As well cast as she was in Almost Famous, that's how badly cast she is here.

(James Berardinelli, Reelviews)

Actress, Raising Helen (2004)

More and more, Kate Hudson's Oscar-winning turn in Almost Famous is looking like a solitary aberration. Someone has evidently told Hudson that she has a lovely smile, and she wastes no opportunity to show it off, however inappropriately.

(Christopher Tookey, Daily Mail)

Actress, Fool's Gold (2008)

Ms Hudson does not convince as an intellectual powerhouse.

(Christopher Tookey, Daily Mail)

If there is a romantic comedy Hell, Matthew McConaughey and Kate Hudson surely stand at the gates waving people in.

(Matt Kelemen, Las Vegas CityLife)

Actress, Bride Wars (2009)

She can not act. Her features have coarsened unpleasantly with age. And she is so badly made up that she looks as though she has jaundice.

(Christopher Tookey, Daily Mail)

ANDY HUMPHRIES

Writer, Director, Sex Lives of the Potato Men (2004)

About as funny as being stabbed repeatedly in the face with a bread knife... How on earth Humphries managed to convince such an impressive cast to take part in his truly awful film should go down as one of the biggest mysteries in Brit flick history. The guy must have had one Helluva lot of favours to call in. Either that or a remarkable array of incriminating photographs.

(Gary Panton, Movie Gazette)

If ever a movie testified to the utter cynicism, tastelessness and moral corruption of those who commission and make British movies, it is this abomination. First-time writer-director Andy Humphries' film is no isolated example, but it is the most shamefully inept, witless and repulsive British comedy I have ever had the misfortune to see. And yes, I do remember Guest House Paradiso.

(Christopher Tookey, Daily Mail)

HELEN HUNT

Actress, As Good As It Gets (1997)

Helen Hunt won the Oscar by weighing less than the statuette itself.

(Paul Rudnick, aka Libby Gelman-Waxner, Premiere)

ELIZABETH HURLEY

Actress, Beyond Bedlam (1994)

Elizabeth Hurley follows up her ignominious big-screen debut in
Passenger 57 by being the least convincing movie scientist since Zsa
Zsa Gabor in Queen of Outer Space (1958).

(Christopher Tookey, Daily Mail)

Actress, Mad Dogs and Englishmen (1995)

La Hurley plays the whole thing as though suffering from an overdose
of Night Nurse.

(Christopher Tookey, Daily Mail)

Actress, Bedazzled (2000)

There is nothing so unsexy as bad acting: Liz has a ruinous on-screen
confidence matched only by Madonna's. It's like watching a Roedean
head girl gamely having a go at the house play.

(Jason Solomons, Mail on Sunday)

The stills camera loves Liz, but not the movie camera. I swear that
there are moments in this film when Hurley, with her masculine jaw
line, over made-up cheekbones and husky voice, looks like a blowsy
transvestite.

(Cosmo Landesman, Sunday Times)

It's a tribute to Brendan Fraser that he's unfazed by the diabolical acting
going on within his eye-line. The way Elizabeth Hurley recites her lines
is atrocious but mesmerising. She's so scarily camp, she's like Joan
Collins auditioning to replace Christopher Lee in a Hammer horror
movie.

(Christopher Tookey, Mail on Sunday)

Actress, Bad Boy/ Dawg (2002)

Hurley plays one of the least convincing lawyers in screen history, and the embarrassingly predictable plot requires her to fall for a womanizing millionaire playboy. Not much of a stretch for her after Steve Bing, you might think, but on screen she can't do it.

(Christopher Tookey, Daily Mail)

ANJELICA HUSTON

Actress, A Walk With Love and Death (1969)

There is a perfectly blank, supremely inept performance in the feminine lead by Huston's daughter, Anjelica, who has the face of an exhausted gnu, the voice of an un-strung tennis racket, and a figure of no describable shape.

(John Simon, National Review)

DANNY HUSTON

Actor, 30 Days of Night (2007)

Danny Huston is the vampire leader. Who knew that vampires look like traveling salesmen, belly up to the bar at the Holiday Inn by the highway in Poughkeepsie?

(Mark Ramsey, Moviejuice)

RHYS IFANS

Actor, Rancid Aluminium (1999)

Rhys Ifans was ideally cast in Notting Hill as a Welsh slob and in Twin Town as a Welsh yob. Here, he ill-advisedly tries to play a weedy, hysterical, Cockney businessman who is supposed to be irresistible to women. As Sadie Frost, Tara Fitzgerald and Dani Behr hurl themselves at this lugubrious loser with ever-increasing sexual abandon, it is hard to keep one's jaw from hitting the floor.

(Christopher Tookey, Daily Mail)

The main actor is (snarl) Rhys Ifans. This man is a cancer eating away at British film-making. Every film he touches becomes infected with his satanic presence and total inability to act or be funny. Apparently he is one of Britain's most talented actors - if this is the case then God help us all.

(Punkass, eFilmCritic.com)

Actor, Once Upon a Time in the Midlands (2002)

The adult characters are uniformly dislikeable, and the uniquely dreadful Rhys Ifans hams so charmlessly that I kept wishing he would leave town as quickly as possible. It's quite late on that the awful realisation dawns that we're actually meant to want him to get the girl.

(Christopher Tookey, Daily Mail)

JEREMY IRONS

Actor, The House of the Spirits (1994)

Splendidly suicidal as a whip-brandishing South American patriarch. Invited to act an age range of about fifty years, he opts early on for a

hilarious wig that makes him look Mahatma Gandhi with a Kevin Keegan perm. His choice of accent is equally perplexing: a cross between a Robert Maxwell growl and Winston Churchill mumbling a cover version of I Was Born Under A Wandering Star.

(Christopher Tookey, Daily Mail)

Actor, Dungeons and Dragons (2000)

Jeremy Irons hams it up like Richard III on speed.

(Jack Garner, Rochester Democrat and Chronicle)

Jeremy Irons chews the carpet and leaves toothmarks all over the furniture, not to mention his wooden fellow actors… Spouting dialogue of preposterous inanity (my favourite was Irons' cry "Now is the hour to act!" which brought mutters of agreement from this particular critic), Irons succeeds in sabotaging further a once glittering career that seemed to have reached an all-time low with Lolita.

(Christopher Tookey, Daily Mail)

This performance will haunt Irons for the rest of his career or put an abrupt end to it.

(Louis B. Hobson, Jam! Movies)

AMY IRVING

Actress, Benefit of the Doubt (1993)

The heroine's reaction, on finding herself threatened with rape and death is not to call the police, naturally, but to rush off to the most lonely, inaccessible area possible. Later, she has the perfect opportunity to finish off the villain when he's lying stunned, but chooses instead to go off on a motorboat excursion. The film ends with Amy Irving weeping. Whether it's for her demented daddy or her prospects as an actress, is hard to say.

(Christopher Tookey, Daily Mail)

EDDIE IZZARD

Actor, The Avengers (1998)

Eddie Izzard, an actor with the grace and physique of a collapsing sack of potatoes, is ludicrously cast as the chief heavy.

(Christopher Tookey, Daily Mail)

Actor, The Cat's Meow (2001)

Eddie Izzard is miscast as Charlie Chaplin: nothing like him facially, too broad in the beam, too lacking in grace and, above all, too camp. Whatever else Charlie was, he was certainly heterosexual; and Izzard's languidly effeminate manner constantly jars with Chaplin as an aficionado of (very) young women. This Chaplin looks infinitely more likely to make a pass at William Randolph Hearst.

(Christopher Tookey, Daily Mail)

Actor, Ocean's Thirteen (2007)

Eddie Izzard, wittily cast as a technological master-criminal, decides to play one scene as American, and the next as English – and why not? What do you expect in a film without characters? Characterisation? Continuity? Intelligence?

(Christopher Tookey, Daily Mail)

GLENDA JACKSON

Actress, Women in Love (1969)

Glenda Jackson has a face to launch a thousand dredgers.

(Jack de Manio, BBC Radio)

Actress, The Music Lovers (1970)

Her thunderous, full-frontal, carpet-clawing caricature is a calamity of mistiming.

(Mark Whitman)

One can't really blame Tchaikowsky for preferring boys. Anybody might become a homosexualist who had once seen Glenda Jackson naked. Since she has been kind enough to show it to us, I must remark that she has a most unusual configuration in her pubic hair. It seems to grow in a narrow tuft, like the hairstyle of the Last of the Mohicans. I wonder if Ms Jackson has any Red Indian blood. If so, it might explain why there are no more Mohicans.

(Auberon Waugh)

DEREK JACOBI

Actor, Revengers Tragedy (2003)

Jacobi minces through the whole ghastly shambles as a semi-embalmed Frankie Howerd.

(Christopher Tookey, Daily Mail)

KEVIN JAMES

Actor, I Now Pronounce You Chuck and Larry (2007)

Somewhere there's a world where Kevin James is funny, at least so says the Hubble space telescope which just spotted this world in a galaxy far, far away. But on our world, any bald dude who combs his hair like Emperor Nero is usually judged to be more sad than comical. And by "his" hair I mean the hair that he possesses – regardless of its horse of origin.

(Mark Ramsey, Moviejuice)

Actor, Paul Blart: Mall Cop (2009)

To call this Kevin James comedy fatuous might be misinterpreted as an attack on the star's girth - so how about inane, tepid, lazy, puerile, phony, and unfunny?

(Andrea Gronvall, Chicago Reader)

DEREK JARMAN

Writer, Director, The Garden (1990)

The film takes the form of a vacuous and seemingly never-ending nightmare. "I want to share this emptiness with you..." begins the narration, unpromisingly and only too accurately. "I offer you a journey without direction." The director himself appears early on, and falls asleep. It is not long before members of his audience have joined him. The film raises, according to the publicity blurb, "important ecological issues". It's true that I did catch myself wondering why the planet's resources are being wasted on making such self-pitying, self-sanctifying garbage.

(Christopher Tookey, Sunday Telegraph)

JIM JARMUSCH

Director, The Limits Of Control (2009)

"Part of me wanted to make an action film with no action in it, whatever the hell that means," explains Jim in the director's notes. What it means for us is a ruddy boring two hours in the cinema, matey.

(Robbie Collin, News of the World)

DON JOHNSON

Actor, Guilty as Sin (1993)

A preposterous plot is made insufferable by Don Johnson's inability to portray any emotion more threatening (or interesting) than galloping narcissism.

(Christopher Tookey, Daily Mail)

Actor, Born Yesterday (1993)

Don Johnson, with his perma-tan and dimply come-on, is like a gigolo impersonating a professor.

(Owen Gleiberman, Entertainment Weekly)

ANGELINA JOLIE

Actress, Lara Croft, Tomb Raider: The Cradle of Life (2003)

If you thought the first Lara Croft was bad, you won't believe how appalling this one is. What is there to say about Angelina Jolie other than big lips, big breasts and small talent? Never mind her lack of grace or athleticism, she's just not sexy.

(Cosmo Landesman, Sunday Times)

Actress, Alexander (2004)

Cast hilariously as Alexander's mum, Angelina Jolie looks, at the most, two years older than him. She adopts a mysterious Mediterranean accent and a kind of absent-minded haughtiness among the Irish-accented Macedonians, rather like Nancy Dell' Olio put out to find herself in a room full of National Hunt jockeys. She amuses herself, if not us, by throwing tantrums and caressing a multitude of snakes in a suggestive fashion. The unintended effect is to make us aware all the more that we are watching a load of old cobras.

(Christopher Tookey, Daily Mail)

THE JONAS BROTHERS

Actors, The Jonas Brothers: The 3D Concert Experience (2009)

Thanks to 3D, you feel like you can almost reach out and touch the Jonas Brothers, grab them by the neck, and strangle the everlasting life out of them.

(Mark Ramsey, Moviejuice)

TERRY JONES

Actor, Writer, Director, The Wind in the Willows (1996)

Jones himself is scriptwriter, director and Toad, a hat trick in ineptitude.

(Brian Case, Time Out)

ASHLEY JUDD

Actress, Twisted (2004)

The problem with being asked to name the worst Hollywood thriller starring Ashley Judd is that you first have to be able to tell them apart.

(Todd Gilchrist, FilmStew.com)

Ashley Judd needs to climb out of this rut or retire.

(Laura Clifford, Reeling Reviews)

Judd is even less likeable than ever, and seems to be countering those accusations of humourlessness by developing the most horrendously hearty, Honoria Glossop-style laugh.

(Catherine Shoard, Sunday Telegraph)

TOMMY LEE JONES

Actor, Man of the House (2005)

The comedy is meant to arise from Tommy Lee's being a fish out of water among these sexy young girls, and it's possible to see why Hollywood executives bought the pitch: see Tommy Lee fall over while roller-skating! see Tommy Lee have a facial! See Tommy Lee gawp as the girls leave their lingerie hanging in the bathroom! On the screen, however, absolutely none of this is funny, and when we get to the stage where Tommy Lee is supposed to be learning life-lessons from the girls about opening up emotionally and becoming a better father to his 17 year-old daughter, you will find yourself struggling to control your gag reflex. Tommy Lee comes across as understandably bad-tempered throughout. When, towards the end, he groans "I'm in deep shit", I found myself nodding in heartfelt agreement.

(Christopher Tookey, Daily Mail)

VINNIE JONES

Actor, Mean Machine (2001)

Vinnie Jones as a soul in torment is an improbable concept, especially since he has only two or three working expressions.

(Tom Aitken, Tablet)

The campaign to convince us that Vinnie Jones is a movie star continues. Unfortunately, in his new film - his first as a leading man - he fails to convince even as a former footballer.

(Christopher Tookey, Daily Mail)

MILLA JOVOVICH

Actress, Ultraviolet (2006)

Jovovich is bad, and not in a good way. She turns in an epically expressionless performance (maybe she thought it was one of her modeling gigs?).

(Jonathan Perry, Boston Globe)

Actress, Resident Evil: Extinction (2007)

Milla Jovovich vividly demonstrates what the world would look like if Miss Teen South Carolina was licensed to kill.

(Mark Ramsey, Moviejuice)

JEFFREY KATZENBERG

Producer

Jeffrey Katzenberg is the eighth dwarf – Greedy.

(Alec Baldwin)

CHARLIE KAUFMAN

Writer, Adaptation (2005)

The dismally overrated non-writer Charlie Kaufman wins critical praise for writing incoherent movies about why he can't write coherent movies.

(Rex Reed, New York Observer)

Writer, Director, Synecdoche New York (2008)

No matter how bad you think the worst movie ever made ever was, you have not seen Synecdoche, New York. It sinks to the ultimate bottom of the landfill, and the smell threatens to linger from here to infinity.

(Rex Reed, New York Observer)

Kaufman's not nearly as bright or original as he wants to be. His film is about the way life transmutes into art, but the art he creates is so lifeless as to be alienating. It's a piece poking fun at morbid self-indulgence, that becomes morbid and self-indulgent itself. "No one wants to hear about my misery because they have their own," wails a priest, speaking out loud what Kaufman fears is true, and he's right. Fatally for its commercial prospects, Synecdoche is something that no previous Kaufman picture has been: depressive, pretentious, overlong and supremely unattractive in its self-pity.

(Christopher Tookey, Daily Mail)

DIANE KEATON

Actress, Annie Hall (1977)

Her work, if that is the word for it always consists chiefly of a dithering, blithering, neurotic coming apart at the seams — an acting style that is really a nervous breakdown in slow motion - but it has never before been allowed such latitude to deliquesce in. It is not so much an actress playing a role as a soul in torment crying out for urgent therapy — in bad taste to watch and an indecency to display. Miss Keaton is allowed to top her acting by singing two songs, which she does even less endurably: to compensate for her lack of vocal endowment, she goes in for even heavier mugging — it might as well be Central Park after dark.

(John Simon, National Review)

Actress, Because I Said So (2007)

Thirty years after Annie Hall, the beloved actress is scraping below the bottom of the barrel with this desperately unfunny farce, in which she mugs and pratfalls in the worst performance of her entire career.

(Lou Lumenick, New York Post)

Playing a ditzy control freak of a mother with serious boundary issues, Keaton comes across as such a screeching, flailing flibbertigibbet that you want to give her costars tranquilizer dart guns.

(Timothy Knight, Reel.com)

Diane Keaton's decades-long grip on audiences' affections continues to weaken; her shrill portrayal of Daphne, an anxiety-plagued L.A. mother, bypasses neurosis and enters the territory of mental derangement.

(David Gretton, Daily Telegraph)

MICHAEL KEATON

Actor, First Daughter (2004)

The least convincing US President in screen history - that's Michael Keaton, with the scary grin of a serial killer and the eerie, semi-embalmed cadaverousness of Robert Kilroy-Silk.

(Christopher Tookey, Daily Mail)

Michael Keaton appears to have fashioned his hairpiece out of a squirrel.

(Tim Robey, Daily Telegraph)

FELICITY KENDAL

Actress, Parting Shots (1999)

The one intended exception to the parade of tarts and harpies is Felicity Kendal as the girl-friend who finds the hero's serial-killing habits charming and sexy. Winner clearly intends her to be sweetly supportive, like Barbara in The Good Life. Instead, she comes across as hideously grotesque, a homicidal troll.

(Christopher Tookey, Daily Mail)

JAMIE KENNEDY

Actor, Son of the Mask (2005)

Instead of Jim Carrey, we have a young American comedian called Jamie Kennedy, who's even more abject when pulling faces than that poor sap who played Carrey in Dumb and Dumberer.

(Christopher Tookey, Daily Mail)

How far down the Hollywood food chain do you have to go before you get stuck with Jamie Kennedy as the star of your movie? Did Ben Affleck turn down Son of the Mask? Was Carrot Top busy? Did Pauly Shore refuse to return your calls?

(Willie Waffle, Wafflemovies.com)

PATSY KENSIT

Actress, The Blue Bird (1976)

Patsy Kensit is a cute Mytyl, but not much of an actress, and further cursed with reminding one of Goldie Hawn. Let us pray that she outgrows it.

(John Simon, National Review)

Actress, Blame It On The Bellboy (1992)

Ms Kensit has all the comic timing and subtlety of an aircraft carrier.

(Christopher Tookey, Sunday Telegraph)

Actress, Angels and Insects (1995)

"It has not done me any good to look pretty, to be admired" whimpers poor Patsy Kensit, once a promising actress. It certainly hasn't.

(Christopher Tookey, Daily Mail)

LANCE KHAZEI

Writer, Son of the Mask (2005)

Remember the name of writer Lance Khazei. This is his screenwriting debut, and if he gets a second chance, be afraid, be very afraid. It's hard

to know when Khazei is being more pathetic – when he's desperately trying to be zany, or when he's plucking at our heartstrings like a brain-damaged gorilla with boxing gloves.

(Christopher Tookey, Daily Mail)

NICOLE KIDMAN

Actress, The Portrait of a Lady (1996)

Poor Nicole Kidman has features that cannot support an upswept hairdo, and looks like a disgruntled provincial librarian.

(John Simon, National Review)

Actress, Birthday Girl (2001)

Nicole Kidman "does" sexy with all the erotic charge with which one "does" the washing up. Frankly, I'd rather gargle battery acid than have to watch Birthday Girl again.

(Sukhdev Sandhu, Daily Telegraph)

BEEBAN KIDRON

Director, Amy Foster (1997)

Beeban Kidron directs at the speed of fossil formation.

(Anne Billson, Sunday Telegraph)

Beeban Kidron's direction is unimaginative when it is not being hysterical.

(Christopher Tookey, Daily Mail)

VAL KILMER

Actor, The Saint (1997)

The trick with multiple roles, as Alec Guinness proved in Kind Hearts and Coronets, and as Chevy Chase didn't in Fletch, is not to show off. Kilmer has many qualities, but the wholesale abandonment of ego is not one of them.

(Anthony Lane, New Yorker)

Kilmer looks as petulantly smug as ever, relishing his own gratuitous performance as if he deserved an Oscar. And I know just where he should put it.

(Neil Norman, Evening Standard)

Actor, At First Sight (1999)

Kilmer, never good, is getting worse.

(Jason Solomons, Mail on Sunday)

Actor, Alexander (2004)

As King Philip of Macedonia, here portrayed as a crazed, drunken, one-eyed rapist, Val Kilmer gives us a curious mixture of Brendan Behan on a very bad day, and Long John Silver. Philip appears puzzlingly schizophrenic towards his son, cuddling him one moment, banishing him the next. Kilmer seems to have decided that, since the script doesn't give much of a clue how to accommodate these two extremes, he may as well play the movie as though he's too drunk to care.

(Christopher Tookey, Daily Mail)

Actor, MacGruber (2010)

MacGruber's arch-enemy is played by Val Kilmer, a man who's now so fat, if they remade Top Gun he'd sink the aircraft carrier.

(Robbie Collin, News of the World)

ZALMAN KING

Writer, Director, Wild Orchid (1989)

Mr King's sensual imagery is as depressingly detumescent as ever (waves crash, motorbikes throb, waterpipes spurt), and his dialogue is not so much sexually depraved as intellectually deprived.

(Christopher Tookey, Sunday Telegraph)

BEN KINGSLEY

Actor, The Love Guru (2008)

Ben Kingsley's eyes are crossed in a desperate attempt to vanish off-screen even if it means different sides of the screen at the same time. The temptation to follow his eyes out both exits at once is overwhelming.

(Mark Ramsey, Moviejuice)

MIA KIRSHNER

Actress, Anna Karenina (1997)

The pretty Canadian actress Mia Kirshner seems to have been misled by the name of her character, Princess Kitty, into thinking that she is starring in a Judith Krantz mini-series. Such a misapprehension is pardonable in view of the excruciatingly banal dialogue. Rose's adaptation is dim-witted when attempting to be deep, and chuckle-making when attempting to evoke the cadences of nineteenth century Russia. I particularly treasured Princess Kitty's account of her character-forming convalescence – "I learned how to healthcare for the other patients".

(Christopher Tookey, Daily Mail)

CHRIS KLEIN

Actor, Rollerball (2002)

I'd say Klein was out of his depth, if he had any depth to be out of.

(Gary Susman, Boston Phoenix)

Leading actor Chris Klein is hopelessly miscast as a tough guy, and carries all the physical menace of Kylie Minogue at a convention of Hell's Angels.

(Christopher Tookey, Daily Mail)

KEIRA KNIGHTLEY

Actress, King Arthur (2004)

King Arthur is badly let down by some woeful acting. Knightley undoes every scrap of good that The Pirates of the Caribbean did for her career by turning Guinevere into a bored-sounding suburban teenager.

(Matthew Bond, Mail on Sunday)

Ah yes, the Woads. Anglo-Saxon scholars will be interested to know

that for Hollywood purposes all indigenous tribes of Britain south of Hadrian's Wall have been merged into one, the Woads, who fight under the aforementioned Guinevere (Keira Knightley), who seems by her accent just to have left Woadean.

(Christopher Tookey, Daily Mail)

Actress, Pirates of the Caribbean: At World's End (2007)

Keira Knightley, who has proved in Pride and Prejudice that she really can act, gives a truly horrible performance of pitiful shallowness. Her attempt to deliver a climactic, Henry V-style speech to her assembled army of pirates is an especially woeful embarrassment. She sounds like an ineffectual prefect at Benenden, and the wardrobe department makes her looks like a little girl playing dress-up, with a tea cosy on her head.

(Christopher Tookey, Daily Mail)

ELIAS KOTEAS

Actor, Crash (1996)

Vaughan is the Canadian director's most egregious error. In the novel, he is a grubby, pockmarked weirdo who re-stages celebrity car crashes for audiences of like-mindless fanatics. In the film, he is played by Elias Koteas, an actor yet more repellent, so that no one - in his wrong mind even - would want to get involved with him, psychically or sexually, as James and Catherine do. Still, the only vaguely titillating scene has the couple in bed fantasizing intercourse with Vaughan - Koteas, which strikes me as sicker than humping a hood ornament.

(John Simon, National Review)

KRIS KRISTOFFERSON

Actor, Millennium (1989)

The other star of the movie is alleged to be Kris Kristoffersen; but his performance suggests that time-travellers have long since replaced him with an animatronic doll of the same name.

(Christopher Tookey, Sunday Telegraph)

Actor, Welcome Home (1989)

The only conceivable interest lies in the chance it offers to observe at close quarters the continuing transformation of Kris Kristofferson from an actor into a Thunderbirds puppet.

(Christopher Tookey, Sunday Telegraph)

ASHTON KUTCHER

Actor, Just Married (2003)

Brittany Murphy has no comic timing and Kutcher overcompensates. His mistimed pratfalls and superfluous gurning are a means to distract you from their otherwise banal interaction. If nobody says anything vaguely amusing within five minutes, chances are, Kutcher will fall on his face. And Murphy will register open-mouthed surprise. Followed by: mock frown. The script fits in a few decent wisecracks but Kutcher overplays these with his incessant mugging, and Murphy reacts with Canderel sweetness - artificial and obvious. Watching Just Married is like watching your drunken dad on the dance floor. Embarrassing.

(Stella Papamichael, BBCi)

Actor, The Butterfly Effect (2004)

Eric Bress's time-travel travesty stars Ashton Kutcher (of Dude, Where's My Car? and Demi Moore fame) as a tormented maths genius - brave casting, that.

(Catherine Shoard, Sunday Telegraph)

Actor, A Lot Like Love (2005)

As for Kutcher, the less said the better. He has yet to give a performance that isn't a dude-acious commentary on his own unwillingness to give a performance, and what once looked like slacker irony is more and more plainly lack of ability.

(Ty Burr, Boston Globe)

Actor, What Happens in Vegas (2008)

Little did I dream when seeing Ashton Kutcher play a brainless, sexist dork in his first movie, Dude, Where's My Car?, that I was witnessing his best ever performance. Eight years on, he still looks cute, but continues to confuse pulling faces with acting. He is one of the few Hollywood stars who might actually be improved by Botox.

(Christopher Tookey, Daily Mail)

Actor, Spread (2009)

Of all the actors to have played the lady-killer role - Warren Beatty in Shampoo, Richard Gere in American Gigolo - Ashton Kutcher is the least qualified to engage an audience's sympathies: he struts through the bedroom like the most odious of fratboys.

(Mike McCahill, Sunday Telegraph)

Actor, Killers (2010)

Kutcher is surprisingly anticharismatic as a star. A smarmy grin and looking good while shirtless does not equal screen presence, dude.

(David Fear, Time Out New York)

Professional prankster Ashton Kutcher plays – and I can hardly believe that I'm writing these words - a suave, debonair, multilingual assassin working for the CIA. He is as well suited to the role as Rupert Grint would be, giving us his James Bond. Mr Kutcher makes his unlikely bid to be the new Cary Grant by adopting a cheesy grin, often when inappropriate, and stripping to the waist. Since Mr Kutcher is credited as producer, presumably his leading lady was contractually obliged to say that he has "physical godlike perfection". A more objective reviewer might note that he looks like an exceptionally dumb narcissist with the comic timing of a corpse.

(Christopher Tookey, Daily Mail)

Here's a film where an entire town of people want to kill Ashton Kutcher. Yes, it's a bit far-fetched. I mean, just the one town?

(Robbie Collin, News of the World)

Yeah, Ashton Kutcher's a CIA agent. And I'm Pauline Kael.

(Thomas Leupp, Hollywood.com)

Actor, Valentine's Day (2010)

"It's Valentine's Day," says Ashton. "I can talk about love to total strangers and no-one will think I'm a moron." Wanna bet?

(Robbie Collin, News of the World)

CHRISTOPHER LAMBERT

Actor, Highlander III: The Sorcerer (1995)

The Gallic actor Christopher Lambert is about as Gaelic as a crouton; if he's a Highlander, Kenny Dalgleish is a Dutchman.

(Christopher Tookey, Daily Mail)

ANGELA LANSBURY

Actress, The Three Musketeers (1948)

Angela Lansbury wears the crown of France as though she had won it at a county fair.

(New Yorker)

CYNDI LAUPER

Actress, Off and Running (1992)

Cyndi Lauper has another go at becoming a movie star with this silly caper movie. There are fish with more talent in their fingers.

(Simon Rose)

JUDE LAW

Actor, Sleuth (2007)

Law can't stay still for a second: playing a struggling thesp, he too often embodies one.

(Tim Robey, Daily Telegraph)

Actor, Sherlock Holmes (2009)

As Watson, Jude Law is dull, which in the light of his recent screen performances is a step up for him. But he's still weirdly lightweight, like The X Factor's Joe McElderry attempting to give us his Disraeli.
(Christopher Tookey, Daily Mail)

MARTIN LAWRENCE

Writer, Director, Actor, A Thin Line Between Love and Hate (1996)

The leading lady (Lynn Whitfield) is not convincing for a second, mainly because she has to appear attracted to a leading man with all the charm of primordial slime. Complaints about the coarse direction and misogynistic script, a never-ending fusillade of four-letter words and obscenities, should be addressed to the film's would-be star.
(Christopher Tookey, Daily Mail)

Actor, National Security (2003)

Is there anything worse than a Martin Lawrence movie?
(Kevin N. Laforest, Montreal Film Journal)

Lawrence has to be the singularly most untalented, most obnoxious, most misogynistic and most racist comedian working in movies today. That's a lot of mosts, but "most overpaid" can be added with his $20 million price tag for this.
(Ken Hanke, Mountain Xpress)

GEORGE LAZENBY

Actor, On Her Majesty's Secret Service (1969)

Lazenby is as wooden as Pinocchio.

> (Alan Frank, Frank's 500)

As Agent 007, Lazenby is about as animated as Westminster Abbey.

> (Steven H. Scheuer)

DAVID LEAN

Director, Doctor Zhivago (1965)

Imperceptibly, David Lean has evolved into the middlebrow's answer to the late Cecil B. DeMille.

> (Andrew Sarris, Village Voice)

JASON LEE

Actor, Alvin and the Chipmunks (2007)

Jason Lee adopts a panic-stricken smile and shouts a lot as a songwriter who becomes the chipmunks' father figure. He has a frightened look, as though fearful of the effect this is going to have on his career. He is wise to be worried.

> (Christopher Tookey, Daily Mail)

SPIKE LEE

Director, Writer, She Hate Me (2004)

When a Spike Lee film doesn't fly, it sinks like a stone. This one is Gibraltar.
(Peter Travers, Rolling Stone)

Lee combines his usual humourless hectoring with a brand-new inability to make any of his points coherently.
(Christopher Tookey, Daily Mail)

SHELDON LETTICH

Writer, Director, Double Impact (1991)

Director Sheldon Lettich directs the sex and slugging like the less talented brother of Walter and Benny Hill.
(Christopher Tookey, Sunday Telegraph)

LIBERACE

I've done my bit for motion pictures. I've stopped making them.
(Liberace)

Actor, Sincerely Yours (1955)

My big try for stardom in the movies, but no one noticed it or me. Maybe I should have worn my candelabra on my head, Carmen Miranda style.
(Liberace)

Liberace seems beside himself with joy just to be in a movie. He's so

happy, in fact, that he can't stop smiling, even in serious scenes. And there you have it. Sincerely Yours is insipidly sentimental, hopelessly hokey, stiflingly hothouse-flowery. But what takes it from bad to worse is the star. The man. The movie's whole reason for being.

> (Michael Sauter, The Worst Movies of All Time)

A competent set of supporting actors looks on in bewilderment.

> (Derek Winnert, Radio Times Film Guide)

MAUREEN LIPMAN

Actress, Captain Jack (1998)

Maureen Lipman, Mr Rosenthal's real-life spouse, loyally wades on to this sinking ship-movie as Mr Hoskins's love interest and tries without success not to look nine inches taller than him. Though she's meant to be the proprietor of a caravan site, she patrols it with politely feigned interest, like the Queen visiting the Chelsea flower show and being tricked by Esther Rantzen into inspecting an indelicately shaped cucumber.

> (Christopher Tookey, Daily Mail)

LUCY LIU

Lucy Liu continues to find work despite being the worst actress in the solar system.

> (Joe Queenan)

Actress, Charlie's Angels (2000)

Lucy Liu displays a grasp of comic timing unseen since the oratorical heyday of John Redwood.

> (Christopher Tookey, Daily Mail)

ANDREW LLOYD WEBBER

Composer, Jesus Christ, Superstar (1973)

Nobody can sing. Of course, if you had to wrap your tongue around Tim Rice's banal lyrics and Lloyd Webber's Vegas-style orchestrations, you'd have trouble singing too.

(Michael Sauter, The Worst Movies of All Time)

Composer, Evita (1996)

I doubt any director could have made a good movie from Andrew Lloyd Webber's baffling and shallow musical… Those who enjoy his brand of pompous pop may not mind the numbingly repetitive Evita; at times, I felt as if I were trapped inside a jukebox that only plays three songs.

(Rob Gonsalves, eFilmCritic.com)

Writer, Composer, Producer, The Phantom of the Opera (2005)

Lord Lloyd Webber's thorough acquaintance with the canon of 18th- and 19th-century classical music is not in doubt, but his attempt to force a marriage between that tradition and modern musical theater represents a victory of pseudo-populist grandiosity over taste - an act of cultural butchery akin to turning an aviary of graceful swans and brilliant peacocks into an order of Chicken McNuggets.

(A.O. Scott, New York Times)

Andrew Lloyd Webber is the Mozart of mediocrity, the Beethoven of bland, and a shallow, giftless dilettante whose hackneyed McOperas are an embarrassment to the art form. And as much as I loathe his entire pedestrian oeuvre, The Phantom of the Opera in particular appalls me as both a horror fan and a music lover.

(John W. Bowen, Rue Morgue Magazine)

Quite possibly the worst thing I've ever seen in my entire life, Andrew Lloyd Webber's The Phantom of the Opera represents everything that's wrong with much of today's musical theater. Like overpriced costume jewelry, this tacky Broadway version of Gaston Leroux's 1910 novel — with its soulless histrionics set to music and pedestrian lyrics Hilary Duff could have written during a bad break-up (sample contrivance: "We never said our love was evergreen") — seems to appeal to the same people who like Celine Dion and Meatloaf albums.

(Ed Gonzalez, Slant Magazine)

LINDSAY LOHAN

Actress, Just My Luck (2006)

Looking tired and sallow and drained of her customary glow, Lindsay Lohan marches grimly through this mechanical tween comedy as if it were a particularly tedious homework assignment. Which it is.

(Ella Taylor, LA Weekly)

Actress, I Know Who Killed Me (2007)

Even before recent tabloid events exploded across the cultural wasteland, Lindsay Lohan's movie future was in dire straits. After viewing her latest big screen adventure, I Know Who Killed Me, who could've predicted a bust for alleged cocaine possession, vocational self-destruction, and a general display of young Hollywood stupidity would be the career highlight of her weekend?

(Brian Orndorf, Film Jerk)

Lohan's appearance in I Know Who Killed Me may ultimately work in her favor. Given her latest legal troubles, it could provide her with sufficient grounds for an insanity defense.

(Steve Davis, Austin Chronicle)

JENNIFER LOPEZ

Actress, Out of Sight (1998)

She is not the most plausible US marshal I have ever seen. The way she holds her shotgun during the jailbreak suggests someone trying to prod a spider with a broomhandle.

(Anthony Lane, New Yorker)

Actress, Gigli (2003)

Jennifer Lopez and Ben Affleck should fire their agents. Or take a long, hard look at themselves in the mirror.

(Jane Stevenson, Jam! Movies)

Lopez wanders through the film looking glisteningly, adoringly, rapturously in love with herself. When she finally allows Ben to liberate her from lesbianism, accompanied by John Powell's cheesy score, it's like watching two expensive cars crashing into each other. There isn't a sign of life after the collision, and you wonder if the best solution to their problem might not involve jump-leads and several thousand volts.

(Christopher Tookey, Daily Mail)

Actress, Monster-in-Law (2005)

Lopez reacts amateurishly to Fonda's brittle, furious overacting, and it's laughable, even obscene, to see her playing yet another working girl when she looks like the most indolent, pampered woman on the planet.

(Dan Callahan, Slant Magazine)

Actress, An Unfinished Life (2005)

I'd love to understand the casting mentality that leads some power in

Hollywood to think "Our leading lady is an abused, guilt-ridden single mother with low self-esteem – I know: let's get Jennifer Lopez!" Even less convincing than when she was playing another abused woman, in the aptly titled Enough, J-Lo comes across as slightly less vulnerable than Nancy Dell' Olio.

(Christopher Tookey, Daily Mail)

Actress, The Back-Up Plan (2010)

The mystery of Jennifer Lopez: how can someone with such a beautiful face be quite so unappealing as a presence? Every role she touches just withers and dies.

(Anthony Quinn, Independent)

Jennifer Lopez has never looked better or acted worse.

(Christopher Tookey, Daily Mail)

The Back-Up Plan represents a major comeback for Jennifer Lopez. Unfortunately, she's come back to making crap.

(Mike McGranaghan, Aisle Seat)

JOSEPH LOSEY

Director, The Assassination of Trotsky (1972)

Losey succeeds in making fact seem like lurid fiction.

(Judith Crist)

We get lots of crazy acting and lots of the aimless camera movement which director Joseph Losey passes off as style.

(Richard Schickel, Life)

GEORGE LUCAS

Writer, Director, The Empire Strikes Back (1980)

Lucas should stop contributing to the sappiness of nations. [His film is] malodorous offal, stale, limp, desperately stretched out, and pretentious. Infantile is the operative word. This witless banality is made even less bearable by the nonacting of the principals. The program lists five and a half pages of credits; it would take at least twice that space to list the debits.

(John Simon, National Review)

Writer, Director, Star Wars II: Attack of the Clones (2002)

Lucas is a toymaker and merchandising mogul who has long since lost the human touch.

(Scott Von Doviak, Culturevulture.net)

The dialogue is so wooden that you can use it for batting practice.

(Nell Minow, Movie Mom)

BELA LUGOSI

Actor Bride of the Monster (1955)

Lugosi's fight with a rubber octopus (for which Lugosi must wrap the tentacles around himself) is truly hilarious.

(Danny Peary, Guide for the Film Fanatic)

JOANNA LUMLEY

Actress, Prince Valiant (1997)

It would be kinder not to name anyone involved, but connoisseurs of ham-acting will not wish to miss Joanna Lumley as Morgan Le Fay, in the eye make-up Dusty Springfield rejected.

(Christopher Tookey, Daily Mail)

Actress, Parting Shots (1999)

A special word of commiseration must go to Joanna Lumley, wretchedly miscast as the proprietor of a gangland pub. She's about as convincing as Lady Olga Maitland, trying to play Dot Cotton in EastEnders.

(Christopher Tookey, Daily Mail)

DOLPH LUNDGREN

Actor, Masters of the Universe (1987)

After Arnold Schwarzenegger, Dolph Lundgren is a bit of a disappointment. At least Arnold looks as if he comes supplied with batteries.

(Adam Mars-Jones, Independent)

Actor, The Shooter (1995)

The dated, B-movie script is further undermined by the once-talented Ted Kotcheff's turgid direction and a leading actor (Dolph Lundgren) with all the charm and fluidity of a Sixties tower-block.

(Christopher Tookey, Daily Mail)

JOHN LYDON

Actor, Order of Death (1983)

The only miscalculation is the casting of Lydon (aka Johnny Rotten), who seems as threatening as a wet poodle.

(Chris Peachment, Time Out)

KELLY LYNCH

Actress, The Desperate Hours (1987)

Kelly Lynch plays the high-powered lawyer in love with Mr Rourke, as though auditioning for the role of a deranged hooker in a John Waters movie.

(Christopher Tookey, Sunday Telegraph)

Kelly Lynch, as a micro-skirted bimbo whose blouse keeps flapping open, is the cinema's least convincing lawyer since Cher in Suspect.

(Simon Rose)

Actress, Three of Hearts (1993)

The film's view of lesbianism is laughably crude. Lynch's idea of playing butch is to walk like a chimpanzee on a rolling ship.

(Christopher Tookey, Daily Mail)

ADRIAN LYNE

Director, 9 ½ Weeks (1986)

It only seems that long.

(Simon Rose, Essential Film Guide, 1993)

Lyne directs as though advertising something, possibly sado-masochism, but it might equally well be the hi-fi equipment and furniture in Rourke's apartment.

(Christopher Tookey, Sunday Telegraph)

ANDIE MACDOWELL

Actress, Four Weddings and a Funeral (1994)

Andie MacDowell looks ravishing enough for anyone to be smitten at first sight, but as a light comedienne she is disastrous. Her idea of sprightly repartee is to pronounce every syllable, and she can't quite hide the furrow of perplexity around her eyes - she doesn't seem to grasp her own witticisms. She is not helped, either, by having to pretend that she has fallen for someone who looks like a chipmunk.

(Caren Myers, Sight and Sound)

ALI MACGRAW

Actress, Love Story (1970)

Ali McGraw is horribly smug and smirky. If you share my impulses, whenever she gets facetious you'll probably want to wham her one.

(Pauline Kael, New Yorker)

What can you say about a twenty-five year-old girl who died? That she loved Mozart, Bach, The Beatles... and Ryan O'Neal. Sadly, this movie's about her love for O'Neal, who'd be the worst actor in the movie if it weren't for co-star Ali McGraw. Staring at each other all dewy-eyed, the two handle lame dialogue with all the style and grace of the leads in as junior high-school play.

(Michael Sauter, The Worst Movies of All Time)

KYLE MACLACHLAN

Actor, Show Girls (1995)

Show Girls has the distinction of being the first movie about Las Vegas that is actually more vulgar than Las Vegas. Zack is played by Kyle MacLachlan, a real actor, who, for the purposes of the movie, graciously sinks to the level of the other performers.

(Anthony Lane, New Yorker)

SHIRLEY MACLAINE

To read Shirley Maclaine's autobiography is to encounter one of the most inflated airheads ever to break free of her moorings.

(John Preston, Sunday Telegraph)

The oars aren't touching the water these days.

(Dean Martin)

Actress, Sweet Charity (1969)

I like Miss MacLaine, but one thing is certain: she's not touched by a stroke of genius. She is not a great actress, she dances only adequately, and her singing voice is pleasant without any trace of power or presence.

(Rex Reed)

Actress, The Evening Star (1997)

Unwisely revisiting the role which won her an Oscar, MacLaine gives a performance of exasperating coarseness and egotism. There's an

exceptionally distasteful sexual liaison between MacLaine and Bill Paxton, playing a psychotherapist young enough to be her grandson. Yes, I know there's a sexual double standard - Sean Connery does get away with wooing women a third of his age - but he still looks pretty good; MacLaine here has all the allure of Albert Steptoe.

(Christopher Tookey, Daily Mail)

MADONNA

She has her defenders, and I suspect she loathes them even more than she scorns her enemies. She is disappointed about something, and hugely driven by resentment.

(David Thomson, A Biographical Dictionary of Film)

Actress, The Next Best Thing (2000)

So lean and toned that she resembles a watchful whippet, Madonna displays all the charm of a third world police state.

(Christopher Tookey, Daily Mail)

Madonna can barely muster even the rudiments of human expression.

(Steve Daly, Entertainment Weekly)

Actress, Swept Away (2002)

What Madonna does here can't properly be called acting - more accurately, it's moving and it's talking and it's occasionally gesturing, sometimes all at once.

(Rick Groen, Toronto Globe and Mail)

If there is one thing worse than a Guy Ritchie movie, it's a Guy Ritchie movie with Madonna in it.

(Rex Reed, New York Observer)

The film's a vehicle for Madonna, who, as everyone but her husband knows, has the acting talent of a pickled egg.

(Fiona Sturges, The Independent)

NORMAN MAILER

Actor, Eild 90 (1967)

I cannot say that Mailer was drunk the whole time he was on camera. I can only hope that he was drunk.

(Stanley Kauffmann, New Republic)

JOHN MALKOVICH

Actor, Dangerous Liaisons (1988)

Valmont is portrayed by Mr John Malkovich as a leering satyr, launching himself at women with a vulgar abandon that would get him banned from every respectable drawing-room in the land. Valmont had his faults, certainly, but lack of savoir faire was not one of them.

(Anne Billson, Film Review)

Actor, Of Mice and Men (1992)

Somewhere along the line the story of two friends on the road has become the Malkovich acting workshop roadshow. No sooner have Lenny and George walked into their new lodgings than, uh-oh, Malkovich has spotted a bed on which he can bounce up and down in an endearingly simple way. And who the hell let that puppy on the set? Too late, Malkovich has his hands on it and, well, he's mewling at it in this wonderfully simple way as well. Sinise does his best as the exasperated and occasionally irate George. But perhaps because he also directed the

movie he has made the mistake of being too self-effacing. You do your best to concentrate on him every now and again but, here we go again, Malkovich has just spotted another fold in his dungarees to fiddle with.

(Tom Shone, Mail on Sunday)

Actor, Mary Reilly (1996)

As for John Malkovich, he is so obviously the same man whether playing Dr Jekyll or Mr Hyde (to play Hyde, he simply shaves and puts on a Max Wall wig) that it's impossible to understand why his domestic staff don't spot the similarity or the fact that he's a modern method actor from New York.

(Christopher Tookey, Daily Mail)

Actor, Eragon (2006)

The only entertainment value lies in watching Malkovich, Irons and Carlyle compete to give the worst performance of 2006. Malkovich, at his laziest, seems to have turned up for only a couple of days during the shoot, never leaving his single set, and plays the thing as high camp, mincing about like Dale Winton as King Rat. "I am not interested in being challenged!" lisps this once acclaimed stage actor. How true.

(Christopher Tookey, Daily Mail)

I wish that I could push aside a filing cabinet somewhere and crawl through a secret passageway into Malkovich's brain for 15 minutes, just so I could learn what he was thinking when he signed on for this movie.

(Mike McGranaghan, Aisle Seat)

Actor, Mutant Chronicles (2008)

Note to John Malkovich: when reading your dialogue off highly visible cue-cards, try not to glance down before speaking each line.

(Tim Robey, Daily Telegraph)

TERRENCE MALICK

Writer, Director, The Thin Red Line (1998)

What Malick does is just a higher form of advertising art. He's not
exploring emotion; he's conceptualizing it, and not very clearly. There's
no there there in Malick's filmmaking, no horror to the battle scenes,
no sense that anything we're watching has a present tense, or any
dramatic weight, or anything requiring us to care.

(Charles Taylor, Salon Entertainment)

Malick has evidently decided to make a poetic art-house picture, one
that ignores the importance of narrative, characterisation or a sense of
period. The story is background for the scenery and New Age
philosophising that has nothing to do with the novel, World War II, or
the psychology of those who fought. Malick has never seen a tree he
didn't like, and though this might be admirable in a photographer for
Gardens Illustrated, it's downright weird in a war movie, and plays
havoc with pacing and plot. A novel notable for its variety of
character and brutal honesty has become a one-paced mood piece with
a Zen-like detachment from its subject-matter.

(Christopher Tookey, Daily Mail)

JANE MARCH

Actress, Color of Night (1994)

You know the film's really in trouble when Jane March, the erstwhile
"sinner from Pinner", turns up in her second bad movie, and claims to
be playing a "struggling actress". Actress is wrong, struggling is right;
for in this role (which a Jodie Foster or Debra Winger would have
found an insuperable challenge), she sinks without trace. Like another

Worst Actress of All Time, Pia Zadora, Miss March has taken the precaution of marrying her film's producer; but it must be doubtful whether even this can save a career which already looks dead in the jacuzzi.

(Christopher Tookey, Daily Mail)

JAMES MARCUS

Writer, Director, Tank Malling (1988)

Writer-director James Marcus's naivety makes the works of Daisy Ashford seem like the last word in sophistication. His inattention to detail would be sad, were it not laughable. The plot has the air of having being scrawled on a succession of beermats, several of which have got lost. Other movies have been almost as incompetently scripted, crudely directed and badly acted; but, in view of the way Tank Malling combines all these qualities with grotesque sexism, gratuitous violence and subnormal intelligence, there can be little doubt that this marks a new low in cinema.

(Christopher Tookey, Sunday Telegraph)

GARRY MARSHALL

Director, Pretty Woman (1990)

Critics have described it as a fairy tale, and I guess it is, if you can imagine the brothers Grimm confabbing poolside at the Beverly Hills Hotel with a gaggle of box- office-obsessed Touchstone execs... The first thing you should know about it is that it was directed by a man who became famous for doing the impossible - namely lowering the intellectual level of the television sitcom. This romantic comedy will do nothing to tarnish his reputation as a shlockmeister par excellence. It is the very model of the slick, formulaic contemporary star vehicle, the sort of glossy, diverting, outrageously synthetic picture that nobody involved could possibly take seriously, a picture whose every last line feels as if it has been test-marketed. Next to Marshall, Steven Spielberg is an Italian neo-realist.

(Bruce Bawer, American Spectator)

Director, Valentine's Day (2010)

Suffice to say, the mysteries of the human heart aren't solved by Garry Marshall's Love Actually-style ensemble rom-com. It's more like an all-star perfect teeth and hair convention you'd like to firebomb.

(Tim Robey, Daily Telegraph)

DEAN MARTIN

Actor, The Ambushers (1967)

Martin at times becomes a caricature of himself playing himself, and comes across as a male Mae West.

(Art Murphy, Variety)

Martin's acting is so inept that even his impersonation of a lush is unconvincing.

(Harry Medved, The 50 Worst Movies of All Time)

STEVE MARTIN

Actor, My Blue Heaven (1990)

About as hilarious as a hernia.

(Christopher Tookey, Sunday Telegraph)

Actor, The Pink Panther (2006)

As Inspector Clouseau, Steve Martin is so dead behind the eyes nowadays that he resembles an assassin, which in a way he is. He slaughters every potential laugh, as surely as he joylessly mutilates the memory of Peter Sellers.

(Christopher Tookey, Daily Mail)

Actor, Baby Mama (2008)

Steve Martin has a truly awful cameo as Tina's hippy boss, which only goes to prove that Steve Martin with a pony tail doesn't really look any more or less of a twerp than Steve Martin without a pony tail.

(Robbie Collin, News of the World)

Actor, The Pink Panther 2 (2009)

A creaky Martin, now so dead behind the eyes that he could be mainlining Nurofen, hams haplessly as the clumsy cop, and the body-doubles for his stunts are painfully obvious. Peter Sellers would be funnier turning in his grave, and probably livelier.

(Christopher Tookey, Daily Mail)

LEE MARVIN

Actor, Paint Your Wagon (1969)

Marvin sounds like a bullfrog and looks like one too.

(Michael Sauter, The Worst Movies of All Time)

MARCELLO MASTROIANNI

Actor, A Place for Lovers (1969)

Marcello Mastroianni displays all the zest of a man summoned up for tax evasion.

(Time)

WALTER MATTHAU

Actor, Cactus Flower (1969)

Walter Matthau, a modestly pleasant but vastly overrated actor who looks and acts like Smokey the Bear sleeping through a four-alarm fire, continues to draw top salaries by walking through his roles as though in an advanced state of hypnosis; Frankly, I don't blame him. Helps to get through movies like Cactus Flower without wincing.

(Rex Reed, Holiday)

PAUL MATTHEWS

Writer, Director, Merlin: The Return (2000)

Paul Matthews claims a triple credit as Producer, Director and Writer. His is a name to remember. Compared with this guy, Edward D. Wood was talented.

(Christopher Tookey, Daily Mail)

VICTOR MATURE

Actor, Samson and Delilah (1949)

First film I ever saw where the leading man had bigger tits than the leading lady.

(Groucho Marx)

RIK MAYALL

Actor, Drop Dead Fred (1991)

Mr Mayall, at his least disciplined, gives a laughter-freezing performance that makes one yearn for the sophistication of Pee Wee Herman.

(Christopher Tookey, Sunday Telegraph)

Writer, Actor, Guest House Paradiso (1999)

There is an audience for this film. There is for every film. It's just a little difficult to imagine who it might be but they would have to satisfy the following criteria: They would think watching endless projectile vomiting is hysterically funny. That silly voices are funny. That grown men hitting each other over the head and torturing every body part is funny. That bashing old women is funny. That the threat of rape is funny. That the names of Italian characters like Gina Carbonara and Gino Bolognese are funny. That jokes you can see coming an hour before they're delivered are funny. That the type of material that made The Young Ones funny a very, very long time ago can still be funny. That a gem such as Fawlty Towers can be made funnier. That a comedy doesn't need a plot. That a man running around in women's spiky rubber underwear is funny.

(Lee Gough, Urban Cinefile, Australia)

Why, though, when he has already made a fool of himself in monstrosities as ghastly as Drop Dead Fred and Bring Me The Head of Mavis Davis, does Mayall take pains to come across as even more imbecilic than usual? The worst sights of the year are Mayall showing off his protruding paunch in underpants and red rubber bondage gear, apparently trying to look as much as possible like a perverted pig. At one point, he pulls faces in order to impersonate someone who's mentally ill. Did he really think this was necessary?

(Christopher Tookey, Daily Mail)

Rik Mayall and Adrian Edmondson were sharing a dish of sick one morning, when Rik said, 'Why don't we make the worst film in the world?' Ade said, 'Why?' Rik said, 'It would be reeeally annoying.' Ade said, 'You mean, worse than Mad Cows?' Rik said, 'Worse than Final Cut.' Ade said, 'That bad?' Rik said, 'Worse!' And so they went down to Ealing Studios and shot the film. Dead. Ade directed. Rik stuck out his bum and minced. The jokes ranged from punching Fenella Fielding in the face, having Rik's testicles squeazed in a nut cracker, beating up Ade with an iron frying pan, feeding hotel guests radioactive fish, watching Rik run around in a spikey red rubber bikini and projecting vomit down a corridor with the force of a fire hose.

(Angus Wolfe Murray, Eye for Film)

Actor, Merlin: The Return (2000)

Heading the cast as King Arthur's elderly adviser, Rik Mayall is neither believable nor amusing, capering about and leering like an especially annoying paedophile.

(Christopher Tookey, Daily Mail)

You get the feeling that Rik Mayall was under some sort of Crap Acting Spell.

(Total Film)

MATTHEW MCCONAUGHEY

Actor, Reign of Fire (2002)

If you thought Matthew McConaughey lost his mind a while back when he was caught playing the bongos naked in his home, wait until you see him in Reign of Fire.

(Josh Larsen, Sun Publications)

Actor, Failure To Launch (2006)

The pairing of Sarah Jessica Parker and Matthew McConaughey generates as many sparks as a soaked match in a rainstorm.

(James Berardinelli, Reelviews)

Actor, Fool's Gold (2008)

If there is a romantic comedy Hell, Matthew McConaughey and Kate Hudson surely stand at the gates waving people in.

(Matt Kelemen, Las Vegas CityLife)

Just how long will it be before Matthew McConaughey finally fulfills his destiny by dropping out of Hollywood and opening a chain of nudist colonies? His heart clearly isn't in acting right now, so when it was time to make Fool's Gold, he asked his abs to do the job for him.

(Elizabeth Weitzman, New York Daily News)

McConaughey bravely rips off his shirt, throws himself in front of the women and selflessly absorbs the camera's leers.

(Josh Larsen, Sun Publications, Chicago)

No amount of gratuitous McConaughey ab-flashing (he never stops) or the parading of Kate Hudson in a weeny bikini can scrape this one off the sea bed. Plankton would be insulted.

(Julia Raeside, Film 4)

Actor, The Ghosts of Girlfriends Past (2009)

He simply has no gift for comedy – physical or verbal – because he always seems to be looking past the camera, winking at the audience, whether he's dropping cheesy pick-up lines or ineptly managing a bit of slapstick involving a collapsing wedding cake, during which he whinnies like one of the Three Stooges...Who is it exactly that thinks Matthew McConaughey is funny?

(Marshall Fine, Hollywood and Fine)

Any film starring the self-regarding, teak-veneered charisma vacuum that is Matthew McConaughey has more to overcome than most.

(Wendy Ide, Times)

The whole concept founders on McConaughey's unalterable cheesiness.

(Edward Porter, Sunday Times)

In the worst performance of his career – and he was rightly ridiculed for Fool's Gold and Failure To Launch - McConaughey plays Connor as so insufferable that Jenny would obviously be much better off with somebody else. Anybody else. Even Russell Brand would be an improvement.

(Christopher Tookey, Daily Mail)

MCG

Director, Charlie's Angels (2000)

The director so underestimates his audience, he all but stands in the aisles and tells us what morons we are.

(Robert Wilonsky, New Times Los Angeles)

Director, Charlie's Angels: Full Throttle (2003)

This is not merely one of the worst films in recent memory but it could well go down as one of the worst things ever conceived by human hands - that is, if it gave any evidence that was actually made by human beings instead of by robots hell-bent on destroying humanity by turning human minds to mush.

(Peter Sobczynski, Critic Doctor)

Director, Terminator: Salvation (2009)

Lives up to his nickname by showing off all the directorial skills of your average bacon double cheeseburger.

(Robbie Collin, News of the World)

ALI MCGRAW

Actress, Love Story (1970)

I can never remember seeing a movie where I wanted someone to die as much as Ali McGraw in Love Story.

(Joe Queenan)

EWAN MCGREGOR

Actor, Star Wars Episode 1 – The Phantom Menace (1999)

Ewan McGregor announced around the time he was making this film that he was going to give up acting for a while; my feeling is that he should have waited until after appearing in this movie to go on sabbatical. Playing the young Obi-Wan Kenobi, this normally sparky actor gives a cowed, constipated imitation of Alec Guinness. For much of the movie, he seems to be heavily sedated, which makes Liam Neeson's description of him as "headstrong" seem over-optimistic.

(Christopher Tookey, Daily Mail)

As for Ewan McGregor, what happened? He looks as if he just sat on the sharp end of his lightsabre. It must have taken some nerve to drain the charisma out of this cheerful Scotsman and force him to speak like Noel Coward. McGregor may well be laughed off the screen when the movie opens in Britain - an unthinkable turn of events. His first words in the film are "I have a bad feeling about this". Yes, laddie, and you've got two more episodes to go.

(Anthony Lane, New Yorker)

Actor, Star Wars II: Attack of the Clones (2002)

Ewan McGregor still soldiers on as the Jedi knight to whom Anakin is apprenticed, Obi-Wan Kenobi. He has a bit more to do than in the first movie, where he seemed to spend most of his time standing slightly behind Liam Neeson's left ear, as though inspecting it for psoriasis. He's saddled with a lot of wisecracks that are intended to show how cool he is under pressure. He delivers these with a passable imitation of Sir Alec Guinness's accent, but they just make him sound like Roger Moore in the darker period of the James Bond franchise. This most boyishly mischievous of actors seems ground down by the cares of looking after an apprentice. It's a terrible waste.

(Christopher Tookey, Daily Mail)

Actor, Star Wars III: Revenge of the Sith (2005)

McGregor manages to be simultaneously stiff and lightweight, a kind of balsa-wood sage with a sandy beard that has apparently been ripped untimely from the visage of Bjorn from Abba.

(Jenny McCartney, Sunday Telegraph)

If Hayden Christensen is poor, Ewan McGregor is abysmal. So flat are his line-readings that at one point it crossed my mind that he had fallen out with George Lucas and was deliberately trying to show how terrible his lines are. Even when threatening others ("You won't get away with this, Dookus!") he sounds as uninterested as it is possible to be. And his timing when delivering Han Solo-style wisecracks is way, way off. Much of his dialogue sounds as if it's been revoiced by Keanu Reeves. And in a climactic sequence taking place on molten lava, McGregor forgets even to look slightly warm.

(Christopher Tookey, Daily Mail)

Actor, Angels & Demons (2009)

Ewan McGregor can also be seen acting, in a way, as Camerlengo Patrick McKenna, a character apparently modelled on Father Ted's Most Boring Priest In The World. Possibly the first man in film history, is Ewan, to be out-acted by the statues.

(Robbie Collin, News of the World)

As the second most important character in the movie, Camerlengo Patrick McKenna, the late Pope's confidante and adopted son, the pitifully lightweight Ewan McGregor affects an Oirish accent, which is more of an attempt to act than he's made in any of his last twenty movies. Unsurprisingly, he fails to make sense of a character whose actions and speeches throughout are papal bull.

(Christopher Tookey Daily Mail)

SIOBHAN MCKENNA

Actress, King of Kings (1961)

As the Virgin Mary, Siobhan McKenna looks like somebody's aunt impersonating the Mona Lisa.

(Dilys Powell, Sunday Times)

NORMAN Z. MCLEOD

Director, Panama Hattie (1942)

This film needs a certain something. Possibly burial.

(David Lardner)

SHANE MEADOWS

Writer, Director, Dead Man's Shoes (2004)

Though Meadows shoots in a cinema-verite style, the transparent lack of realism – the police are nowhere to be seen, and the crooks are unbelievably useless at defending themselves – means that the film becomes tediously predictable extremely quickly. A few critics have long been touting Shane Meadows as the Great White Hope of British cinema, but I'm afraid I still see him more as the Great White Hype.

(Christopher Tookey, Daily Mail)

Writer, Director, This Is England (2008)

The film descends into a risibly belated example of Thatcher-bashing, as Mr Meadows strives to draw a glib and spurious parallel between the rise of the National Front and the then Prime Minister's reconquest of the Falklands. Hardly a Shane Meadows film comes out with someone hailing it as a masterpiece by one of Britain's finest directors, but the poor plotting, sledgehammer symbolism and sheer ugliness of his work continue to leave me less than impressed.

(Christopher Tookey, Daily Mail)

This is England is a vile exercise in nihilism that goes nowhere fast.

(Rex Reed, New York Observer)

BETTE MIDLER

Actress, Stella (1989)

Bette Midler, showed a talent for melodrama in Beaches and The Rose, but here she's so far over the top that the director should have brought her down to earth, if necessary with anti-aircraft fire. The final scene, where she turns up anonymously in a plastic mac, headscarf and varicose-veined leg-pads to watch her daughter marry, warm and safe from the rainstorm outside, is a memorable acting tour de farce.

(Christopher Tookey, Sunday Telegraph)

Midler, who probably cannot spell "subtle", plays the sacrificing mom as an emotional terrorist, and doesn't notice that her co-stars steal scenes simply by being attentive. Unbelievably bad.

(John Harkness, Film Review)

Actress, Jinxed (1982)

She's got big tits but thank God she's got them, because she hasn't got anything else.

(Divine)

ANTHONY MINGHELLA

Writer, Director, The English Patient (1996)

The problem with the English Patient is that to enjoy it, you have to be either English or patient.

(Joe Queenan)

LIZA MINNELLI

I always thought Liza Minnelli's face deserving of first prize in a beagle category.

(John Simon, National Review)

Actress, Cabaret (1972)

The film's irredeemable disaster is its Sally Bowles: changing her into an American was bad enough; into Liza Minnelli, catastrophe. Miss Minnelli cannot act any part without calling attention to how hard she is working at it and how far she is from having worked it out. She cannot even move right - in this case, like a sexy cabaret artiste and thriving nymphomaniac; instead, she rattles around gawkily and disjointedly, like someone who never got over being unfeminine and unattractive. Plain, ludicrously rather than pathetically plain, is what Miss Minnelli is. That turnipy nose overhanging a forward-gaping mouth and hastily retreating chin, that bulbous cranium with eyes as big (and as inexpressive) as saucers; those are the appurtenances of a clown - a funny clown, not even a sad one. And given a matching figure - desperately uplifted breasts, waist indistinguishable from hips - you just cannot play Sally Bowles. Especially if you have no talent. In fact, Miss Minnelli has only two things going for her: a father and a mother who got her there in the first place, and tasteless reviewers and audiences who keep her there.

(John Simon, National Review)

Actress, Lucky Lady (1975)

Age cannot wither, nor make-up stale, her infinite sameness. She is herself a perfect ménage a trois in which lack of talent, lack of looks, and lack of a speaking voice cohabit blissfully. Stanley Donen sensibly concentrates on her best feature, her legs, but he unfortunately can't wrap them around her face.

(John Simon, National Review)

Actress, New York, New York (1977)

Liza Minnelli, difficult to like at best, comes out looking like a giant rodent en route to a costume ball.

(Stanley Kauffmann, New Republic)

ROBERT MITCHUM

Listen, I've got three expressions: looking left, looking right and looking straight ahead.

(Robert Mitchum)

Actor, Out of the Past (1947)

Mitchum's curious languor, which suggests Bing Crosby supersaturated with barbiturates, becomes a brand of sexual complacency that is not endearing.

(James Agee, Time)

ALFRED MOLINA

Actor, Anna Karenina (1997)

In the role of Constantin Levin, supposedly an intellectual, gentleman farmer (whom Rose ultimately reveals, in a farcically misjudged postscript, to be none other than Leo Tolstoy himself), Alfred Molina plays the whole thing as though operating a dodgy mini-cab service out of Edgware.

(Christopher Tookey, Daily Mail)

MARILYN MONROE

She's a vacuum with nipples.

(Otto Preminger)

She's an arrogant little tail-twitcher who learned to throw sex in your face.

(Nunnally Johnson)

She's the original good time that was had by all.

(Bette Davis)

She was good at playing abstract confusion in the same way that a midget is good at being short... As far as talent goes, Marilyn Monroe was so minimally gifted as to be unemployable, and anyone who holds to the opinion that she was a great natural comic identifies himself immediately as a dunce.

(Clive James, Observer)

Actress, Some Like It Hot (1959)

She has breasts of granite and a mind like a Gruyere cheese.

(Billy Wilder)

Acting with her was like kissing Hitler.

(Tony Curtis)

DEMI MOORE

I like Demi Moore. But that's because I have no taste.

(Joe Queenan)

Actress, The Butcher's Wife (1991)

An innocent young clairvoyant from the sticks (Demi Moore) disrupts the life of a pompous New York shrink (Jeff Daniels). It doesn't help that Moore wears one of the world's worst wigs and looks about as innocent as Robert Maxwell.

(Christopher Tookey, Sunday Telegraph)

Actress, The Scarlet Letter (1995)

Demi Moore is nobody's idea of a 17th century Puritan, and languorous shots of her caressing herself in a bath look like something designed for the Playboy channel.

(Christopher Tookey, Daily Mail)

Actress, Striptease (1996)

In addition to Moore's non-gifts as an actress, she displays a galloping narcissism that is horrible to behold. Striptease resembles one of those Joan Collins mini-series where the supporting actors are obliged every few moments to say how beautiful she is. Perhaps Ms. Moore's body conforms to some people's idea of femininity; but the last time I saw thighs like that, they were on Daley Thompson. And most men probably prefer to see a bosom that moves when the rest of its owner does. Moore's idea of a come-on is to look at men as though they're cockroaches and tear off her clothes as though they're hand grenades. With her "go thither" eyes, iron-hard torso and breasts like Scud missiles, she has all the warmth and sensuality of Saddam Hussein.

(Christopher Tookey, Daily Mail)

Actress, Mr Brooks (2007)

These days watching Moore act, all you can think is: 'Wow, look at all that plastic surgery!"

(Cosmo Landesman, Sunday Times)

Demi manages the difficult feat of looking simultaneously wooden and plastic. Cut into strips by a careful serial killer, she would make marvellous decking.

(Christopher Tookey, Daily Mail)

MICHAEL MOORE

Nobody outside of Hollywood seriously believes that Moore likes or cares about working-class people, and, for their part, working-class people are either oblivious to his existence or despise him. Nor is anybody fooled by the faux prole headgear any more: a young man in a red baseball cap is an imp; a middle-aged man in a baseball cap is a buffoon.

(Joe Queenan)

Writer, Director, Bowling For Columbine (2002)

Moore is telling enemies of America what they want to hear, so the usual range of kneejerk liberals and gullible idiots will happily confuse Bowling for Columbine with crusading journalism. Really, it's carefully selective propaganda – smug, unscrupulous self-promotion by a man who oozes fake sympathy for those he bullies, and mistakes superior smirking for satire. Michael Moore is a shameless fake, the Gilderoy Lockhart of the Loony Left.

(Christopher Tookey, Daily Mail)

Moore's bag of tricks is familiar from Roger & Me - smirking, oozing false sympathy, insinuating, fiddling with facts - and it works best the first time you see it.

(Jim Lane, Sacramento News & Review)

ROGER MOORE

If I kept all my bad notices, I'd need two houses.

(Roger Moore)

Playing James Bond? Sometimes I wear a white dinner jacket, sometimes a black one.

(Roger Moore)

I may not be as good as Olivier but I'm taller than he is.

(Roger Moore)

Actor, Moonraker (1979)

Roger Moore is dutiful and passive as Bond, his clothes are neatly pressed and he shows up for work, like an office manager who is turning into dead wood but hanging on to collect his pension.

(Pauline Kael, New Yorker)

Actor, For Your Eyes Only (1981)

Roger Moore fronts for a succession of stunt men with all the relaxed, lifelike charm of a foyer poster of himself.

(Sunday Times)

Actor, A View to a Kill (1985)

Roger Moore as James Bond: not so much like a piece of plastic as something embalmed but moving.

(David Shipman)

I was only about 400 years too old for the part.

(Roger Moore)

SAMANTHA MORTON

Actress, Code 46 (2003)

Mr. Robbins and Ms. Morton are not the warmest actors. He can be mannered and smug, and she often seems to beam her performances from a strange, private mental universe.

(A.O. Scott, New York Times)

As in Morvern Callar, it's just possible to glimpse that she has extraordinary talent, but yet again she seems perversely determined to misapply it. She drifts through this film like a neurotic marmoset, blissed out on her own close-ups.

(Christopher Tookey, Daily Mail)

JOSH MOSTEL

Actor, Jesus Christ, Superstar (1973)

As Herod, young Mr Mostel, who manages the difficult feat of reaching the grotesque while totally bypassing the funny, has not inherited any of the Mostel from his father, only the Zero.

(John Simon, National Review)

ZERO MOSTEL

Actor, The Producers (1968)

Zero Mostel rolls his eyes on the screen as if he were running a bowling alley in his skull.

(Andrew Sarris, Village Voice)

Actor, The Front (1976)

Hearing Mostel speak these days is like having him fall on you, repeatedly.

(Stanley Kauffmann, New Republic)

EDDIE MURPHY

Actor, Beverly Hills Cop (1984)

With Murphy bursting his sides guffawing in self-congratulation, and the camera jammed into his tonsils, damned if the audience doesn't whoop and carry on as if, yes, this is a wow of a comedy. Murphy's aggressive oneupmanship through most of the film kills your interest in him as a performer.

(Pauline Kael, New Yorker)

Actor, Writer, Director, Harlem Nights (1989)

In Harlem Nights, Eddie Murphy continues his one-man war against the female gender. Those women he doesn't kill outright are punched, maimed and slugged with garbage cans. But apparently they deserve it - there isn't a single female character in the film who isn't a prostitute.

(Dave Kehr, Chicago Tribune)

The most horrible indictment of the Hollywood star system since Barbra Streisand's Yentl. The opening titles say it all: Paramount pictures have made 'in association with Eddie Murphy Productions' a 'film by Eddie Murphy', starring Eddie Murphy, executive produced by Eddie Murphy, written and directed by... Eddie Murphy. The picture which follows is the cinematic equivalent of vanity publishing: a lame-brain rip-off of 1930s gangster films, and an embarrassing failure in virtually every department. The plot is risible, the execution without wit. The language is that of the gutter, and an extremely filthy, modern gutter at that. As if to compensate for being so up-to-the-moment verbally, the film's morality - in particular, its attitude towards women - is neanderthal. All complaints should be addressed to Eddie Murphy.

(Christopher Tookey, Sunday Telegraph)

Actor, The Adventures of Pluto Nash (2002)

Murphy's latest comedy, The Adventures of Pluto Nash, takes place in the year 2087, which is about the earliest he can hope to be forgiven.

(Jack Mathews, New York Daily News)

Actor, The Haunted Mansion (2003)

Nowadays, folks say "remember when Eddie Murphy could make you laugh" the same way they say "remember the Alamo."

(Mark Ramsey, Moviejuice)

Actor, Norbit (2007)

Murphy is back in the laugh-free doldrums with Norbit. He co-scripted and produced it and he plays three roles (a nerd, his fat wife and an elderly Chinese restaurateur). Most of the jokes concern obesity, which Murphy evidently believes to be ipso facto funny.

(Philip French, Observer)

Actor, Meet Dave (2008)

On just about every occasion in Meet Dave, Murphy appears to be on the verge of cracking himself up. This is good news. At least someone found him funny.

(Wesley Morris, Boston Globe)

MIKE MYERS

Actor, Writer, So I Married an Axe Murderer (1993)

Myers, who plays both the hero and his father very badly, is the least charming comedian in movies since Jerry Lewis. And his compulsion to expose his bottom in every movie he makes strikes me as unwise, unhealthy and aesthetically ill-advised.

(Christopher Tookey, Daily Mail)

Actor, Writer, Austin Powers: The Spy Who Shagged Me (1999)

A stronger directorial hand was needed than Jay Roach's to stop the film from becoming grossly distended by Myers' antics, which suggest a dangerously high level of inane self-satisfaction.

(Christopher Tookey, Daily Mail)

MIKE MYERS

Actor, The Cat in the Hat (2003)

Never before has a title character sucked the energy and humor out of a project the way Myers does when he prances across the screen. His black cat is a Roach Motel of comedy. Jokes go in, but the laughs don't come out.

(Sean O'Connell, Filmcritic.com)

Actor, Writer, The Love Guru (2008)

Like a kid with a mallet and a toy that makes noise, Mike Myers just keeps hitting his audience over the head until they're so delirious that maybe they'll laugh. One of the least funny movies in years, The Love Guru could be used as a torture device to get enemy combatants to talk.

(Videohound's Movieretriever.com)

The always creepily self-indulgent Myers has written about three good jokes for the first five minutes, but then repeats them over and over and over again until you have lost the will to live. His habit of laughing uproariously at himself may also make you want to murder him, especially when he comes up with such witticisms as "I think I just made a happy wee-wee" or "I'm making diarrhoea noises in my cup" and giggles in a way that he clearly believes is boyishly winsome. An all too obviously tragic victim of celebrity self-love, Myers doesn't seem to know if his character is an idiot savant, or merely an idiot. Amazingly, he does seem to think he's sexy.

(Christopher Tookey, Daily Mail)

MIKE NEWELL

Director, The Awakening (1980)

It is difficult to imagine a film more likely to send you to sleep.

(Guardian)

Director, Prince of Persia: Sands of Time (2010)

Newell directs it all like a jolly uncle at Christmas time, hogging the kids' new PlayStation, and doing so enthusiastically enough that no one has the heart to tell him he's holding the controller upside down.

(Tim Robey, Daily Telegraph)

ANTHONY NEWLEY

Actor, Writer, Director, Can Hieronymus Merkin Ever Forget Mercy Humppe and Find True Happiness? (1969)

Anthony Newley has now cornered the market on Hollywood-style pornography. I'm not sure he'll ever work again, and quite frankly, I'm not sure he deserves to. He dances in the nude, performs cunnilingus on a naked girl under-water, sings a song called What a Son of a Bitch I Am and, for the crowning blow, actually allows a dirty old letch to run his hand up his own baby daughter's dress in a scene that has to win some kind of award for the penultimate in rotten bad taste. If I'd been Anthony Newley I would have opened it in Siberia during Christmas week and called it a day.

(Rex Reed)

A rather seedy monument to Anthony Newley's totally uninteresting sex life, and to the talent which he obviously thinks he possesses. The few mildly amusing moments are not provided by him.

(Leslie Halliwell, Halliwell's Film Guide)

PAUL NEWMAN

Actor, The Silver Chalice (1954)

Paul Newman, a lad who resembles Marlon Brando, delivers his lines with the emotional fervor of a Putnam Division conductor announcing local stops.

(John McCarten, New Yorker)

Actor, Sweet Bird of Youth (1962)

Something will have to be done about Mr Newman. He is simply not an actor and possibly not even alive; seems to be carved from wood, his movements stiff and jerky as a marionette, his one expression an agonized grimace as of wood trying to smile.

(Dwight Macdonald, Esquire)

ROBERT NEWTON

Actor, This Happy Breed (1944)

Although he doesn't roll his eyes as much as he did as Long John Silver in Treasure Island, he is clearly lost without his wooden leg and his parrot.

(Ken Russell, 1993)

THANDIE NEWTON

Actress, The Truth About Charlie (2003)

She wanders through Charlie completely unaware she needs to show some presence and star quality.

(Victoria Alexander, Filmsinreview.com)

OLIVIA NEWTON-JOHN

Actress, Xanadu (1980)

Newton-John is as close to non-existent as a pretty girl can be. Her acting is one-dimensional, her singing hardly better, and try as she might, she simply can't dance. She visibly loses her footing during one big production number. Very embarrassing for a modern-day Terpsichore.

(Michael Sauter, The Worst Movies of All Time)

JACK NICHOLSON

Actor, The Shining (1980)

In making The Shining Jack Nicholson told of how Stanley Kubrick had pushed him into an acting style beyond naturalism. Clips of Jack in action proved that there is no acting style beyond naturalism except ham.

(Clive James, Observer)

Actor, Batman (1989)

Jack Nicholson's performance has the unselfish, self-effacing quality of Sir Donald Wolfit upstaging a performance of Hamlet by riding a unicycle across the Niagara Falls in lurex hot pants.

(Christopher Tookey, Sunday Telegraph)

DAVID NIVEN

Actor, Dodsworth (1935)

In this picture we are privileged to see Mr Samuel Goldwyn's latest "discovery". All we can say about this actor is that he is tall, dark and not the slightest bit handsome.

(Detroit Free Press)

Actor, Bonnie Prince Charlie (1948)

David Niven rallying his hardy Highlanders to his standard in a voice hardly large enough to summon a waiter.

(New Yorker)

Actor, The Elusive Pimpernel (1950)

Niven plays the Scarlet Pimpernel with the sheepish lack of enthusiasm of a tone deaf man called upon to sing solo in church.

(Daily Express)

CHISTOPHER NOLAN

Writer, Director, Inception (2010)

Director Christopher Nolan is such a master movie technician - a combination of engineer, architect, game designer and God - that it's startling to realize how constricted his vision is and how clumsily he tells stories... Inception is a handsome, clever and grindingly self-serious boy-movie, shorn of imagination, libido, spirituality or emotional depth.

(Andrew O'Hehir, Salon)

None of this prattling drivel adds up to one iota of cogent or convincing logic. You never know who anyone is, what their goals are, who they work for or what they're doing.

(Rex Reed, New York Observer)

Nolan's modus operandi here is to present a muddle at such a breakneck speed that it gets mistaken for profundity.

(Jenny McCartney, Sunday Telegraph)

NICK NOLTE

Actor, The Deep (1977)

With his attenuated forehead and befogged eyes, his prognathous and semicretinous aspect, he looks very much like one of those late and degenerate Hapsburg monarchs of Spain whom not even the brush of Velasquez could, or would, whitewash. Not only can he not act, he cannot even look and sound halfway intelligent during the rare moments when the screenplay calls for it.

(John Simon, National Review)

Actor, The Good Thief (2002)

Nick Nolte has always had that look euphemistically described as "lived in"; he now looks as though squatters have moved in, trashed the place and left.

(Christopher Tookey, Daily Mail)

CHRIS O'DONNELL

Actor, In Love and War (1997)

Richard Attenborough's weakest film casts Chris McDonnell, with extreme improbability, as the young Ernest Hemingway. What next: Patsy Kensit as Virginia Woolf? As a casting decision, it's as weird as Attenborough's original intention of casting Albert Finney as Gandhi. McDonnell is so cockily obnoxious that I spent the entire film hoping that his lovely leading lady (Sandra Bullock, who acts charmingly but doesn't look in period) would see sense and have nothing more to do with him.

(Christopher Tookey, Daily Mail)

O'Donnell can't handle any nuance subtler than boyish hurt. He doesn't even wear a beard convincingly.

(Tom Gliatto, People Weekly)

MAUREEN O'HARA

Actress

She looked as though butter wouldn't melt in her mouth – or anywhere else.

(Elsa Lanchester)

MICHAEL OLIVER

Actor, Problem Child 2 (1992)

Oliver makes Macaulay Culkin look like Gene Hackman.

(Suzi Feay, Time Out)

LAURENCE OLIVIER

Actor, Othello (1965)

Larry's Othello looked like Al Jolson with palsy.

(Allison Pearson, Independent on Sunday)

Actor, Inchon (1981)

Wearing what looks like dance hall makeup, Olivier [playing General Macarthur at the time of the Korean war] presents the camera with a truly bizarre countenance, especially in closeup. His nose is altered with putty. His dyed black hair, augmented by a toupee, is plastered to his head. His eyes are lined with mascara. He's possibly wearing rouge. He's definitely wearing lipstick. He looks like a drag queen in an open casket.

(Michael Sauter, The Worst Movies of All Time)

ASHLEY & MARY-KATE OLSEN

Actresses, New York Minute (2004)

Have Ashley and Mary-Kate any talent? Well, they bear exactly the same relationship to acting as Tara Palmer-Tompkinson does to TV presenting. They share an enormous enthusiasm for pulling faces, a liking for pubescent clothes that show off their extreme skinniness, and an iron determination to be centre-screen at all times. I hated every moment of this deeply sinister, uniquely repellent exercise in child exploitation. Clearly this film is not aimed at me, but I suspect that even the audience for whom this tripe is being marketed as harmless fun may baulk at its money-grubbing cynicism. It makes Spiceworld: The Movie look like a work of shining creative integrity. Junk food causes obesity. This kind of junk cinema is more likely to encourage eating disorders and rampant consumerism in teenage girls who really, really wish to become, just like the Olsen girls, commodities.

(Christopher Tookey, Daily Mail)

RYAN O'NEAL

Actor, What's Up, Doc? (1972)

So stiff and clumsy that he can't even manage a part requiring him to be stiff and clumsy.

(Jay Cocks)

Actor, Barry Lyndon (1975)

Kubrick's lack of concern with his protagonist is underscored by his casting of Ryan O'Neal as Barry. This lump, this noodle, is meant to embody youth and high spirits, daring and deviltry, courage and susceptibility to the ways of cunning, all with a heart of at least some gold underneath, as shown by his love for his little son and his grief when the boy is killed. For all these qualities O'Neal supplies one expression through most of the picture, occasionally varied. Yes! You actually see the expression change sometimes! And as the O'Neal features are not very striking to begin with, we can only assume that Kubrick's concern lay elsewhere - an assumption heightened by the sound of O'Neal's accent, pure American only slightly disguised, juxtaposed with the accents of the several good Irish and English actors in the cast.

(Stanley Kauffmann, New Republic)

Actor, Driver (1978)

O'Neal is as bland as bleached bread.

(Alan Frank, Frank's 500)

WILLIAM OSBORNE

Writer, Fat Slags (2004)

Quite simply, everyone involved in making this truckload of tripe should be lined up against a wall and shot. It's hard to believe that William Osborne, the man responsible for penning this worst-film-of-all-time, once wrote the reasonably entertaining Twins.

(Gary Panton, Movie Gazette)

The awe-inspiringly inexpert screenplay is by William Osborne, whose previous offences against humanity include the Thunderbirds movie and Sylvester Stallone's stinker Stop, or My Mom Will Shoot! I say, chaps - enough is enough. Will somebody please confiscate his word processor before he can do any more damage?

(Christopher Tookey, Daily Mail)

PETER O'TOOLE

Peter O' Toole has a face that is not so much lived in as infested.

(Paul Taylor)

Peter O'Toole looks like he's walking around just to save the funeral expenses.

(John Huston)

Actor, Lawrence of Arabia (1962)

If Lawrence was corny, naively romantic and absurd, then I congratulate Mr O'Toole on a masterly portrait.

(Cassandra, Daily Mirror)

O'Toole's tormented hermaphrodite (his cerebral tensions conveyed by such a fierce working of cheek musculature it's as if his nerves were on fire) would have had a hard time directing a revolt of disaffected palace eunuchs - let alone a military campaign.

(Roger Sandall, Film Quarterly)

Actor, Fairytale: A True Story (1997)

Peter O' Toole's performance as Sir Arthur Conan Doyle reminds us that just because something has been captured on camera, it isn't necessarily believable.

(Edward Porter, Sunday Times)

CLIVE OWEN

Actor, I'll Sleep When I'm Dead (2004)

You'll sleep while it's on. It contains the worst performance ever by a near-robotic Clive Owen.

(Christopher Tookey, Daily Mail)

Actor, King Arthur (2004)

Owen has his first blockbuster lead here, but you could hardly accuse him of enjoying it much. Barely raising his voice above the usual Estuary monotone, he approximates the mien of a rattled maths teacher.

(Tim Robey, Daily Telegraph)

All this might not have been quite so laughably inane had the film's hero been even slightly charismatic. Screenwriter David Franzoni, amazingly the same man who wrote the excellent Gladiator, seems to have had Russell Crowe in mind for some would-be stirring battle-

scene rants. Clive Owen vocally just doesn't have the equipment. His wooden delivery of admittedly lousy lines evokes not so much a charismatic leader as an embarrassed south London copper giving false evidence on a witness stand. Instead of impressing us with his heroism, he comes across as a tedious nonentity. This is a career-destroying performance.

(Christopher Tookey, Daily Mail)

Actor, Derailed (2005)

The semi-alert Owen and the leaden Aniston go together like sausages and syrup.

(Lawrence Toppman, Charlotte Observer)

AL PACINO

Actor, Looking for Richard (1996)

Pacino is a terrible Richard, which makes the entire movie an arrogant and extremely annoying waste of time. Does he understand Shakespeare? Pacino either honks the lines ("A hawse! A hawse! My kingdom for a hawse!") or lets them dribble out. This Richard, bleary-eyed and charmless, could not connive his way past a nightclub bouncer.

(Tom Gliatto, People Weekly)

Actor, Gigli (2003)

Just as you think things can't get worse, Al Pacino comes on as a Godfather figure and shouts a lot, emphasising ALL THE wrong WORDS as only he can DO when totally out of DIRECTORIAL CONTROL, while sensitive members of the audience try to cover their eyes and ears simultaneously.

(Christopher Tookey, Daily Mail)

ALAN PARKER

Actor, 88 Minutes (2007)

Interestingly, the more overblown and insincere a performance Pacino delivers in a film, the more self-important and bouffant his hair gets. Here, it's so towering it takes up 90 per cent of the screen.

(Wendy Ide, Times)

ALAN PARKER

Director, Bugsy Malone (1976)

The film's gimmick is to turn the kids into appallingly realistic scale models of full-grown brutes and trollops for the amusement of whom, I wonder? Pederasts and child molesters certainly, who may find something deliciously provocative about tots got up as delinquent adults; some backward children, no doubt, who think this film exalts them; and adults benighted enough to perceive this offal as a lovable masquerade… What could Alan Parker & Company do for an encore? The history of the Campfire Girls performed entirely by androgynous Oriental giants? A movie about horse racing with all the horses played by kangaroos?

(John Simon, National Review)

The almost pornographic dislocation, which is the source of the film's possible appeal as a novelty, is never acknowledged, but the camera lingers on a gangster's pudgy, infantile fingers or a femme fatale's soft little belly pushing out of her tight satin dress, and it roves over the pubescent figures in the chorus line.

(Pauline Kael, New Yorker)

Writer, Director, Come See The Paradise (1990)

Like his fellow writer-director John Boorman, Alan Parker's biggest failing is that he can't write. The movie constantly grinds to a halt, to

make room for tracts of exposition. Dennis Quaid speaks more like a man who has undergone therapy during the 1980s than a working man in the 1940s. Worse still, Parker seems to think that subtext is dialogue in a submarine.

(Christopher Tookey, Sunday Telegraph)

SARAH JESSICA PARKER

Actress, Smart People (2008)

Sarah Jessica Parker's face, always equine in repose, keeps getting longer and longer, as though she's morphing into Edvard Munch's The Scream.

(Christopher Tookey, Daily Mail)

Actress, Sex & The City 2 (2010)

Sarah Jessica Parker's Carrie should be a cautionary tale of perpetual adolescence; her character should be out dating any number of Hollywood's graying beer bellied frat boys. But no. Instead, we are asked to identify and sympathize with a person who gets everything she wants, but complains anyway.

(John DeVore, Premiere)

When Carrie asks Big, "Am I just a bitch wife who nags you?" I could hear all the straight men in the theater - all four of us - being physically prevented from responding.

(Andrew O'Hehir, Salon)

If this is what modern womanhood means, then just fucking veil me and sew up all my holes. Good night.

(Lindy West, The Stranger, Seattle)

DEV PATEL

Actor, The Last Airbender (2010)

Poor Dev Patel, from Slumdog Millionaire, struggles to appear evil and masterful as fire prince Zuko while barking out instructions on ethnic cleansing that appear to have been compiled by someone not very scary at all, possibly Vince Cable. I especially enjoyed his order to some not terribly frightened villagers to "BRING ME ALL YOUR ELDERLY!"

(Christopher Tookey, Daily Mail)

JASON PATRIC

Actor, Speed 2 - Cruise Control (1997)

I left the theatre drenched in disappointment and missing Keanu Reeves. What is Jason Patric, after all, but Keanu without the passion, fire and intellect?

(Anthony Lane, New Yorker)

An actor who is like an action-man doll but without the facial mobility. Bullock starts bickering with him, in a way which is probably meant to evoke memories of Doris Day teasing Rock Hudson, but reminded me rather more of that edition of Have I Got News for You, where Paul Merton attempted conversation with a tub of lard.

(Christopher Tookey, Daily Mail)

Actor, Incognito (1997)

Jason Patric displays even less charisma than he did in Speed II, and his idea of playing a brilliant French art forger is to put on a beret.

(Christopher Tookey, Daily Mail)

GREGORY PECK

Actor, The Most Dangerous Man in the World (1969)

Peck plays the whole thing as though he is posing for a face-lift on Mt Rushmore.

(Rex Reed)

Actor, The Omen (1976)

As for Peck, he worries and suffers as nobly as only a piece of granite can.

(John Simon, National Review)

Mr. Peck expresses every emotion simply by raising his left eyebrow. It is a silken and elegantly arched eyebrow indeed, and it surely must have benefited from the work- out it received in this film. Is Mr. Peck shocked at the antics of his adopted son? Up goes the eyebrow. Is he pained at the loss of his wife? Up goes the eyebrow. Is he pursuing Damien in a murderous rage? Keep that eyebrow up there. Since the canine theme runs so prominently throughout this film, the analogy is inescapable: his left eyebrow plays the same expressive role for Mr. Peck as a wagging tail does for man's best friend.

(Harry Medved & Randy Dreyfuss,
The Fifty Worst Films of All Time)

Actor, Macarthur (1977)

To tell his years, in fact, you would have to saw him in two and count the rings. The actor tries to be granite but never gets beyond walnut. Maybe MacArthur really was like this; if so, he, also, could have been converted very nicely into a coffee table.

(John Simon, New York)

SAM PECKINPAH

Director, Writer, The Wild Bunch (1969)

Phony, pretentious piece of throat-slashing slobber... which goes around announcing good anti-violent intentions while exploiting and glorifying violence to the happy jungle of box-office coins... Peckinpah's philosophy of life appears to be that the world is totally corrupt, that there is no decency or morality left in society, and therefore the best thing to do is blow everyone's head off and have a great time doing it. He's a man to be pitied, not admired.

(Rex Reed)

ROBIN WRIGHT PENN

Actress, Message in a Bottle (1999)

Robin Wright Penn always reminds me of one of those fuzzy computer-composites of beautiful people, stuck on the neck of an ox.

(Anne Billson, Sunday Telegraph)

SEAN PENN

Actor, We're No Angels (1989)

De Niro's co-star, Sean Penn, succeeds in being even less impressive, method-acting his way through the proceedings with an anguished expression as though wishing he were somewhere else: a sentiment which will be shared by anyone foolhardy enough to sit through the entire fiasco.

(Christopher Tookey, Sunday Telegraph)

Actor, All The King's Men (2006)

Penn comes across like a grotesque, battery-driven 'Sean Penn' merchandising doll, grinning and gesticulating, flailing and fist-pumping, a terrible mix of the friendly autistic he played in I Am Sam (2001) and his hollering vigilante in Mystic River (2004). He's playing Willie Stark, a God-fearing New Orleans local politician who turns into a raving despot the minute he's made Governor. A good part, then. But this is a performance of such hopping hamminess that Willie seems not just inhuman but positively plastic, like the sort of awful novelty figurine you might see bobbing up and down on someone's dashboard. The way he looks doesn't help. Penn's hair is swept skywards in the style as worn by those little rubber trolls that still seem so popular. Nor does his voice – a caterwaul so effortlessly colourful half his lines are incomprehensible. But what makes Penn's performance most excruciating is its misplaced confidence.

(Catherine Shoard, Sunday Telegraph)

CLARE PEPLOE

Writer, Director, The Triumph of Love (2001)

Ever since Clare Peploe penned the so-called script to one of the most pretentious films of all time, Zabriskie Point, I have considered her one of cinema's outstanding bores, with a grotesquely inflated idea of her own artistry. Nothing in this picture causes me to reverse that opinion; indeed, her over-use of irritating jump-cuts and pointless shots of a present-day audience (intended, I would guess, to impress with how post-modernist she is) made me wonder instead why on earth anyone funds her. Far too much of this film resembles some long-lost series of costume playlets, written and directed by the late, great Ernie Wise.

(Christopher Tookey, Daily Mail)

PIPER PERABO

Actress, Coyote Ugly (2000)

Piper Perabo, who already used The Adventures of Rocky and Bullwinkle to prove she can't act, solidifies it here.

(Eric D. Snider, The Daily Herald)

Just about everything in Coyote Ugly is hard to believe, the most unbelievable being the fact that a worldwide talent search resulted in the casting of Perabo.

(Michael Dequina, themoviereport.com)

Actress, Imagine Me and You (2006)

Ms Perabo is too bland an actress. To call her "vanilla" would be an insult to ice cream.

(Christopher Tookey, Daily Mail)

ROSIE PEREZ

Rosie Perez's voice would drive me back to heroin.

(Charlie Sheen)

Actress, It Could Happen to You (1994)

Rose Perez has always been a one-note actress, and here settles for an irritating screech that sounds like a cat sliding down a blackboard.

(Christopher Tookey, Daily Mail)

Actress, Perdita Durango (1998)

The screeching Rosie Perez, an actress with the charm and sex appeal of a decomposing gerbil.

(Christopher Tookey, Daily Mail)

MATTHEW PERRY

Actor, The Whole Nine Yards (2000)

If you bottled Matthew Perry's talent and tried to sell it as cologne, it would smell like the innards of a rotting corpse and come in an eyedropper.

(Mr. Cranky, Mr Cranky Rates The Movies)

Almost everybody wants Matthew Perry dead in The Whole Nine Yards. This would be a good thing if it were to stop him from making more movies.

(Peter Howell, Toronto Star)

Actor, Serving Sara (2002)

I have tried to come up with reasons why Matthew Perry and Elizabeth Hurley would agree to appear in something like this. My guess is that Perry's judgment was, at the time, severely impaired by alcohol and/or drugs. Such an explanation seems entirely reasonable, since he doesn't even do a credible imitation of a competent actor.

(James Berardinelli, Reelviews)

MICHELLE PFEIFFER

Actress

I look like a duck.

(Michelle Pfeiffer)

RAIN PHOENIX

Actress, Even Cowgirls Get the Blues (1994)

Rain Phoenix, the awesomely untalented sister of the ill-fated River, turns out to be more of a slow drizzle.

(Christopher Tookey, Daily Mail)

HAROLD PINTER

Writer, Accident (1967)

This former and, occasionally, present actor has worked out a three-part program for himself. (1) Use dialogue with cryptic laconism; make it mostly commonplaces but surround these with an indefinable, lurking, omnipresent nastiness and have the most banal utterance bulge with an ill-concealed threat. (2) Stick in as many ugly jokes and befogging ambiguities as possible; even a sophomoric jape in a tart sauce of ambivalence strikes the gullible palate as haute cuisine. (3) When asked about your work, keep smilingly silent, or practice every form of put-down or put-on you can muster. (Being an actor helps.) You will thus shroud yourself in a tantalizing mystery and be a sort of intellectual Greta Garbo. With a measure of talent and mastery of this trio of tricks, you become the Kierkegaard of the kindergarten.

(John Simon, National Review)

Writer, The Comfort of Strangers (1991)

Pinter's script is a good example of how not to write a screen adaptation. As usual, Pinter's dialogue is repetitive, abstruse and literary. His stagey structure suggests not only that he has never written a film before, but also that he has never seen one.

(Christopher Tookey, Sunday Telegraph)

Writer, Sleuth (2007)

Pinter's inane, self-parodying script, which doesn't allow either character to do anything believable – would have defeated even Daniel Day Lewis or Johnny Depp. It's so lazy that Milo denies being a hairdresser in one act, then acknowledges without explanation that he is one in another. Pinter famously isn't fond of rewriting; it would help, though, if he could be bothered at least to re-read. This insultingly poor work suggests that not only has Pinter not seen Anthony Shaffer's stage play (a fact of which he boasts in the press notes), he seems not to have seen a feature film for around 30 years, nor met another sentient human being.

(Christopher Tookey, Daily Mail)

BILLIE PIPER

Actress, Spirit Trap (2005)

Billie Piper's accent wanders from Roedean to Romford, and she acts throughout as though recently stunned by falling masonry.

(Christopher Tookey, Daily Mail)

BRAD PITT

Actor, Interview With The Vampire: The Vampire Chronicles (1994)

As for Brad Pitt, different vampires may tell him he's beautiful, but actually he looks awkward in period costume - an unsmiling, inhibited actor with puffy lips and a dead voice.

(David Denby, New York)

Watching Pitt, about all we register is his stony simian stare: the thick lips and zombie eyes, the look of vague dyspepsia that could be anything from fear to constipation. Through it all, however, one thing remains constant: the guilty, whiny agony of Brad Pitt's Louis - the vampire as eternal killjoy. He looks like he could use a transfusion, and so, by the end, could the entire movie.

(Owen Gleiberman, Entertainment Weekly)

Actor, Troy (2004)

The wrath of Brad looks more like a migraine. His physique is more than up to it, but in every other respect it's a painfully misconceived performance: mumbled, cold, alienating. He huffs and puffs, frowns and glowers, but never remotely inhabits the part, massively overdoing Achilles's pride and egotism at the expense of his tragic, thwarted nobility.

(Tim Robey, Daily Telegraph)

Pitt isn't a demigod, just a fabulously buff 40 year-old in a leather skirt.

(Will Self, Evening Standard)

Pitt's long, lank hair is not good: it combines with his pronounced jaw muscles, pouty lower lip and snub nose to make him look like an overgrown pekinese.

(Edward Porter, Sunday Times)

MICHAEL PITT

Actor, Silk (2007)

Should Michael Pitt ever quit acting - and God knows there must be some petitions going round - it's hard to know what he might attempt as an alternative. Other than as a cure for insomnia, or a special kind of vacuum designed to suck the life out of everything around him, Pitt seems strikingly ill-equipped for employment. In fact, on the basis of Silk, one is inclined to think he's not just slow, slack-jawed and sulky, as he appeared in The Dreamers and Last Days. He seems less man, more plankton.

(Catherine Shoard, Sunday Telegraph)

Pitt was last observed moping around in Gus van Sant's pretentious biopic of Kurt Cobain contemplating suicide, Last Days. Pitt does not appear to have rediscovered the will to live; until he does, I doubt if I will rediscover my will to watch him.

(Christopher Tookey, Daily Mail)

ROMAN POLANSKI

Director, Rosemary's Baby (1968)

Make a film like Rosemary's Baby? I wouldn't touch it with a five-foot Pole.

(Billy Wilder)

STEPHEN POLIAKOFF

Writer, She's Been Away (1989)

The actors can not rescue a negative and depressingly mean-spirited screenplay, by Stephen Poliakoff. I would not dream of recommending to him that he adopt a sunnier disposition, or try to write sympathetically about merchant bankers, or become any less hostile towards Thatcher's Britain. However, if he ever wants to write a movie which is not itself smug and parochially English, he could go back to the basics of story-telling, and consider how to involve his audience and where he is leading it. His critique of society might have more impact, or even some impact, if he could stop thinking in 70s cliches, snap out of a kind of generalised grumpiness, and express a single positive view on where we should be heading.

(Christopher Tookey, Sunday Telegraph)

Writer, Director, Food of Love (1997)

Stephen Poliakoff, who wrote and directed, should be stood against a wall and shot, but I daresay British producers are even now queuing up to fund his next project. Heaven help us.

(Anne Billson, Sunday Telegraph)

No less than £800,000 of Lottery cash was invested by the demented generosity of the Arts Council's awards panel to part-fund this £2.1 million disaster written and directed by Stephen Poliakoff in the manner of a Harrods doorman vainly trying to control the crowds on the first day of the sales. What is Film Four thinking of, even distributing it?

(Alexander Walker, Evening Standard)

Writer, Director, Glorious 39 (2009)

Poliakoff has won numerous awards and a CBE for his writing, which makes the direness of his dialogue all the more exasperating. Far too much of it is patronisingly clunky, repetitive exposition... As a director of child actors, Poliakoff is hopeless. Worst of all, he seems not to have seen many movie thrillers of the past twenty years, for the pacing is pedestrian and the camerawork static, more redolent of bad episodes of Midsomer Murders than modern cinema. Poliakoff's obsession with

anti-semitic cover-ups of the past looks more and more like a reluctance to address the rather more pressing scandals of the present. A revealing film might be made of how yesterday's enfants terribles become today's pillars of the establishment, fatally dependent for financial assistance on the BBC and the Lottery Panel.

(Christopher Tookey, Daily Mail)

SYDNEY POLLACK

Director, Random Hearts (1999)

Sydney Pollack directs in his sleep, and the audience's.

(Christopher Tookey, Daily Mail)

IGGY POP

Actor, Dead Man (1996)

The most memorable moment is one when pop-star turned actor Iggy Pop, in a stained gingham frock, retells the tale of Goldilocks. I only wish it were memorable in a good way.

(Christopher Tookey, Daily Mail)

NATALIE PORTMAN

Actress, Star Wars II: Attack of the Clones (2002)

Hopelessly stiff - not helped by several zillion hairstyle and costume changes, that suggest that when traveling round the galaxy the lovely Senator must carry a packing case the size of the Death Star.

(Christopher Tookey, Daily Mail)

Actress, V For Vendetta (2006)

Portman has her hair shaved off and starts nodding earnestly at the idea of the greater good. This might play better if her performance didn't have all the fluency of a preliminary script-read by a cockatoo.

(Tim Robey, Daily Telegraph)

PARKER POSEY

Actress, The Misadventures of Margaret (1998)

Imagine Erica Jong with the sex appeal of a decomposing squirrel.

(Christopher Tookey, Daily Mail)

SALLY POTTER

Director, Writer, Yes (2005)

The more serious Potter gets (there are several earnest soliloquies about dirt), the harder it is not to laugh.

(Kyle Smith, New York Post)

This is the kind of movie that nice people call ambitious. Let's just leave it at that.

(Allison Benedikt, Chicago Tribune)

Long, painful experience has taught me to beware any drama in which the protagonists are called He and She, any piece not written by Shakespeare that claims to be in rhyming iambic pentameters, any film that's Lottery-funded, and anything that's written and directed by Sally Potter. Yes fulfils all four criteria. Sally Potter has never fulfilled the promise of her debut, the 1992 Orlando, and her biggest problem is the terrifying banality of her writing. When she attempts a form as literary as the rhyming iambic pentameter, it would help if she understood at least the basics of rhyming and scansion. The actors do their best with her limping doggerel, but no actor on earth could disguise the illiteracy of statements such as "I did not mean to infer that you were over-large" (meaning "I did not mean to imply that you were fat", which may not be an iambic pentameter but has the merit of at least making sense).

(Christopher Tookey, Daily Mail)

GARY PREISLER

Director, National Lampoon's Gold Diggers (2004)

This is the spectacularly inept directing debut of writer-producer Gary Priesler, who is said to have 12 other movies in development. God help us.

(Lou Lumenick, New York Post)

There's no sense of comic timing and director Gary Preisler wouldn't know screwball from a set of anal beads.

(Erik Childress, eFilmCritic.com)

If National Lampoon's Gold Diggers... had a single laugh in it, that laugh would die of loneliness.

(Roger Moore, Orlando Sentinel)

If you're given the choice between seeing National Lampoon's Gold Diggers and death, you'd be wise to choose death.

(Jeff Vice, Deseret News, Salt Lake City)

OTTO PREMINGER

Director, Hurry Sundown (1967)

Nobody has accused Otto of any particularly noticeable talents in recent years, but this time the Big O (as he is called by his co-workers) has pulled out all the stops in supreme bad taste... A slimy, crawling, pitiful obscenity.

(Rex Reed)

To criticize it would be like tripping a dwarf.

(Wilfrid Sheed, Esquire)

Director, Skidoo (1968)

Curiously, in his private life Otto Preminger is the most tasteful of men. Unfortunately, none of that taste seems to turn up in his pictures.

(Arthur Knight, Saturday Review)

For those who can't just get their kicks by watching other people turn on in a film, Skidoo offers plenty of good old-fashioned titillation passing as the latest thing in fun and games: Mr Preminger is really in there swinging, and I wouldn't be surprised if he next produced the Timothy Leary Story, a sort of inspirational film along the lines of The Cardinal .

(Dan Wakefield, Atlantic Monthly)

I thought Otto Preminger had touched rock bottom with Hurry Sundown but this time he is digging well below the substrata.

(Tom Milne, Observer)

Otto Preminger's direction would make an elephant doing the frug look light-toed by comparison.

(Alexander Walker, Evening Standard)

DENNIS QUAID

Actor, Flight of the Phoenix (2004)

Real stars are conspicuous by their absence and we have to make do with B-list actors like Dennis Quaid as the pilot on whom everyone depends for their lives. His performance consists largely of looking rugged. His acting is, in effect, limited to turning the corners of his mouth down, like someone tasting tea made with urine.

(Ben Davis, Morning Star)

KATHLEEN QUINLAN

Actress, The Hills Have Eyes (2006)

Kathleen Quinlan, once Tom Hanks' wife in Apollo 13, her forehead now retaining Botox like the Hoover Dam retains the mighty Colorado.

(Mark Ramsey, Moviejuice)

ANTHONY QUINN

Actor, A Walk in the Clouds (1996)

Anthony Quinn, the heroine's cheerfully drunken, suspiciously Zorba-like grandfather, spouts platitudes under the mistaken impression that he is being lovable, and gives his most tiresome performance in years.

It's proof that only he who dares, Quinns; and he who Quinns, loses.

(Christopher Tookey, Daily Mail)

The most fun to be had with the film is in watching Reeves struggle through his dialogue — that and attempting to figure out what in heaven's name Anthony Quinn, who plays Victoria's sagacious grandfather, is trying to do. With his hands fluttering wildly around his face like a belly dancer's, Quinn looks at times as if he were actually trying to achieve liftoff.

(Hal Hinson, Washington Post)

DANIEL RADCLIFFE

Actor, Harry Potter and the Goblet of Fire (2005)

Radcliffe's performance as Potter is the film's weakest link. Yes, he can grunt and groan with the best of them, but conveying any kind of mood, be it fear or happiness, is just beyond his grasp.

(Cosmo Landesman, Sunday Times)

Actor, Harry Potter And The Half-Blood Prince (2009)

To my eye, Radcliffe still looks like the teenage offspring of Hitler and a gay owl.

(Robbie Collin, News of the World)

CHARLOTTE RAMPLING

Actress, Farewell, My Lovely (1975)

A poor actress who mistakes creepiness for sensuality.

(John Simon, National Review)

Actress, Orca... Killer Whale (1977)

At the end, when the whale has lured Harris north with a come-hither flick of its tail, Miss Rampling is caught on the icefloes, leaping from one to t'other and clad in thigh boots, homespun poncho and a turban, as if she expected David Bailey to surface and photograph her for Vogue's Arctic number.

(Alexander Walker, Evening Standard)

CHRIS REA

Writer, La Passione (1996)

How on earth did pop star Chris Rea managed to finance this self-written, self-produced vanity production? Rea is all too evidently influenced by Fellini and Terence Davies, but has absolutely none of their talent. La Passione may be a labour of love but it is entirely devoid of drama and most politely described as "intensely personal," since it's so awful that I can't imagine anyone except Mr Rea having the patience to sit through it. The most treasurable sequence is a gloriously banal production number featuring Shirley Bassey, entitled Shirley, Do You Own a Ferrari? – some kind of all-time low in both movie song-writing and cinematic fantasy sequences.

(Christopher Tookey, Daily Mail)

Actor, Parting Shots (1999)

Bad singer, worse actor.

(Jason Solomons, Mail on Sunday)

Rea treats everything - the bad news from his doctor, his killing of numerous innocent people, the revelation that he isn't going to die after all - with the same expression, a quizzical bewilderment that suggest overlong exposure to the films of Roger Moore.

(Christopher Tookey, Daily Mail)

STEPHEN REA

Actor, Feardotcom (2003)

Bad news is that the cackling, demonic webmaster is none other than our old pal Stephen Rea, trying to persuade us that he's a scalpel-wielding maniac called Dr Pratt, who loves to terrorise young women by performing autopsies on them while they are alive. It's a horrifying concept in every way, but involuntarily hilarious since Rea looks like Leo Sayer attempting an impersonation of Hannibal Lecter.

(Christopher Tookey, Daily Mail)

Actor, The Reaping (2007)

The runner's up prize for outrageous thespianism goes to an exaggeratedly woebegone Stephen Rea as an Irish priest, who has nothing to do except ring up the leading lady with awful warnings and useless advice. Yes, he literally phones in his Godawful performance.

(Christopher Tookey, Daily Mail)

VANESSA REDGRAVE

Actress, Camelot (1967)

All the horses wear $6,000 suits of armor; this is helpful in that it enables us to distinguish them from Vanessa Redgrave, who has never been shot to look so equine before.

(John Simon, National Review)

Actress, Sparrow (1993)

Vanessa Redgrave's performance as a mad nun is tragic, but not in the way she meant it to be.

(Christopher Tookey, Daily Mail)

Actress, Wilde (1997)

Vanessa Redgrave gives one of her increasingly eccentric performances as Oscar's mother, Speranza, with Oirish accent, mad cackle and wig like a red setter - more than enough to turn any son off women for life, one would imagine.

(Anne Billson, Sunday Telegraph)

PEYTON REED

Director, Down With Love (2003)

Shot like the Doris Day-Rock Hudson movie from Hell, and acted with an archness that kills every laugh stone dead, the film makes Renee Zellweger look plain and puffy. Ewan McGregor comes across as a talentless amateur. Ugly, unfunny and utterly devoid of charm, it flopped in the States, and no wonder: it's painful to watch - a smirky turkey.

(Christopher Tookey, Daily Mail)

Director, Yes Man (2008)

Too bad Yes Man is directed by Peyton Reed, a tone-deaf, buzz-kill comedy specialist. You've never seen Jim Carrey flail like he does under Reed's incompetence.

(Armond White, New York Press)

KEANU REEVES

Actor, Point Break (1991)

You've got to love any suspense movie that asks us to buy Keanu Reeves, player par excellence of clueless dudes, as Johnny Utah, a football supernova whose career was detoured by a busted knee. Considering that Reeves suggests a guy who scored too many tackles without a helmet, that's already pushing it, but Reeves's character is also supposed to have won a law degree and graduated at the top of his class.

(Edward Margulies & Stephen Rebello, Bad Movies We Love)

Actor, Much Ado About Nothing (1993)

Keanu Reeves, as Don Pedro's bastard brother, Don John, isn't as bad as one might reasonably expect (given his lackluster track record), principally because he doesn't have many lines.

(James Berardinelli, Reelviews)

As for Reeves, such lines as 'Come, come let us thither' do not fall trippingly off this surfer dude's tongue.

(Peter Travers, Rolling Stone)

Actor, Johnny Mnemonic (1995)

Keanu Reeves, an actor of exceptionally limited scope, plays the title character with about as much wattage as a pen flashlight.

(James Berardinelli, Reelviews)

As played by Reeves (not the most expressive actor to begin with), Johnny may as well be the walking dead. No dialogue is really necessary, just a few motor skills and the rest of the story will surely

follow. And when you are being upstaged by the likes of Ice-T, Henry Rollins, Udo Kier, and god help us, Dolph Lundgren, you know you are in trouble.

(Ned Daigle, Bad Movie Night)

The idea of casting Keanu Reeves as someone suffering from cerebral overload may sound like a callous joke. What makes matters worse is the way he tries to deepen his voice, so that he sounds like a college kid impersonating John Wayne. Most of the time, he acts as if he has misheard the title and is trying to be Jolly Moronic.

(Christopher Tookey, Daily Mail)

Actor, The Devil's Advocate (1997)

A fixed fight: putting Keanu Reeves up against Al Pacino is a bit like throwing wood on to a fire to see if it burns.

(Tom Shone, Sunday Times)

Actor, The Matrix (1999)

When he's not delivering lines and is supposed to be reacting, his face freezes, like a computer screen that's crashed because you're trying to enter too much data at once. Then someone must reboot him or something, because he talks, albeit slowly as though he is being operated by very primitive speech-recognition software. The amazing truth which gradually dawns about Keanu over the course of the movie is that HE ISN'T SUPPOSED TO BE PLAYING A FAULTY PIECE OF MACHINERY. He's meant to be not only a real person, but a brilliant computer criminal and The One Who Is Going To Save The World. He struck me as the least likely Messiah since Olivia Newton-John saved humanity in one of 1983's worst turkeys, Two of a Kind.

(Christopher Tookey, Daily Mail)

Actor, Hardball (2001)

In Hardball, he really, really tries to act - with lots of awkward, irrelevant hand signals, as though he is hoping some day to replace John McCririck on Channel 4 horse-racing. In the absence of any sporting excitement or character depth, the film ladles on the sentiment as one of the small boys is killed in a heavily foreshadowed drive-by shooting, and Keanu gets to deliver his funeral eulogy, complete with hand movements. This deeply felt speech was greeted at the national press screening with tears, I regret to say, of hilarity. Keanu Reeves trying to emote is like Big Ron Atkinson reciting Rilke, or a moose trying to compete in the finals of a world figure-skating championship. It is bizarre, surreal and somehow deeply uncalled for.

(Christopher Tookey, Daily Mail)

Actor, Constantine (2005)

The film's pretensions are rendered even more ludicrous by Keanu's lovingly detailed impersonation of a sleep-walking plank.

(Christopher Tookey, Daily Mail)

Actor, A Scanner Darkly (2006)

An animated Keanu Reeves is quintessentially a contradiction in terms.

(Christopher Tookey, Daily Mail)

Actor, Street Kings (2008)

It's hard to know whether Keanu Reeves has finally been replaced with an animatronic version of himself, been hit on the head by a massive tub of Botox, is under heavy sedation with horse tranquillisers, or has been persuaded to try to reinvigorate his career with a double eye transplant from a stuffed moose. Whatever the

explanation, as a latterday Dirty Harry, he is even more facially inert than usual.

(Christopher Tookey, Daily Mail)

Actor, The Private Lives Of Pippa Lee (2009)

Keanu Reeves does a nice job of playing a vacant, musclebound dimwit. Funny, that.

(Robbie Collin, News of the World)

Actor, The Day The Earth Stood Still (2009)

Keanu Reeves plays Klaatu with all the expressiveness of a wok. I have never seen a wok better portrayed.

(Victor Olliver, Teletext)

TARA REID

Actress, Van Wilder (2002)

For each chuckle there are at least 10 complete misses, many coming from the amazingly lifelike Tara Reid, whose acting skills are comparable to a cardboard cutout.

(Citysearch)

Tara Reid – not altogether convincingly cast as a hotshot student journalist – looks like the winner of a Midwest beauty pageant who's won a chance of Hollywood stardom, and is now trying to smile at the camera and remember her lines at the same time.

(Christopher Tookey, Daily Mail)

Actress, Alone in the Dark (2005)

I've heard of the suspension of disbelief, but Tara Reid as an archaeologist?
(Thomas Delapa, Boulder Weekly)

Reid delivers her lines as though she is calling for another round of Mai Tais for the house.
(Nell Minow, Movie Mom)

You need an actor who can make the words SOUND smart, and Reid won't be winning a Nobel Prize anytime soon. She's proof that alcohol kills brain cells… with a vengeance.
(Willie Waffle, WaffleMovies.com)

Reid seems to have learned each long sentence in segments, so she wouldn't be overtaxed.
(Lawrence Toppman, Charlotte Observer)

Think of the lamest horror movie you've ever seen. Now think of Tara Reid in the lamest horror movie you've ever seen. See how much worse it could have been?
(Janice Page, Boston Globe)

Note to Tara: It's not pronounced New-FOUND-land.
(Greg Maki, Star Democrat)

ALAIN RESNAIS

Director, Providence (1977)

For Resnais himself, it's no longer possible to hope. He's consumed with artiness… And under artiness there is always at least a whiff of stupidity.
(Stanley Kauffmann, New Republic)

BURT REYNOLDS

Actor, At Long Last Love (1975)

As for Burt Reynolds as a jaded millionaire playboy, there is in Funny Lady a buffalo named Charles, whom Billy Rose insists on displaying in a musical, where, on opening night, he creates havoc by improvising a one-buffalo stampede. Well, put a dinner jacket on Charles, and you've got Reynolds in At Long Last Love, except that he never musters enough animation for a stampede.

(John Simon, National Review)

Burt Reynolds sings like Dean Martin with adenoids and dances like a drunk killing cockroaches.

(John Barbour, Los Angeles)

Starring Cybill Shepherd and Burt Reynolds, who have, between them, four left feet and who sing with a gallantry that reminds me of small children taking their first solo swim across the deep end.

(Vincent Canby, New York Times)

Actor, Lucky Lady (1975)

Burt Reynolds's face looks like an armored car made, inexplicably, out of meat.

(John Simon, National Review)

Actor, Striptease (1996)

In a movie in which absolutely nothing works, Burt Reynolds manages to not work more than anything else.

(Bob McCabe, Daily Express)

Actor, The Dukes of Hazzard (2005)

The grinning Reynolds looks Botoxed into immobility.

(Lawrence Toppman, Charlotte Observer)

The movie's villain is named Boss Hogg, and he's played by someone calling himself Burt Reynolds, though it is impossible to recognize the once-famous star of the same name. He has either been replaced by his own Madame Tussaud's waxwork, or he has been drowned in some sinister new embalming fluid by a maniacal mortician.

(Christopher Tookey, Daily Mail)

Actor, In The Name of the King: A Dungeon Siege Tale (2008)

When King Burt Reynolds says, 'What kind of joke do the gods play on me?,' we feel the pain of a downslide that took him from No. 1 box-office star to appearing in an Uwe Boll schlockfest.

(Chuck O'Leary, FulvueDrive-in.com)

RYAN REYNOLDS

Actor, Van Wilder (2002)

As the eternal student party-giver Van, Ryan Reynolds strolls about lugubriously like a younger, even more meaningless Chevy Chase.

(Christopher Tookey, Daily Mail)

Actor, Waiting… (2005)

The leading clown, Ryan Reynolds, gives a smug, inert performance. His deadpan expression would be ideal as the look of somebody who's just been whacked in the face with a plank, but that's the limit of its comic potential.

(Edward Porter, Sunday Times)

Ben Affleck without the brains, Adam Sandler without the subtlety, Reynolds – creepily overgroomed, preternaturally smug – is the last word in inept sarkiness. He's rubbish in horror (The Amityville Horror). He's rubbish in action thrillers (Blade: Trinity). He's rubbish as a leading man (Just Good Friends). And he's rubbish in comedy (National Lampoon's Van Wilder).

(Catherine Shoard, Sunday Telegraph)

CHRISTINA RICCI

Actress, Miranda (2002)

Even when shot sympathetically, Christina Ricci has a curious kind of beauty. As photographed here, her protruding saucer eyes, flat face and dank complexion make her look uncannily like Gollum.

(Christopher Tookey, Daily Mail)

Actress, Monster (2003)

Ricci, meanwhile, makes the best of an underwritten part, though she has the misfortune of looking like wee Jimmy Krankie.

(Sukhdev Sandhu, Daily Telegraph)

TIM RICE

See Andrew Lloyd Webber.

JOELY RICHARDSON

Actress, Shoreditch (2003)

A disastrously gawky and miscast Joely Richardson comes across like Joyce Grenfell having a valiant stab at impersonating Jessica Rabbit.

(Christopher Tookey, Daily Mail)

ALAN RICKMAN

Actor, Blow Dry (2001)

Alan Rickman plays the humiliated husband as though recently stunned by falling masonry. He makes all the wrong acting choices for a comedy and behaves as though he is the lead in a Strindberg play, glowering and brooding upon a lifetime of sexual jealousy and female mistreatment. Yet, at the same time, he seems dimly aware that there is fun going on around him, and that hairdressing may strike some people as a louche career choice. So he adopts a faintly camp Yorkshire accent. It comes as a major surprise when the twist in the tale is not that he's a closet homosexual. While Rickman gives his disastrous impersonation of David Hockney playing Othello, the others have to get on with supplying the intentional laughs.

(Christopher Tookey, Daily Mail)

NOAH RINGER

Actor, The Last Airbender (2010)

The lead actor, Noah Ringer, is 13 years old and was plucked from obscurity after a talent search. A talent search that came up empty, apparently.

(Eric D. Snider, Film.com)

In a role that required the mystical gravitas of a young Dalai Lama, the depressingly earth-bound Caucasian Noah Ringer speaks the lines as though he has learnt them phonetically. His one talent seems to be that he can flare his nostrils. There are far too many opportunities to study this phenomenon in close-up.

(Christopher Tookey, Daily Mail)

GUY RITCHIE

Director, Writer, Swept Away (2002)

Maybe his decision to make Swept Away proves that love really is blind. Let's hope his future filming schedule with Madonna is restricted to home videos with Lourdes and Rocco.

(Almar Haflidason, BBCi)

Not only does the story, script and direction seem to have been arranged by a committee of cretins, but even the lighting seems to be designed to make Madonna look as stringy, old, and sexless as possible.

(Julie Burchill, Guardian)

Director, Writer, Revolver (2005)

Revolver is no ordinary turkey. If it is to be likened to any large, flightless bird, it resembles most of all a pea-brained ostrich that has forgotten to hide its head in the sand at the first sign of attack, and has chosen instead to insert its head all the way up its own fundament. Ritchie's gangsterish wisecracks, so lively in his first two movies, are cringe-makingly feeble in this; his attempts at religious symbolism are clunkingly banal; his pronouncements about "ego versus the light" will be wearisomely opaque to anyone who isn't intimately acquainted with his wife's Kabbalah sect; and his annoyingly repetitive attempts to quote other people's aphorisms on warfare and the "art of the con" convey an impression of an intellectual featherweight trying to punch at least 30 IQ points above his intellectual capacity.

(Christopher Tookey, Daily Mail)

TIM ROBBINS

Actor, Code 46 (2003)

Tim Robbins doesn't look like a man consumed by lust, but a Hollywood actor feeling superior about finding himself in an incomprehensible art-house movie. He's smug, smirky and smackable.

(Christopher Tookey, Daily Mail)

Actor, Catch a Fire (2006)

The problem with Tim Robbins' dreadful turn as a South African "anti-terrorist" official in Catch A Fire - and it was also a problem with his sniveling Bill Gates impersonation in Antitrust - is that he can't hide his distaste for his own character.

(Scott Tobias, The Onion)

Robbins's banal performance makes knee-jerk racism look indistinguishable from constipation.

(Tim Robey, Daily Telegraph)

JULIA ROBERTS

Actress, Hook (1992

J.M. Barrie's Tinkerbell was all brain and no body, whereas Julia Roberts...

(Jill Parkin, Daily Express)

Actress, The Pelican Brief (1993)

Abysmal. She is not remotely credible as a law student; she poses rather than acts; and some of the things she does on the run are frankly bird-brained. Would someone in fear of an assassin's bullet really perch, beautifully lit, in front of a window at night with the curtains open?

(Christopher Tookey, Daily Mail)

Actress, I Love Trouble (1994)

On the evidence of her last few films, one can only deduce that it is in Miss Roberts's contract that someone has to compliment her character every so often on her intellectual brilliance (in the same way that supporting actors always used to have to congratulate Joan Collins on her extraordinary youthfulness). It has to be doubted, however, whether Miss Roberts's reputation as Beverly Hills' answer to Dame Mary Warnock can survive another embarrassment on this scale.

(Christopher Tookey, Daily Mail)

Actress, Mary Reilly (1996)

Julia Roberts, whose Irish accent is so dodgy I assumed it was meant to be Scottish, suppresses her natural charms - her millions of teeth, her tumbling red hair, her endearing way with a baggy jumper - to play a skivvy who unaccountably fails to spot that her master, Dr Jekyll, and his assistant, Mr Hyde, are both played by the same actor.

(Anne Billson, Sunday Telegraph)

In a role which required an actress who could hint at forbidden, sado-masochistic passions, Julia Roberts behaves like Bambi on tranquillisers.

(Christopher Tookey, Daily Mail)

JAY RODAN

Actor, The Triumph of Love (2001)

Rodan is such an inept actor and dull leading man that it's hard to know why our heroine goes to so much trouble to seduce him. In order to survive a harsh winter, he looks as if he would need creosoting.

(Christopher Tookey, Daily Mail)

KATHARINE ROSS

Actress, Butch Cassidy and the Sundance Kid (1969)

Katharine Ross is rapidly losing her youthful bloom without sprouting any compensatory growth in artistic stature.

(John Simon, National Review)

Actress, Stepford Wives (1975)

It was hard to tell Katharine Ross playing a robot from Katharine Ross playing a normal housewife.

(Les Keyser)

TERRY ROSSIO

See Ted Elliott and Terry Rossio.

ELI ROTH

Director, Hostel (2005)

I am worried about Eli Roth. His debut movie Cabin Fever was a misconceived, misguided, stupid, and schlocky hodgepodge of horror and comedy that was neither scary nor funny. That movie was ultimately harmless, but his new feature Hostel seems to me a cry for help. Why no one during the process of making the movie saw that Roth's sadistic, homophobic, and overall misanthropic tendencies in filmmaking were clearly evidence that the man needs at least some major therapy is a great mystery.

(Mark Dujsik, Mark Reviews Movies)

Eli Roth (whose only previous film was another low-budget shocker, Cabin Fever) is virtually talent-free and seems motivated entirely by a desire to make money and make cinema more graphically, sleazily, pornographically violent than ever before.

(Christopher Tookey, Daily Mail)

Director, Hostel: Part II (2007)

Compared to this Eli Roth fetish video, the Saw films are Oscar bait. Certainly, porn-torture is what passes for horror these days, and Hostel gleefully pushes the envelope. If this movie is any indication, Roth's career goal is to make a snuff film. And he comes close, with scenes of gratuitous gore, including a naked woman being drained of her blood, a man being castrated, and children playing soccer with a severed head. But what really undermines this sequel is not its mean spirit, but plain old poor filmmaking. For a movie that wants to make you squirm, Hostel evokes unintended laughs… The movie ends so abruptly, one has to think the filmmakers ran out of either money or prosthetic body parts.

(Scott Bowles, USA Today)

It's a free country. Just don't go preaching that this desensitized crap reflects our current sociopolitical climate like Vietnam-era slashers did, which just so happens to be something Roth attempted to do recently in the Los Angeles Times.

(Aaron Hillis, Premiere)

Might please its target audience of ugly young men who are not getting any sex. Others will leave not so much nauseated as depressed at the sheer cynical hatred of humanity that films like this display.

(Peter Whittle, Sunday Times)

Oh, do grow up.

(Mark Kermode, Observer)

Roth's main preoccupations remain as infantile and paranoid as before. Abroad is hell, and Americans are constantly under threat from sinister Europeans with bad teeth... I gather that Mr Roth is trying to argue that having a female character castrate and axe-murder two of her attackers (in a kind of revenge torture porn) somehow turns this into a female empowerment movie. It doesn't. More misogynistic even than its predecessor, the second Hostel takes violence towards (and by) women to hitherto unexplored extremes. It is an astonishingly depraved, sleazy piece of work, and I regret that I can not un-see it.

(Christopher Tookey, Daily Mail)

TIM ROTH

Actor, Four Rooms (1995)

As the bellhop who links all four episodes, Tim Roth gives the worst performance of his career, twitching and overacting in a way that Jim Carrey might find unseemly.

(Christopher Tookey, Daily Mail)

MICKEY ROURKE

Actor, Homeboy (1988)

Rourke's performance is a classic: an unconsciously ridiculous parody of method acting. He out-mumbles Sylvester Stallone; his lopsided, vacant expression could pass as a vicious send-up of Dustin Hoffman in Midnight Cowboy; while his shuffling gait evokes not so much pathos as fond memories of Richard Dreyfuss's camp, off-off-Broadway Richard III in Neil Simon's more intentional comedy about egotistical actors, The Goodbye Girl. Rourke's excesses might not matter so much, if the rest of his performance didn't render the plot nonsensical. The star's evident pride in his own boxing ability and physique (he used to be a boxer in his youth) ensures that this character – exaggeratedly unable to stand, talk, think, hear or see straight – becomes transformed in the ring, as it were miraculously, into a mean fighting machine who can take on the best.

(Christopher Tookey, Sunday Telegraph)

Actor, Wild Orchid (1989)

The film's central male performance - which struck this observer, at least, as having all the animal magnetism of a dead dog - is tragic confirmation that Mickey Rourke's head needs examining. Who can say whether nature or vanity has played a cruel trick on him, but he has acquired high cheekbones precipitately and rather late in life, so that he now looks like Michael Jackson trying to turn himself into Mount Rushmore. Meanwhile, the cheeks below have gained that stretched, latex sheen hitherto seen only on cinematic aliens whose heads are about to explode. And goodness knows what's happening inside the head of this once-promising method actor. Rourke's lamebrain boxing movie of last year, Homeboy, was dreadful enough to be the nadir of any ordinary actor's career, but after Wild Orchid there lingers the disturbing possibility that his next film may be even more humiliating.

(Christopher Tookey, Sunday Telegraph)

GENA ROWLANDS

Actress, A Woman Under The Influence (1974)

As Isabel, Gena Rowlands lets it all hang out ubiquitously and continually; if feelings were laundry, she'd be the city of Naples.

(John Simon, National Review)

KEN RUSSELL

Writer, Director, Actor, The Secret Life of Arnold Bax (1992)

Ken Russell casts himself in the title role of his own film, The Secret Life of Arnold Bax, and gives a portrayal so dire that I suspect he may have had to perform sexual favours for himself on the casting couch in order to get the part.

(Victor Lewis-Smith)

Writer, Director, The Devils (1970)

Russell's swirling multi-colored puddle… made me glad that both Huxley and Whiting are dead, so that they are spared this farrago of witless exhibitionism.

(Stanley Kauffmann, New Republic)

A garish glossary of sado-masochism… a taste for visual sensation that makes scene after scene look like the masturbatory fantasies of a Roman Catholic boyhood.

(Alexander Walker, Evening Standard)

Ken Russell doesn't report hysteria, he markets it.

(Pauline Kael, New Yorker)

Writer, Director, Mahler (1974)

Whether the title of the opus happens to be Strauss or Tchaikowsky or Elgar or Brubeck, the real title is always Russell.

(Benny Green, Punch)

Vulgarity so self-confident, so unrepentant wins a kind of horrified respect. Ken Russell stands on his own, a mixture, at once frightening and preposterous, of Benjamin Robert Haydon, Hieronymus Bosch and the propaganda-poster artists of the Third Reich.

(Dilys Powell, Sunday Times)

Exuberant but supremely vulgar. If there's ever a Society For The Preservation of Famous People's Reputations, Russell's in for a lot of trouble.

(Steven H. Scheuer)

MEG RYAN

Actress, Proof of Life (2000)

If your husband had been kidnapped at machine-gunpoint and held to ransom by a bunch of drug-smuggling, South American revolutionaries, how often would you have your highlights done? Would it be a) not until you knew he was going to get released, b) not until Russell Crowe pitched up at the front door promising to help, or c) once a month? The answer I was looking for was a). The most popular answer, I suspect, is b) which, post-Gladiator, I suppose, is fair enough. But that still doesn't excuse Meg Ryan for going for c), perfectly preserving her gold-streaked and maddeningly floppy hair-do throughout her husband's four-month long incarceration. Goodness, she's an annoying actress.

(Jason Solomons, Mail on Sunday)

Actress, Against the Ropes (2004)

Ryan looks very uncomfortable, as though all the (obvious) nips and tucks on her features have left her with a face she doesn't have a clue how to use.

(Antonia Quirke, Islington Tribune)

WINONA RYDER

Actress, The Private Lives Of Pippa Lee (2009)

In a small role as a sensitive poet, Winona Ryder steals a few scenes. Force of habit, I suppose.

(Robbie Collin, News of the World)

ADAM SANDLER

Actor, Writer, Little Nicky (2000)

Sandler proved in The Wedding Singer that he can be likeable. Here, though, he resorts to the shambling gait of Quasimodo, a silly nasal whine of a voice, seemingly based on Dustin Hoffman's in Midnight Cowboy, and the lop-sided mouth of a stroke victim. His performance is even more annoying and offensive than the crude and remarkably unhumorous jokes he helped to write.

(Christopher Tookey, Daily Mail)

Sandler's performance brings to the screen the most intentionally irritating character since Jerry Lewis used to insist on wearing fake buck teeth.

(Jay Stone, Ottawa Citizen)

Actor, Mr Deeds (2002)

Adam Sandler is to Gary Cooper what a gnat is to a racehorse.

(Robert W. Butler, Kansas City Star)

What's next? Rob Schneider, Dana Carvey and Sarah Michelle Gellar in The Philadelphia Story? David Spade as Citizen Kane?

(Robert Wilonsky, New Times Los Angeles)

The awful Adam Sandler is a bad Deeds in a naughty world.

(Philip French, Observer)

Actor, The Hot Chick (2003)

Executive producer Adam Sandler, playing a dope-smoking bongo-player, turns up in what must surely be the least funny, most self-congratulatory cameo role of the year (narrowly beating George Clooney in Welcome to Collinwood). Not content with being unfunny once, he turns up again and is even less amusing. Right at the end, he treats us to a reprise so laughter-freezing that it makes the first two efforts look uproarious by comparison.

(Christopher Tookey, Daily Mail)

Actor, Click (2006)

Be honest now: haven't we all had quite enough of Adam Sandler? The heart sinks when his name appears on a screen, a harbinger of tiresome fratboy humour, wilful ignorance and pointless outbursts of violence.

(Paul Arendt, BBCi)

Actor, Reign Over Me (2007)

Mike Binder's schlockfest Reign Over Me offers the unedifying spectacle of Adam Sandler in a dramatic role. He plays Charlie Fineman, a dentist who lost his family on one of the planes involved in 9/11.He now roams the streets of New York in a near-catatonic state. Some of the time, he behaves like Dustin Hoffman in Rain Man, at others like a stoned Bob Dylan, but mostly he resembles Adam Sandler begging for an Oscar.

(Christopher Tookey, Daily Mail)

Actor, Writer, Grown Ups (2010)

The new Adam Sandler comedy has all the charm of a home movie that does not star your own family, which means it's overly sentimental, filled with you-had-to-be-there moments, bad jokes and even worse camera angles.

(Betsy Sharkey, Los Angeles Times)

It's like The Big Chill made by morons.

(Bill Goodykoontz, Arizona Republic)

Sandler's recent career is a cautionary tale in self-mutilation.

(Brandon Fibbs, Brandonfibbs.com)

The good news for Adam Sandler is that people may finally stop razzing him about Little Nicky. The bad news is that any dramatic street cred he may have built up with Punch-Drunk Love or even Funny People will be as forgotten as Hitler's penmanship.

(Mike Ward, Richmond.com)

JULIAN SANDS

Actor, Boxing Helena (1993)

Julian Sands is a horse-faced British actor with a shoulder-length blond

mane, whose voice drips with castor oil and whose manner is so mawkish and languid that the most pacific spectator would want to kick him.

(John Simon, National Review)

Julian Sands plays the central role as though anaesthetised and about to throw up. Perhaps someone did, and he was - and who can blame him? For some unexplained reason, he plays most (though not quite all) of his scenes with cotton wool in his left ear: this is by far the most interesting aspect of his performance.

(Christopher Tookey, Daily Mail)

Actor, The Medallion (2003)

They even decided to cast Julian Sands as the baddie, despite his reputation (here maintained) as the world's worst actor

(Edward Porter, Sunday Times)

The incomparable Julian Sands is a reliably awful performer who has perfected the art of intoning his lines as though they are being fed to him via an earpiece by a poorly serviced speak-your-weight machine.

(Christopher Tookey, Daily Mail)

Actor, Ocean's Thirteen (2007)

Just as you think things can't deteriorate further, along comes the worst actor of all time, Julian Sands – and if you think I'm being harsh, treat yourself, if you dare, to a triple-bill of him in Gothic (1986), Boxing Helena (1993) and The Medallion (2003). Here is a man so inept that he can't speak, move or even stand in a remotely believable fashion. Cast as a technological genius, he has all the conviction of Norman Wisdom attempting to play Gandalf.

(Christopher Tookey, Daily Mail)

JOHN SCHLESINGER

Director, Billy Liar! (1963)

Schlesinger is obviously a man to watch for future awards. Everything he does is so wrong that the accumulation of errors resembles a personal style.

(Andrew Sarris, Village Voice)

Director, Day of the Locust (1975)

Schlesinger has never shown much originality in his direction, but he has shown taste, sympathy and control. Gone.

(Stanley Kauffmann, New Republic)

Director, The Next Best Thing (2000)

It's almost impossible to believe that the director, John Schlesinger, was once the sure hand behind Midnight Cowboy. Did he do this one by telephone?

(Peter Howell, Toronto Star)

John Schlesinger should be forcibly retired from filmmaking before his reputation as a world-class director is completely shot to hell.

(Robert Payne, Reel.com)

ROB SCHNEIDER

Writer, Actor, Deuce Bigalow, Male Gigolo (2000)

A refugee from American TV's Saturday Night Live, Rob Schneider, co-wrote the thing, possibly after or even during a pub crawl. He mugs

charmlessly in the leading role, which comes across as one that was probably offered to Hollywood's gross-out comedy star Adam Sandler. Sandler had the good sense to turn it down, but why he chose instead to executive-produce the ostentatiously untalented Mr Schneider in this movie must remain a private grief best explored by Mr Sandler with his therapist.

(Christopher Tookey, Daily Mail)

Actor, The Animal (2001)

I'm no fan of injury-based humor, but I guess if there were any actor I'd like to see pummeled, it'd be Rob Schneider.

(Chris Hewitt, St. Paul Pioneer Press)

Actor, The Hot Chick (2003)

Schneider bounces around with limp wrists, wearing tight tummy tops and hip huggers, twirling his hair on his finger and assuming that's enough to sustain laughs.

(Rob Blackwelder, Splicedwire)

The film gives Schneider the chance, but not unfortunately the ability, to act like a teenage girl. The effect is of someone who's watched too many Jerry Lewis films giving a sadistic imitation of a mentally retarded homosexual. Schneider is so completely devoid of charm and subtlety that I found myself thinking back to Deuce Bigalow, Male Gigolo and The Animal, and realising that those stinkers may yet turn out to be the highlights of his career. The only hope of this guy ever making a funny movie is for him to switch brains with someone who's actually talented.

(Christopher Tookey, Daily Mail)

Actor, Writer, Deuce Bigalow: European Gigolo (2005)

Deuce Bigalow: European Gigolo makes a living prostituting himself.

How much he charges I'm not sure, but the price is worth it if it keeps him off the streets and out of another movie... Speaking in my official capacity as a Pulitzer Prize winner, Mr. Schneider, your movie sucks.

(Roger Ebert, Chicago Sun-Times)

Actor Grow Ups (2010)

Schneider is just a parasite on Adam Sandler's butt.

(Bob Grimm, Reno News & Review)

He's contractually obligated to appear in every Sandler movie until the end of time in a role that is specifically designed to make you realize that talent plays absolutely no part in 99 percent of Hollywood casting decisions... Rob Schneider, the herpes of Hollywood, is eternal.

(Mr Cranky, Mr Cranky Rates The Movies)

JOEL SCHUMACHER

Director, The Number 23 (2007)

There may be filmmakers who are even worse than Joel Schumacher, but few so talentless have worked so steadily for so long. Now entering his third decade of gainful employment producing flashy garbage on an almost annual basis, Schumacher will always live in infamy as the man who decided to put nipples on the Batsuit, thereby sidelining the Dark Knight to years of cinematic obscurity and bad gay jokes. Schumacher started out as a window dresser, and one could make an argument that he approaches his films in much the same fashion.

(Sean Burns, Philadelphia Weekly)

Joel Schumacher flails around like a drowning man, and takes his picture under with him... Schumacher is infamous for wrecking the Batman franchise and for his mishandling of Andrew Lloyd Webber's

NAMED &

Phantom of the Opera a couple of years ago. In fact, Schumacher should do everyone a favor and never set foot behind a camera again. Everything he handles seems to turn to crap.

(Bob Bloom, Journal and Courier, Lafayette, Indiana)

ARNOLD SCHWARZENEGGER

He looks like a brown condom stuffed with walnuts.

(Clive James, Observer)

His acting is limited. He has an inability to pick up light objects, such as a telephone, in any sort of naturalistic way.

(Nigel Andrews, Financial Times)

Actor, Jingle All The Way (1996)

Schwarzenegger gives the worst comedy performance of his career. In between committing acts of grotesque sadism, he mugs to camera in a way that's so self-consciously cute that he seems to have been taking acting lessons from Macaulay Culkin.

(Christopher Tookey, Daily Mail)

Actor, Batman and Robin (1997)

Perhaps children may find it easier than I did to swallow the idea of Schwarzenegger as a Nobel-prizewinning scientist. As a villain, Mr Freeze is much less chilling than Jack Nicholson's Joker or Jim Carrey's Riddler. His idea of wit is to grunt "Stay cool!" or "Tonight Hell freezes over! Ha ha ha!!!" Neither funny nor frightening, Schwarzenegger delivers these lame laugh-lines with the adroitness of a mastodon performing the mambo.

(Christopher Tookey, Daily Mail)

Actor, The End of Days (1999)

Bad acting honours, however, are reserved ultimately for Arnie himself, who moves like the ice-demon in the lowest ring of Dante's Inferno, with about as much human warmth and slightly less facial expression. Called upon to cry over the loss of his wife and child, he can do nothing more than wince like a constipated man with conjunctivitis.

(Mark Kermode, Sight & Sound)

Any compendium of low points in screen acting would have to include the moment when Arnie goes into a church and attains spiritual enlightenment to the enthusiastic accompaniment of a celestial choir, or the one shortly afterwards when he is possessed by the Devil. Arnie, who even at his peak was never an Oscar contender, seems to think that the same facial expression - Man Bothered By Mild Toothache - will suffice for both. Connoisseurs of camp may also enjoy the experience of seeing Arnie crucified but come down from the cross to save the world. It's good to know that he has remained unspoiled by stardom.

(Christopher Tookey, Daily Mail)

RIDLEY SCOTT

Director, Blade Runer (1982)

If anybody comes around with a test to detect humanoids, maybe Ridley Scott and his associates should hide.

(Pauline Kael, New Yorker)

Director, Robin Hood (2010)

Sitting through Ridley Scott's Robin Hood is rather like being in the presence of a spoilsport, rather humourless history teacher earnestly

shattering the myths of a legend. Merry Men? What was merry about life in 12th-century England, for goodness sake? Stealing from the rich to give to the poor? Sentimental claptrap! Men in tights? You've got to be joking. As Scott might say, if it's daft nonsense you want, watch that rubbish with Kevin Costner.

(Henry Fitzherbert, Sunday Express)

TONY SCOTT

Director, Revenge (1989)

Tony Scott is the whoring technician par excellence. The chic trash of The Hunger, the noisy chases and gunplay of Beverly Hills Cop II and the all-American jingoism of Top Gun create an image of a man who has no ideas and no soul.

(John Harkness, Film Review)

Director, The Fan (1996)

Scott has no feel for losers: he always backed winners and was at his most winning with Top Gun. Scott is far too interested in serving up piping hot fantasy fodder to want to pull back from the trough and check out the feeders. The Fan is Taxi Driver as John Hinckley might have directed it.

(Tom Shone, Sunday Times)

Director, Man on Fire (2004)

Mindless, meaningless violence, rendered all the more objectionable by the fact that we don't know or care about the characters he is torturing and dispatching. Scott further cheapens things with his music-video production values and his cod religious imagery.

(Matthew Bond, Mail on Sunday)

Scott is even more obnoxiously flashy than he was in the days of his first success, Top Gun. He's obviously been watching some of the younger Latin-American directors' work in Amores Perros and City of God, and they've had a disastrous effect. The film is full of meaningless whip-pans, jump cuts and double images that make it hard to know what is going on, except that the director is showing off, and the editor needs to stick to decaffeinated coffee.

(Christopher Tookey, Daily Mail)

STEVEN SEAGAL

If you can make a star out of Steven Seagal, you can make a star out of anyone.

(Mike Bygrave)

He wears the anxious expression of a man who hasn't had a decent bowel movement in more than a week.

(Barry Norman, BBC)

Actor, Marked for Death (1990)

An actor with eyes like anthracite, the facial mobility of an Easter Island statue, and the acting talent of a dead dog.

(Christopher Tookey, Sunday Telegraph)

Actor, On Deadly Ground (1994)

Rarely has such a cruelly inept film been allowed out into the public domain. It is tough luck, really, being an action hero with a squeaky voice. Seagal has other problems too: he has a funny face, the silliest ponytail in show-business and no identifiable acting talent at all.

(Marcus Berkmann, Daily Mail)

Actor, Under Siege 2: Dark Territory (1995)

An actor with the physique of a side of beef and roughly the same acting ability.

(Christopher Tookey, Daily Mail)

Remains one of the modern screen's least prepossessing action stars. With a face the colour and mobility of mahogany, squinty eyes and an inappropriately babyish mouth, he is the George Lazenby of action movies, lacking even the downhome appeal of the charmless Chuck Norris. But at least this is an improvement on his self-directed eco-thriller On Deadly Ground. Dumb, bloody and fairly entertaining, it is an efficient if predictable exercise in controlled demolition.

(Neil Norman, Evening Standard)

A great deal of killing and several mighty explosions may compensate some for the semi-literate script and a leading player with the eloquence of an overfed stoat. But I doubt it.

(Derek Malcolm, Guardian)

Actor, The Glimmer Man (1996)

Oh God, spare us Steven Seagal. You've heard of the ham actor - well, now meet the spam actor.

(Anthony Quinn, Mail on Sunday)

He continues to exhibit less acting ability than the average coffee-table.

(Christopher Tookey, Daily Mail)

This man was surely put upon earth to make Jean-Claude Van Damme look sensitive.

(Anne Billson, Sunday Telegraph)

Actor, Half Past Dead (2003)

This former action star is now so portly that his martial arts skills are reminiscent of a hippopotamus irritably flicking off flies with its ears.

(Christopher Tookey, Daily Mail)

TOM SELLECK

Actor, Christopher Columbus: The Discovery (1992)

Tom Selleck costars as King Ferdinand, and a comical king he is. Looking stiff and stern, and saying things like "I defer to my queen,'" he cuts quite a figure in his shoulder-length wig and brocaded robes. He reminds you of the captain of the football team doing a walk-on in the senior play. You can almost hear him thinking, "Gee, I hope the guys aren't laughing".

(Michael Sauter, The Worst Movies of All Time)

AARON SELTZER & JASON FRIEDBERG

Writers, Directors, Date Movie (2006)

"Comedy is hard," said Steve Martin. For the writers of Date Movie, it's apparently impossible.

(Jack Mathews, New York Daily News)

Writers, Directors, Meet The Spartans (2008)

Words cannot accurately describe what a depressing experience each new film from spoof-laden writer-directors Jason Friedberg and Aaron Seltzer is. These two lucky bastards are the absolute dirges of modern cinema, cobbling together laughless visual and technical monstrosities

NAMED &

that wouldn't pass muster in an amateur filmmaking school for the mentally disabled.

(Dustin Putman, The Movie Boy)

OK, I get it now: Aaron Seltzer and Jason Friedberg are agents of Satan himself, and their recruitment video is Meet the Spartans, the latest in their own private franchise of head-slappingly awful parody product.

(Brian Orndorf, Film Jerk)

Writers, Directors, Disaster Movie (2008)

The filmmakers are idiots.

(Michael Hardy, Boston Globe)

There's no nice way to say this, so I'll just say it: Writer/directors Friedberg and Seltzer are a scourge.

(Josh Rosenblatt, Austin Chronicle)

This carpet-fouling mongrel of a movie no more deserves release than anthrax spores.

(Jim Ridley, L.A. Weekly)

Just as thoroughly unfunny as all of their others. I do wish they'd pack it in.

(Edward Porter, Sunday Times)

It's about as funny as a dog in a lawn mower.

(Robbie Collin, News of the World)

Writers, Directors, Vampires Suck (2010)

Seltzer and Friedberg have the comic timing of a dead rat.

(Dustin Putman, The Movie Boy)

ADAM SHANKMAN

Director, The Pacifier (2005)

The director is the reliably inept Adam Shankman, who mishandled every puerile joke in The Wedding Planner and Bringing Down the House, and proves here that his previous misdemeanours were no fluke.

(Christopher Tookey, Daily Mail)

The film is directed by Adam Shankman, whose CV is a rap sheet to put Al Capone's to shame. The Wedding Planner, A Walk to Remember, Bringing Down the House. And now this. Next up? Cheaper by the Dozen 2, which I look forward to as I might my own evisceration with a potato-peeler. Never see any of them ever.

(Tim Robey, Daily Telegraph)

Director, Cheaper by the Dozen 2 (2005)

Director Adam Shankman's name upon the credits pretty much guarantees unimaginative hackwork. His Bringing Down the House, The Wedding Planner and The Pacifier were three of the most atrocious comedies of recent years. Whatever else can be said about him, he's consistent.

(Christopher Tookey, Daily Mail)

OMAR SHARIF

Actor, Che! (1969)

Omar Sharif can no more interpret the fiery revolutionary than Elvis Presley could portray Lenin.

(Sherwood Ross, Christian Century)

CHARLIE SHEEN

Actor, Navy SEALs (1990)

Charlie Sheen has roughly the dangerousness of a milk shake, without any of a milk-shake's versatility.

(Christopher Tookey, Sunday Telegraph)

CYBILL SHEPHERD

Actress, At Long Last Love (1975)

Cybill Shepherd is a leading lady who can neither sing nor dance and who apparently thinks badinage is something you put on a small cut.

(Vincent Canby, New York Times)

Her singing voice, which is as sing-songy as her speaking voice, causes one to yearn for the days when Marni Nixon dubbed in the songs of every tone-deaf Hollywood leading lady. As for Shepherd's dancing, the best to be said is that it may not be recognizable as such: when this horsey ex-model starts prancing around, she tends to look as if she's fighting off a chronic case of trots.

(Frank Rich, New Times)

Cybill Shepherd, Mr Bogdanovich's inamorata, plays a poor little snotty rich girl with a notion of sophistication that is underpassed only by her acting ability. (I will not even sully my pen by making it describe her singing and dancing.) If it weren't for an asinine superciliousness radiating from her, Miss Shepherd would actually be pitiable, rather like a kid from an orphanage trying to play Noel Coward. In fact, she comes across like one of those inanimate objects, say, a cupboard or a grandfather clock, which is made in certain humorous shorts to act, through trick photography, like people. Well, Bogdanovich is truly in love with Miss Shepherd, so one cannot call his slapping her into the lead of almost every one of his films the casting-couch approach; yet even those crude old-time producers who did have the crassness to use that method at least had the good sense to cast the girl, not the couch.

(John Simon, National Review)

BROOKE SHIELDS

Actress, Endless Love (1981)

Shields and newcomer Martin Hewitt are two dreamy-looking dead weights who'd make better bookends than film stars.

(Edward Margulies & Stephen Rebello, Bad Movies We Love)

Actress, Furry Vengeance (2010)

Brooke Shields, once a chilly child star in Pretty Baby, [is] now a hatchet-faced matron.

(Philip French, Observer)

PAULY SHORE

Actor, Encino Man (1992)

Shore has all the charm of an oil spill.

(Hal Hinson, Washington Post)

Actor, Bio-Dome (1996)

His dim-witted mugging makes Jim Carrey's antics seem creative triumphs by comparison. Vapid, vulgar, and more to the point, not funny.

(David Sterritt, Christian Science Monitor)

Shore seems convinced that the antics of his retarded persona amount to some manner of postmodernist anti-comedy and this makes the resultant boredom seem all the more pathetic.

(John Anderson, Los Angeles Times)

M. NIGHT SHYAMALAN

Writer, Director, The Village (2004)

M. Night Shyamalan has nothing to say, but he's going to keep right on saying it until people make him stop.

(Mick LaSalle, San Francisco Chronicle)

Writer, Director, Lady in the Water (2006)

This cloying piece of claptrap sets a high-water mark for pomposity, condescension, false profundity and true turgidity.

(Joe Morgenstern, Wall Street Journal)

It's as if on some semiconscious level, Shyamalan, who I do not doubt is a serious and self-serious pop-creative original, is calling his own success into question and daring his audience to gulp down larger and spikier clusters of manure, just to see if they will. Or he's lost his mind.

(Michael Atkinson, Village Voice)

The embarrassing excessiveness of Mr S's self-belief is made all the clearer by his performance – which is not so much wooden, as entranced with its own stillness and conviction of its vibrant, inner beauty. Within half an hour, I was rolling my eyes and trying to prevent my finger making little circular notions to one side of my head.

(Christopher Tookey, Daily Mail)

Have you ever been approached by someone who was really drunk, and they tell you some rambling, incoherent story? Well, that's what watching this movie is like.

(Mike McGranaghan, Aisle Seat)

Writer, Director, The Happening (2009)

M. Night Shyamalan's follow-up to his mega-flop Lady in the Water starts with people throwing themselves off tall buildings and shooting themselves. These are presumably the investors. But no. There are too many of them. Not all can work for 20th Century Fox, the company which inexplicably green-lit this turkey... The Happening is like Alfred Hitchcock's The Birds, but without the birds, or the suspense, or Hitchcock... At least John Wyndham, in The Day of the Triffids, got his killer plants on the move; and when Treebeard mobilised the ents in The Lord of the Rings, they too were allowed to run satisfyingly amok. Here, the trees remain obstinately stationary and merely wave around a bit, like ex-Liverpool goalie Jerzy Dudek used to do, while attempting to put off penalty-takers. It's horribly obvious from this movie that Mr Shyarmalan has mislaid more than his sense of the ridiculous.

(Christopher Tookey, Daily Mail)

Writer, Director, The Last Airbender (2010)

If M. Night Shyamalan sold his soul to the devil for the success of The Sixth Sense, I think His Satanic Majesty has finally collected in full with The Last Airbender.

(Lou Lumenick, New York Post)

The current national priorities should be as follows: reduce carbon emissions and stop funding the films of M. Night Shyamalan.

(Cliff Doerksen, Chicago Reader)

Shyamalan's dialogue makes the worst of George Lucas seem like

Billy Wilder. Much of it seems to have been translated through many languages on its way to English by an army of junior civil servants under the tutelage of Lord Prescott. I particularly treasured one bad guy's wondrously stilted attempt to express human sympathy: "Again, I offer my condolences on your nephew burning to death in that terrible accident." It's astonishing that Shyamalan was able to get a project of any size into production after the disasters that were The Lady in the Water and The Happening. Terrifyingly, he is still threatening to make two Airbender sequels. Can no one give this man psychiatric help? Under the circumstances, it's hard to know what more to say, except "Paramount, again I offer my condolences on your motion picture burning to death in this terrible accident."

(Christopher Tookey, Daily Mail)

I see a dead career.

(Robbie Collin, News of the World)

ALICIA SILVERSTONE

Actress, Excess Baggage (1997)

Ungallantly, I should add that Silverstone's puppy jowls have become so heavy that credibility is stretched every time she is asked for her ID. She looks at least 27.

(George Perry, Sunday Times)

Excess Baggage is an unfortunate monicker for a film starring Alicia Silverstone, who looks like a plump troll.

(Anne Billson, Sunday Telegraph)

JESSICA SIMPSON

Actress, The Dukes of Hazzard (2005)

Just make sure you exit the theater before Simpson's god-awful version of These Boots Are Made for Walking starts playing during the end credits, or you may find yourself taking the straw from your drink and puncturing your own eardrums in self defense.

(Pete Vonder Haar, Film Threat)

There's nothing wrong with Simpson's performance that a head transplant wouldn't cure.

(Lawrence Toppman, Charlotte Observer)

Actress, Employee of the Month (2006)

Rarely has an actress exuded such blank nothingness as Simpson, a one-woman vapid delivery system who sucks the energy and joy out of every scene she's in, like some freakishly well-endowed black hole.

(Ann Hornaday, Washington Post)

Jessica Simpson... establishes herself as the most animatronic performer of her generation. When she's called upon to project any emotion more strenuous than 'blonde', it's as though a wire has snapped somewhere.

(Mike McCahill, Sunday Telegraph)

TOM SIZEMORE

Actor, Paparazzi (2004)

Sizemore, pitched halfway between Christopher Walken and the Antichrist, is transfixingly dreadful.

(Tim Robey, Daily Telegraph)

CHRISTIAN SLATER

Actor, Alone in the Dark (2005)

In this chintzy video-game blow-up, Christian Slater battles zombies and transmogrified beasties, revealing the horror of a once-promising career turned miserable.

(Tom Meek, Boston Phoenix)

As for Christian Slater and Stephen Dorff, well, they've been in worse movies - wait a minute, no they haven't.

(Frank Swietek, One Guy's Opinion)

Christian Slater and Tara Reid share quite possibly the most awkward love scene ever recorded on film.

(Larry Ratliff, San Antonio Express-News)

Slater narrates as if reading a restaurant menu.

(Lawrence Toppman, Charlotte Observer)

The three stars have seen better days, but I'd like to think they could still do something classier and more dignified than this. Like gay porn.

(Rob Vaux, Flipside Movie Emporium)

MAGGIE SMITH

Maggie Smith acts like Quentin Crisp in drag.

(James Coco)

Actress, Washington Square (1997)

Maggie Smith seems at times to be indulging in vindictive self-parody.

(Christopher Tookey, Daily Mail)

ZACK SNYDER

Director, Watchmen (2009)

"What has happened to us? What has happened to the American dream?" a character asks. The answer might be: "You, Zack Snyder. Man-boy directors, blessed with skill but no soul, content to peddle enervatingly reverential treatments of soft porn for kidults."

(Sukhdev Sandhu, Daily Telegraph)

TODD SOLONDZ

Writer, Director, Palindromes (2005)

Solondz's best film, Happiness, allowed its dysfunctional characters an element of pathos and redemption. Here, he may think he's being cool, detached and cynical; but instead he comes across as cruel, flippant and smug.

(Christopher Tookey, Daily Mail)

As amusing as lung cancer.

(Rex Reed, New York Observer)

KEVIN SPACEY

Actor, Director, Beyond the Sea (2004)

Hoofing about in a ton of age-defying make-up, director/star Spacey hasn't much idea what to do with the camera except let himself hog it.

(Tim Robey, Daily Telegraph)

Sitting through Beyond the Sea is about as entertaining as watching a two hour episode of Stars in Their Eyes with only one impersonator. Director-star Kevin Spacey clearly admires the hipster smoothness of Bobby Darin, and sings his songs gamely, while not always hitting every note in the middle... The harsh truth is that Spacey is decades too old to play Darin, who died at only 37 – the scenes of Spacey trying to act as though he's in his twenties and pawing a very young Kate Bosworth, as Darin's teenage wife Sandra Dee, are especially hard to watch. And Spacey's many qualities as an actor do not include warmth. He exudes an urbane cynicism about showbiz celebrity and a kind of reptilian wariness, like a snake weighing up whether or not it is likely to catch anything nasty by biting Janet Street-Porter. Those attributes are not the ones you need when you're playing a man head-over-heels in love with show business and Sandra Dee.

(Christopher Tookey, Daily Mail)

JAMES SPADER

Actor, Crash (1996)

Miss Unger is good only in the sexual scenes, but as James, James Spader is, I'm afraid, perfect for all of it. No other actor so oozes spineless, slack-jawed kinkiness even when it is not called for.

(John Simon, National Review)

BRITNEY SPEARS

Actress, Crossroads (2002)

Spears' acting deficiencies go far beyond being unable to utter a line of dialogue with conviction - throughout Crossroads, she resembles a posed Barbie doll, down to the plastic face with the vacuous expression.

(James Berardinelli, Reelviews)

Watching Ms. Spears sing, dance and act can leave you wondering what is meant nowadays by the concept of talent.

(Stephen Holden, New York Times)

THE SPICE GIRLS

Actresses, Spice World (1997)

The Spice Girls are easier to tell apart than the Mutant Ninja Turtles, but that is small consolation: What can you say about five women whose principal distinguishing characteristic is that they have different names? They occupy Spice World as if they were watching it: They're so detached they can't even successfully lip-synch their own songs.

(Roger Ebert, Chicago Sun-Times)

The awful, unavoidable truth about the Spice Girls is this: They're all Ringo.

(Richard Williams, Guardian**)**

SYLVESTER STALLONE

Actor, Rambo: First Blood (1982)

Stallone is to acting what Liberace is to pumping iron.

(Rex Reed, New York Post)

Actor, Tango and Cash (1989)

Wearing spectacles in an attempt to appear intellectual, Mr Stallone displays the comic skills and urbane sophistication of a drowning ox.

(Christopher Tookey, Sunday Telegraph)

Actor, Oscar (1991)

Danny De Vito was to have played the leading role of a gangster trying to reform, but wisely ran for cover when he read the final script. The film is not helped by De Vito's replacement (Sylvester Stallone), who is no Cary Grant, and whose comic timing is more like that of Grant's tomb.

(Christopher Tookey, Sunday Telegraph)

Actor, The Specialist (1994)

Mr Stallone's body looks as if he were trying to make Arnold Schwarzenegger look sissy. Many of the bits that would be on the inside of a normal body are now on the outside. Stallone seems to have been redesigned by Richard Rogers, and now resembles a fleshy Pompidou Centre.

(Christopher Tookey, Daily Mail)

Actor, Get Carter (2000)

Stallone is so artificial, tanned and leathery you could replace his mouth with a zipper and sell him as a pocketbook.

(Desson Howe, Washington Post)

Writer, director, actor, Rambo (2008)

Stallone looks, to all intents and purposes, like somebody shaved a bear.

(Robbie Collin, News of the World)

Writer, Director, Actor, The Expendables (2010)

The Expendables is savage yet inert, and breathtakingly sleazy in its lack of imagination. Stallone, who co-wrote the movie with Dave Callaham, is also listed as the director, but since he appears to be having trouble, in the autumn of his years, getting his eyelids and lower lip to act in consort with the rest of him, I'm hardly surprised that he had no energy left over to command the film.

(Anthony Lane, New Yorker)

Besides wearily sleepwalking through the lead role, Stallone appears to have directed the entire film while wearing a blindfold - and edited it with a roulette wheel.

(Lou Lumenick, New York Post)

Stallone claims that his script went through 100 drafts, in which case I shudder to think what the first 99 were like. The script is borderline incoherent, and not helped by actors whose diction is extremely indistinct. Stallone, never a clear speaker, spends most of his time grunting like a Gloucester Old Spot or barking like a sea lion with a sore throat.

(Christopher Tookey, Daily Mail)

TERENCE STAMP

Actor, Ma Femme Est Une Actrice (2001)

One of the world's great non-actors, Terence Stamp, again recites his lines with slightly less variety and emotion than Clement Freud on valium.

(Christopher Tookey, Daily Mail)

JOHN STANDING

Actor, 8 ½ Women (1999)

Mr Standing in the nude - a vision we are called upon to witness with depressing frequency - resembles a crumpled bag of flour, upon which

someone, in an improbably festive spirit, has hung one of last Christmas's cocktail sausages.

(Christopher Tookey, Daily Mail)

PATRICK STEWART

Actor, Star Trek: First Contact (1996)

Patrick Stewart doesn't so much deliver lines as intone them.

(Quentin Curtis, Daily Telegraph)

BEN STILLER

Actor, Envy (2004)

When it comes to overexposure, Stiller ranks up there with Janet Jackson's right breast.

(Thomas Delapa, Boulder Weekly)

Actor, School for Scoundrels (2007)

An uncredited cameo by Ben Stiller as a discontented old boy from Dr P's academy is as humorous as haemorrhoids.

(Christopher Tookey, Daily Mail)

Actor, Tropic Thunder (2008)

Stiller spends the whole film mugging like a baboon in a hall of mirrors, labouring under the mistaken belief that this is somehow amusing.

(Robbie Collin, News of the World)

ANDREW L. STONE

Director, Writer, Song of Norway (1970)

The movie is of an unbelievable badness; it brings back clichés you didn't know you knew — they're practically from the unconscious of moviegoers. You can't get angry at something this stupefying; it seems to have been made by trolls.

(Pauline Kael, New Yorker)

Godawful... The musical numbers, when not downright ugly, are ludicrous, containing all the conventions of staging that made The Sound of Music so easy to hate. Grieg having apparently lived a life of exemplary dullness, the only issue Stone can trump up for dramatic purposes is his thwarted desire to create an indigenous national music for Norway — hardly a matter to keep us on the edge of our chairs. In the ineptitude of his writing, Mr Stone matches the clumsiness of his direction, unconsciously creating a double parody of both the operetta and biographical forms — truly an amazing work of unintentional humor.

(Richard Schickel, Life)

JOSS STONE

Actress, Eragon (2006)

Teen singing sensation Joss Stone improbably turns up as a non-singing, blind soothsayer, in order to tell Eragon "there is a doom about you" – though it's possible that here she is referring not to him but to the movie in general. There is a doom about you too, Joss, unless you take acting classes.

(Christopher Tookey, Daily Mail)

OLIVER STONE

Oliver Stone is a heavy-handed propagandist, and the women in his films make Barbie look like Sylvia Plath.

(Jane Hamsher)

One of the reasons I retired was so that I'd never have to watch another Oliver Stone movie.

(Pauline Kael)

Writer, Director, Heaven and Earth (1993)

Heaven and Earth is intended to make us muse afresh on the plight of the Vietnamese, and, in an unlikely way, it succeeds. First, they had colonial rule, then the Vietcong, then napalm, and now Oliver Stone trying to be nice to them. Haven't these poor people suffered enough?

(Anthony Lane, New Yorker)

Writer, Director, Natural Born Killers (1994)

A bloody, vulgar exercise in what it purports to condemn. Its moral posture is reminiscent of those Bible epics of the 1920's that feature a 20-minute orgy sequence, followed by a 30-second denunciation by the prophet. A pack of adolescents in the theater roared hysterically at each new murder, little realizing that they, with their delight in movie bloodshed, were precisely the supposed object of Stone's social criticism. What does that say about Stone's clarity as a social critic?

(Richard A. Blake, America)

The idea of a "satire" directed by Oliver Stone does inspire a certain dread. Being a satirist requires a sense of humour and perspective, and anyone who has sat through Mr Stone's work knows that he is about as frolicsome and astute as a wounded bull elephant.

(Christopher Tookey, Daily Mail)

A sustained assault on the senses, shot in MTV style, with all the pinpoint accuracy of an elephant-gun in the hands of an enraged chimpanzee.

(Hugo Davenport, Daily Telegraph)

Writer, Director, Nixon (1995)

Sitting through three and a quarter hours of Stone on Nixon is a tedious, bizarre and more than faintly ridiculous experience - like being harangued about international politics by Forrest Gump's girl-friend.

(Christopher Tookey, Daily Mail)

Director, South of the Border (2010)

As in his Castro documentary of 2003, Stone shows that he likes nothing better than cosying up to left-wing dictators. So Stone calls the thuggish Venezuelan leader Hugo Chavez "Hugo." Chavez calls him "Oliver." Stone's interviewing technique is so toe-curlingly obsequious, he makes Jonathan Ross look like Torquemada.

(Christopher Tookey, Daily Mail)

SHARON STONE

Actress, Basic Instinct (1992)

It's a new low for actresses when you have to wonder what's between her ears instead of her legs.

(Katharine Hepburn)

Actress, Diabolique (1996)

Stone is at her most ridiculous, apparently auditioning for the Joan Crawford role in some inexplicable remake of Mommie Dearest. She

appears in a bizarre succession of skintight costumes, which make her look less like an underpaid algebra teacher than a hooker who's gone berserk after winning the lottery. The one treasurable moment comes when Stone advises Adjani on how to cover up their murder – "We've got to act naturally". In this overwrought melodrama, that's a very forlorn hope.

(Christopher Tookey, Daily Mail)

Actress, Basic Instinct 2 (2006)

At this point, there are inflatable toys that are livelier than Stone, but how can you tell the difference? Basic Instinct 2 is not an erotic thriller. It's taxidermy.

(Kyle Smith, New York Post)

Stone is simply awful, replacing the sexy insouciance from the first film with a beady stare that would seem more appropriate coming from a dead codfish than a calculating nympho adept at playing twisted mind games.

(Matt Brunson, Creative Loafing)

She overplays nearly every line with such over-insinuation that Catherine becomes a caricature of a sexpot, often sounding like Jessica Rabbit in heat. Stone reportedly refused to have Benjamin Bratt cast as the male lead because "he's not a good enough actor." What is it they say about people who live in glass houses, Sharon?

(Chuck O'Leary, Fulvuedrive-in.com)

As for Sharon Stone, her deep-voiced, monotonous and completely unalluring approach suggest that for some incomprehensible reason she has decided to play the whole movie as an over-the-hill transsexual auditioning to play the Wicked Witch of the West in an all-gay remake of The Wizard of Oz.

(Christopher Tookey, Daily Mail)

MERYL STREEP

Oh God! She looks like a chicken!

(Truman Capote)

Actress, The House of the Spirits (1994)

Meryl Streep, whom the more ageist among you may consider an unlikely teenager, skips around the set in a manner disturbingly reminiscent of Bette Davis in Whatever Happened To Baby Jane. Sometimes Streep's character refuses to speak to her husband for years on end, possibly in an attempt to show how right Meryl would have been for Holly Hunter's role in The Piano. After giving birth to Winona Ryder, Streep settles for a beatifically smug expression reminiscent of an ex-hooker accepting an Oscar for humanitarian achievement.

(Christopher Tookey, Daily Mail)

BARBRA STREISAND

Actress, Hello, Dolly! (1969)

I have more talent in my smallest fart than you have in your entire body.

(Walter Matthau to Streisand, on set)

I have no disagreement with Barbra Streisand. I was merely exasperated by her tendency to be a complete megalomaniac.

(Walter Matthau, afterwards)

Actress, What's Up, Doc? (1972)

Miss Streisand looks like a cross between an aardvark and an albino rat surmounted by a platinum-coated horse bun.

(John Simon, National Review)

Actress, A Star is Born (1976)

Starring with Streisand is an experience which may have cured me of movies.

(Kris Kristofferson)

A bore is starred.

(Village Voice)

Streisand's notion of acting is to bulldoze her way from one end of a line to the other without regard for anyone or anything; you can literally feel her impatience for the other performer to stop talking so she can take over again.

(John Simon, National Review)

Actress, Writer, Director, Yentl (1983)

Her face looks as though a truck ran into it.

(Divine)

Actress, Director, The Prince of Tides (1992)

She's a ball-buster. Protect me from her.

(Nick Nolte)

JOSEPH STRICK

Director, Writer, Tropic of Cancer (1970)

Strick has a distinguished record of turning his attention only to genuine works of art and consistently botching them. Genet's The Balcony and Joyce's Ulysses had to bear the brunt of his highminded amateurishness.

(John Simon, National Review)

"A spit in the face of art" is how Henry Miller described this non-book about his life in Paris. Now Joseph Strick has tried but failed to turn it into a movie… Tropic of Cancer is execrable gibberish. The man who wrote it was sick. The people who made it into a movie are whores. The people who pay money to see it are fools.

(Rex Reed)

SARA SUGARMAN

Writer, Director, Mad Cows (1999)

The combination of cheap sensationalism, visual ugliness and atrocious direction of actors suggests that at last Michael Winner has found a protegee.

(Christopher Tookey, Daily Mail)

DONALD SUTHERLAND

Actor, Day of the Locust (1975)

There's nothing specifically wrong with Donald Sutherland's performance. It's just awful.

(Pauline Kael, New Yorker)

Actor, Benefit of the Doubt (1993)

Any doubts as to whether Sutherland is or is not playing The Grandad from Hell are rapidly dispelled by a performance so creepy that he might as well be wearing an "I Love Child Molesting" T-shirt.

(Christopher Tookey, Daily Mail)

PATRICK SWAYZE

Actor, Skatetown USA (1979)

Dolled up in tight-fitting leather pants and vest, Swayze looks like the missing seventh member of the Village People. There's no mistaking who he is, though; you can't miss those trademark blank eyes. If the eyes are the window to the soul, he's got an expanse in there as wide open as Montana.

(Damien Bona, Opening Shots)

Actor, Ghost (1990)

I'm not sure it's intentional that Patrick Swayze has the comic timing of a corpse.

(Christopher Tookey, Daily Telegraph)

QUENTIN TARANTINO

Writer, Director, Actor, Reservoir Dogs (1992)

Here is the ideal date movie, assuming you're dating a psychopathic sadist with a high tolerance for dillydallying.

(Ralph Novak, People)

Writer, Director, Pulp Fiction (1994)

Tarantino is less an ironist than a chronic fetishist; he has cooked up a world where hamburgers matter, and nothing else.

(Anthony Lane, New Yorker)

One cannot help wondering whether the appropriate response to this sort of souped-up trailer-park trash might be to acquire a gun and blow the director's head off. I mean, strictly for laughs, OK? In Tarantino's world, no doubt, it would be a scream. The serious point, however, is not that violence in films is wrong per se, nor that it requires knee-jerk censorship. It's that extremes need a justification beyond being gourmet garbage for jaded gluttons.

(Hugo Davenport, Daily Telegraph)

The consensus among reviewers... seems to be that the new film is even more violent than his Reservoir Dogs, "but at least it's funny". Pardon me while I clutch at comprehension. You mean it is all right to watch people being shot, stabbed, tortured, sodomised or drug-injected if we laugh at it, but not if we take it seriously?

(Nigel Andrews, Financial Times)

Kill Bill: Volume 1 (2003)

This smells like the work of an ageing enfant terrible incarcerated in his malodorous living room, scrabbling among the empty pizza-boxes for fresh ways to shock.

(Jenny McCartney, Sunday Telegraph)

Kill Bill: Volume 2 (2004)

Tarantino mistakes collage for creativity, and, more than ever, his knee-jerk homaging feels cheap and pointless. Take the moment when Uma Thurman stands in the doorway and Tarantino sets up the shot to recall John Wayne in The Searchers. What are we supposed to do with that? Draw parallels? There aren't many, and any you can think of aren't flattering. Just sit there gob-smacked at Tarantino's genius? Presumably. But you don't.

(Catherine Shoard, Sunday Telegraph)

CHANNING TATUM

Actor, Step Up (2006)

A big, lumbering young man who resembles Josh Hartnett crossed with an elephant.

(Christopher Tookey, Daily Mail)

Tatum's an orang-utan with moves.

(Tim Robey, Daily Telegraph)

Actor, GI Joe (2009)

The Joes are led by Channing Tatum, a man with all the emotional range of a dinner plate with a frown painted on.

(Robbie Collin, News of the World)

AUDREY TAUTOU

Actress, The Da Vinci Code (2006)

Tautou maintains a polite demeanor and a quizzical expression, as though she learned her lines phonetically and didn't bother to find out what they meant.

(Andrea Chase, Killer Movie Reviews)

She has no chemistry with Tom Hanks; their vast difference in size sometimes makes her look like his glove puppet.

(Christopher Tookey, Daily Mail)

ELIZABETH TAYLOR

All my life I wanted to look like Liz Taylor. Now I find that Liz Taylor is beginning to look like me.

(Divine)

Liz Taylor says she is retaining water. And so is the Hoover dam.

(Lou Berne)

Actress, A Place in the Sun (1951)

I got so sick of starry-eyed close-ups of Elizabeth Taylor that I could have gagged.

(Raymond Chandler)

Actress, Suddenly Last Summer (1959)

Katharine Hepburn as the matriarch trying to keep the lid on things by persuading Montgomery Clift to lobotomize her niece (Taylor, whose performance suggests that surgery has already taken place).

(Jennifer Selway, Time Out)

Actress, Cleopatra (1963)

Elizabeth Taylor is the first Cleopatra to sail down the Nile to Las Vegas.

(Anonymous)

Overweight, overbosomed, overpaid and under-talented, she set the acting profession back a decade.

(David Susskind)

Actress, The Taming of the Shrew (1967)

Just how garish her commonplace accent, squeakily shrill voice, and the

childish petulance with which she delivers her lines are, my pen is neither scratchy nor leaky enough to convey. The once pretty face has become coarse, though from a distance it can still look good - but only if it avoids any attempt at expression, as, to be sure, it not infrequently does. Only the bosom keeps implacably marching on - or down, as the case may be - but I do not feel qualified to be the Xenophon of this reverse anabasis.

(John Simon, National Review)

Actress, Hammersmith is Out! (1972)

Wobbling her enormous derriere across the screen in a manner so offensive it would bring litigation from any dignified, self-respecting performer, and saying lines like "I'm the biggest mother of them all," [Elizabeth Taylor] inspires pity instead of laughs. She has been announcing plans to retire from the screen. Now is as good a time as any.

(Rex Reed)

SHIRLEY TEMPLE

A swaggering, tough little slut.

(Louise Brooks)

Child star, Wee Willie Winkie (1937)

Infancy with her is a disguise, her appeal is more secret and more adult. Already two years ago, she was a fancy little piece... In Captain January, she wore trousers with the mature suggestiveness of a Dietrich: her neat and well-developed rump twisted in the tap dance: her eyes had a sidelong searching coquetry. Now in Wee Willie Winkie, wearing short kilts, she is a complete totsy.

(Graham Greene, Night and Day)

VICTORIA TENNANT

Actress, All of Me (1984)

Victoria Tennant is stiffer than a frozen pea.

(Elissa Von Pozniak, Girl About Town)

EMMA THOMPSON

Actress, Much Ado About Nothing (1993)

Such is the lack of crackle between Ken [Branagh] and Em that they might as well be tucked up in separate beds drinking a cup of cocoa. In terms of sexual electricity, these two are the filmic equivalents of John and Norma Major.

(Anne Billson, Sunday Telegraph)

Actress, The Remains of the Day (1993)

It's not that she looks too young to be a housekeeper - more that she doesn't look like a housekeeper at all. The Miss Kenton she gives us is quarrelsome rather than bossy, bristling with feeling and slightly bored; she could be one of the Mitford sisters taking charge, just for a lark, on the housekeeper's day off.

(Anthony Lane, New Yorker)

UMA THURMAN

Actress, Adventures of Robin Hood (1991)

A transatlantic Maid Marian, treelike and reciting the lines with an icy

contempt which would get her drummed out of the average school play.

(Christopher Tookey, Sunday Telegraph)

Actress, Batman and Robin (1997)

Ms Thurman does look extremely sexy. But she delivers her sub-Mae West lines as unconfidently as Sister Wendy Beckett compering a stag show.

(Christopher Tookey, Daily Mail)

Actress, The Avengers (1998)

Uma Thurman, struggling to maintain an English accent as Emma Peel, gives the sort of performance that has one examining her anxiously for termite damage.

(Christopher Tookey, Daily Mail)

Uma Thurman obviously wanted to undercut her sex-symbol image by making herself look really stupid.

(Rob Gonsalves, efilmcritic.com)

Actress, Paycheck (2003)

She smiles a lot, even when in mortal danger, which you may not consider very lifelike.

(Christopher Tookey, Daily Mail)

LILY TOMLIN

Actress, The Beverly Hillbillies (1994)

The rest of the cast stop at nothing to demean themselves. As the

Clampetts' efficient secretary, Lily Tomlin works harder than anyone and resembles nothing so much as a runaway horse that has been terrified by something (possibly a reading of the script).

(Christopher Tookey, Daily Mail)

MEL TORME

Actor, Good News (1947)

Mel Tormé reminds me of something in a jar, but is, unfortunately, less quiet.

(James Agee, Nation)

ROBERT TOWNSEND

Director, BAPS (1997)

Congratulations, Robert Townsend, you have made one of the worst comedies in the history of American cinema. I've got to hand it to you. BAPS is so bad that it makes the recent turkeys of Mel Brooks look good. Your film is stupid, inept, amateurish, facile, witless, pathetic - and that's just the first 10 minutes. Later on, things get too awful for words.

(Cosmo Landesman, Sunday Times)

JOHN TRAVOLTA

How difficult can it be to fly a plane? I mean, John Travolta learned how.

(Graham Chapman)

Actor, Battlefield Earth (2000)

Easily the most frightening thing about the Psychlos is Travolta's performance. Audiences will hoot with derision as he cackles demonically, kills off his sidekicks to inspire loyalty, just like Dr Evil in the Austin Powers movies, and takes every opportunity to show off stained teeth and dirty fingernails. These prove that though the Psychlos may have mastered intergalactic flight, they still struggle when it comes to elementary personal hygiene.

(Christopher Tookey, Daily Mail)

Actor, The Taking of Pelham 123 (2009)

Cursed with following in the outsized footsteps of world-class heavy Robert Shaw, Travolta devours the scenery; his performance is 0% inspiration, 100% perspiration.

(Nathan Rabin, The Onion)

Actor, Old Dogs (2010)

Travolta has never been smugger... One of many comedic low points comes when Williams and Travolta accidentally rub bear excrement on to their faces. "Scat happens, man," remarks Travolta, philosophically. Indeed it does.

(Christopher Tookey, Daily Mail)

CHRIS TUCKER

Actor, Money Talks (1997)

A shrieking nincompoop who must be the most obnoxious leading man in modern cinema.

(Christopher Tookey, Daily Mail)

The con man is played by Chris Tucker, the preening clown who yammered his way through The Fifth Element last year. Come to think of it, I should have mentioned his involvement sooner. It would have saved you having to read this far, because, even at this early stage in Tucker's movie career, it has become a rule of thumb that any film starring this actor will be unwatchable.

(Edward Porter, Sunday Times)

Actor, Rush Hour 3 (2007)

Tucker is highly resistible. Screaming his lines, and constantly moving, presumably to cover up the fact that he is not actually funny, his characterisation of the well-meaning but incompetent cop, all rolling eyes and big smiles, is surely as racist as anything pre-Butterfly McQueen.

(Peter Whittle, Sunday Times)

Six years on from Rush Hour 2, during which he has understandably failed to find employment on any other movie, Chris Tucker's high-pitched shrieking and unfounded conviction that he's funny have lost none of their power to infuriate. The fact that he was paid 25 million dollars to repeat his talentless shtick is enough to make anyone despair.

(Christopher Tookey, Daily Mail)

LANA TURNER

Lana Turner could give you an eye-witness account of the Crucifixion and still put you to sleep.

(Herman Mankiewicz)

Actress, The Three Musketeers (1948)

As Lady de Winter, Lana Turner sounds like a drive-in waitress exchanging quips with hotrodders.

(New Yorker, 1980)

LIV ULLMANN

Actress, Pope Joan (1972)

It's just a story of Liv Ullmann looking like George Peppard.

(Anonymous)

Actress, Lost Horizon (1972)

Liv Ullmann registers with all the impact of boiled ham on white bread.

(Vincent Canby, New York Times)

DEBORAH KARA UNGER

Actress, Emile (2003)

Her natural beauty is hidden under a costume of cargo pants and cardigans and, what with her heavily plucked eyebrows, she looks like a transvestite who decided to clear out the garage instead of go on a date.

(Antonia Quirke, Evening Standard)

JEAN-CLAUDE VAN DAMME

Jean-Claude Van Damme exudes the charisma of a packet of Cup-A-Soup.

(Jonathan Romney, Independent on Sunday)

Actor, Kickboxer (1989)

Mr Van Damme is a sensational discovery, combining the balletic grace of Mikhail Baryshnikov with the acting ability of a turnip.

(Christopher Tookey, Sunday Telegraph)

Actor, AWOL - Absent Without Leave (1990)

Further endearing proof that Mr Van Damme is to screen-acting what Saddam Hussein is to humanitarianism.

(Christopher Tookey, Sunday Telegraph)

Actor, Double Impact (1991)

Two Van Dammes for your money is even worse value than one. Here he plays twins, separated when babies. The only interest in this violent actioner is watching Van Damme having trouble trying to remember which brother he's supposed to be playing.

(Simon Rose)

Actor, Maximum Risk (1996)

The soporific and bored-looking Van Damme goes through the motions like a man in an advanced vegetative state. Has the muscles from Brussels turned into the brussel with muscles?

(Cosmo Landesman, Sunday Times)

As palatable as stale bread, leading to some uninvited bursts of laughter as Van Damme tries, really, to do some soul searching stuff, which just doesn't wash. Watching this film will make you want to scrub your skull out with soap.

(Jake Hamilton, Empire)

Actor, Knock Off (1998)

From the halfway point on, nothing in Knock Off matters but the camera work and the size of the explosions. Nothing. Not Van Damme, who thinks he's acting when all he's doing is making faces.

(Edvins Bejtiks, San Francisco Examiner)

GUS VAN SANT

Director, Writer, Last Days (2005)

Seamlessly and rather cleverly, without telling anybody, Gus Van Sant has transitioned out of important filmmaking and has taken up a new career in torture. He's developing a knack. With Gerry (2003), about two guys who get lost in the desert, Van Sant seemed to go as far as anyone could in making a completely inert movie. But with Last Days, about the events leading up to a grunge rocker's suicide, he surpasses himself, making a picture that's in trouble from its first minutes... Before Last Days, his suicide was unquestionably the worst thing that ever happened to Kurt Cobain. But this movie is serious competition.

(Mick LaSalle, San Francisco Chronicle)

This is van Sant at his most creepily complacent and poseurish, and stands alongside his film Gerry as one of the most unbearably boring films I have ever sat through. Its defenders will doubtless call it a mood piece; but the only mood it is likely to engender in a paying audience is profound annoyance.

(Christopher Tookey, Daily Mail)

NIA VARDALOS

Actress, Writer, Connie and Carla (2004)

The phrase "written by Nia Vardalos" should send any self-respecting moviegoer screaming into the night, pursued by the comedienne's frizzy-haired brand of hysteria and the brain meltdown it inevitably induces.

(David Ng, Village Voice)

Vardalos never met a bad joke she doesn't love, never met a stereotype she won't exaggerate to a breaking point and can't seem to get past a sitcom mentality.

(MaryAnn Johanson, Flick Filosopher)

Actress, My Life In Ruins/ Driving Aphrodite (2009)

Nia Vardalos, the star of My Big Fat Greek Wedding, has lost weight, some of it, to judge by Driving Aphrodite, from her brain.

(Nigel Andrews, Financial Times)

Vardalos plays too much of the movie with a smile of feta cheese. She plays Georgia, a superficial, self-obsessed, sex-starved academic turned tour guide, who despises the coach-load of imbeciles she takes round such sights as Mount Olympus, Delphi and the Parthenon... Every so often, one of the actors – clearly wishing they were elsewhere - cracks under the strain and snaps at Vardalos to stop mugging to camera. "You're not funny! Stop trying!" several of them beg. She fails to take their advice.

(Christopher Tookey, Daily Mail)

MATTHEW VAUGHN

Director, Kick-Ass (2010)

Matthew Vaughn, former Guy Ritchie producer, co-wrote and directed, and on this evidence is all flash and no flair.

(Nigel Andrews, Financial Times)

VINCE VAUGHN

Actor, Fred Claus (2007)

Here's a very simple message for Hollywood: Vince Vaughn and sincerity mix about as well as Britney Spears and parenting skill.

(Mr Cranky, Mr Cranky Rates The Movies)

Actor, Four Christmases (2008)

Vince Vaughn and Reese Witherspoon are physically ill-matched. She has never looked tinier, while the always gigantic Vaughn has put on so much weight around the middle that I half-expected the big plot revelation to be that he'd eaten her twin sister.

(Christopher Tookey, Daily Mail)

Actor, Couples Retreat (2009)

This is Vaughn's third stinker in a row, after Fred Claus and Four Christmases, and it's clear the guy doesn't need couples therapy. He needs career advice. Urgently.

(Christopher Tookey, Daily Mail)

JOHNNY VEGAS

Actor, Sex Lives of the Potato Men (2004)

Billed as an 'erotic, testosterone-charged comedy' about a pair of Brummie yobs called Dave and Ferris, who are according to the publicity notes "two good-looking young blokes living by their own rules". The truth is that they live by no rules discernible to the naked eye, and one of these "good-looking blokes" is played by arguably the ugliest, most obese and least sexy comedian in Britain, Johnny Vegas.

(Christopher Tookey, Daily Mail)

This is, I hope, the only movie that has shown, or will ever show, Johnny Vegas, topless, in not one, but two gangbang scenes.

(Ian Waldron-Mantgani, The UK Critic)

LARS VON TRIER

Writer, Director, The Idiots (1998)

Shot with a hand-held camera by someone with an uncertain grasp of focus, it's rambling, formless and depressing, like having to sit through a season of out-takes from the works of Jeremy Beadle. The ideas which lie beneath it - of fragile people's dependency upon groups, of the way actors' roles can take them over - aren't explored. It's a pointless mess - but von Trier may be on to something. The fact that his film was praised by some critics and found funding from bodies in Denmark, France, Italy, Netherlands, Germany and Sweden suggests that in real life too there is no shortage of people bent on acting like idiots.

(Christopher Tookey, Daily Mail)

Writer, Director, Dancer in the Dark (2000)

The scenes at the jail, when Björk sings a ditty to bring comfort to her condemned cellmates, only confirms there should be a Death Row specially reserved for pop singers.

(Alexander Walker, Evening Standard)

The announcement of its win at Cannes inspired boos and hisses from an audience hardened to the inanities of festival juries. If I'd been

there I would have allowed myself a small gasp of incredulity, a cynical chuckle and a quick chorus of The Emperor's New Clothes.

(Christopher Tookey, Daily Mail)

Writer, Director, Antichrist (2009)

Lars von Trier has an inordinately and unjustifiably high reputation. His latest con job, Antichrist, will no doubt be hailed as a masterpiece by his worshippers. Such is not the case for those of us for whom boredom is not synonymous with art, nor violence with profundity... Allegorical in the worst ways, Antichrist is about as profound as a slasher movie.

(Peter Rainer, Christian Science Monitor)

Somehow, a shovel seems a more appropriate implement for dealing with Lars von Trier's Antichrist than any sort of writing utensil. While some critics describe the film as vile and disgusting, that sort of moral judgment seems beside the point when dealing with a bullshit artist like von Trier... Let me state it simply: Lars von Trier is a fraud, who keeps making movies because he has somehow convinced enough people that his delusions or pretensions (the latter, more likely) are art and that his movies are worthwhile. Neither idea could be further from the truth.

(Marshall Fine, Hollywood and Fine)

Lars von Trier, we get it. You really, really don't like women... It's difficult to imagine where von Trier will go next in his career. A graphic onscreen clitorectomy is a tough act to follow. And I can't imagine that actresses will be queuing up to work with him after this.

(Wendy Ide, Times)

Antichrist is a horrible combination of extraordinarily unpleasant elements. It's offensively misogynistic. It's needlessly graphic in its use of violence. And its maker almost certainly needs psychiatric help.

(Christopher Tookey, Daily Mail)

ROBERT WAGNER

Actor, The Pink Panther (1963)

As for Robert Wagner, who plays David Niven's nephew, he is losing his looks and has not acquired the acting ability which would hide it.

(George Millau, Films in Review)

MARK WAHLBERG

Actor, The Truth About Charlie (2003)

Wahlberg, playing the Cary Grant role, is totally miscast and displays the cosmopolitan charm of a wombat.

(Edward Porter, Sunday Times)

No matter how many snazzy camera angles Demme shoves in your face, he can't hide the fact that his leading man has zero acting ability and even less charisma. Forget Cary Grant, Wahlberg isn't even the new George Peppard.

(Catherine Shoard, Sunday Telegraph)

Actor, Max Payne (2009)

This summer, Mark Wahlberg took on a bunch of killer trees in The Happening. And by the look of things, he picked up some acting tips from them along the way, cos the bloke has the same range of emotions as a bit of four-by-two. Wahlberg spends most of the film padding around in the shadows with a pained look on his face. He's aiming for Michael Caine-meets-Humphrey Bogart. He gets Inspector Clouseau-meets-a-fat-fingered proctologist.

(Robbie Collin, News of the World)

Did Wahlberg read the script, or was it hidden under the pile of money that the producers dropped at his doorstep?

(Willie Waffle, wafflemovies.com)

PAUL WALKER

Actor, 2 Fast 2 Furious (2003)

What Paul Walker needed was a stunt double. To stand in for him the entire movie.

(Eugene Novikov, Film Blather)

Paul Walker is probably the worst performer on the planet.

(Joshua Tyler, Film Hobbit)

Actor, Timeline (2003)

The frighteningly talentless nonentity from The Fast and The Furious, Paul Walker, is even drearier and more embarrassing than in his previous movies, making you want to look anywhere on the screen but at him. This guy could actually benefit from having acting lessons from Keanu Reeves.

(Christopher Tookey, Daily Mail)

RACHEL WARD

Actress, Against All Odds (1984)

Ward is so wooden as a femme fatale she should be treated for dry rot.

(Simon Rose)

Actress, After Dark, My Sweet (1990)

The thing which reduces the film to farce, however, is Rachel Ward's embarrassing attempt to play the femme fatale: her idea of how to play an alcoholic is to stand next to an empty wine bottle.

(Christopher Tookey, Sunday Telegraph)

ANDY WARHOL

Director, The Chelsea Girls (1966)

The Chelsea Girls is a testimonial to what happens when a camera falls into the hands of an aesthetic, moral, and intellectual bankrupt.

(John Simon, National Review)

MIA WASIKOWSKA

Actress, Alice In Wonderland (2010)

This girl's got all the warmth of a refrigerated trout, and a face you'd expect to see Blu-Tacked to the inside of a London phone box. She's not a heroine - she looks like she's ON heroin.

(Robbie Collin, News of the World)

JOHN WAYNE

Actor, The Conqueror (1956)

Portrays the great conqueror as a sort of cross between a square-shootin' sheriff and a Mongolian idiot. The idea is good for a couple of snickers, but after that it never Waynes but it bores.

(Time)

John Wayne as Genghis Khan – history's most improbable piece of casting unless Mickey Rooney were to play Jesus in King of Kings.

(Jack Smith, Los Angeles Times)

SIGOURNEY WEAVER

Actress, Imaginary Heroes (2004)

Something terrible has happened to Sigourney Weaver. She's turned into Susan Sarandon. Once a smart and subtle actress, Weaver seems to have been studying Mrs Tim Robbins's withering matriarch routine (see the hellish The Banger Sisters) and somehow, somehow, been inspired... Still sexy but endlessly self-deprecating, she cries a lot, looks wry a lot and is just so wise and quirky it's hard not to hate her.

(Catherine Shoard, Sunday Telegraph)

Actress, Snow Cake (2006)

Weaver's performance is so extravagantly awful, you can't take your eyes off it. When she is happy she gurgles, gurns and waves her arms like a demented mime. When she is upset, she flaps them in a fury, frets over the housework and shrilly orders Alan Rickman to take out the trash. "I don't do garbage!" she roars, although in this case she has gallantly made an exception.

(Xan Brooks, Guardian)

RACHEL WEISZ

Actress, Eragon (2006)

The dragon is called Safira, which sounds regrettably like a people-carrier in the Vauxhall range and, though she's supposedly fierce, she's voiced by Rachel Weisz as though she is an irritatingly over-earnest A-level student at St Paul's Girls School.

(Christopher Tookey, Daily Mail)

RAQUEL WELCH

Actress, Myra Breckenridge (1970)

As an adaptation of Gore Vidal's novel, this is a major travesty. As a Hollywood comedy, it's a major disaster. But as a Raquel Welch movie, it's better than most.

(Tony Rayns, Time Out)

Actress, The Legend of Walks Far Women (1980)

Not a very good singer or dancer, she is not a very good actor either. She looked like Sticks Out Woman.

(Clive James, Observer)

ORSON WELLES

Actor, Jane Eyre (1944)

Welles's Rochester has the studied arrogance, the restless moods of a medieval king carrying his own soul to a halberd and demanding that everybody look at it. We only wish that he spoke more clearly; he so mumbles and macerates his words that half the time we are unable to tell what he was talking about.

(Bosley Crowther, New York Times)

It is possible to enjoy his performance as dead-pan period parody; I

imagine he did. I might have more if I hadn't wanted, instead, to see a good performance.

(James Agee, Nation)

Director, Actor, Macbeth (1948)

Welles doth foully slaughter Shakespeare.

(Life)

Actor, The Immortal Story (1968)

Welles seems unable to do anything these days unless he relates everything and everybody to his own selfish and tortured excessiveness. He belches, he mumbles, he upstages everyone, he chews on his tongue in monosyllabic gibberish. It's all very embarrassing.

(Rex Reed)

Actor, Ten Days' Wonder (1976)

Everybody in the cast looks uncomfortable, particularly Welles, who either has had a very bad makeup job or has let his nose turn gray.

(Vincent Canby, New York Times)

IRVINE WELSH

Writer, The Acid House (1998)

Sitting through this sadistic exercise in sustained puerility is, if I may use an Irvine Welsh-style metaphor, about as pleasurable as having one's head forced beyond the S-bend of an ill-kept public lavatory. Like most films for fashion victims, The Acid House has an ear-splitting soundtrack, but most of all it resounds to the inaudible noise of lottery money being flushed down the drain.

(Christopher Tookey, Daily Mail)

WIM WENDERS

Writer, Director, The American Friend (1977)

A masterpiece for people who think a movie can't be worthwhile unless it makes you suffer. Wenders is not only turgid, he's exhibitionistically turgid. Wenders's unsettling compositions are neurotically beautiful visions of a disordered world, but the film doesn't have the nasty, pleasurable cleverness of a good thriller; dramatically, it's stagnant - inverted Wagnerianism.

(Pauline Kael, New Yorker)

MAE WEST

A plumber's idea of Cleopatra.

(W.C.Fields)

The ultimate female impersonator.

(Divine)

Actress, Myra Breckenridge (1970)

Mae West, close to eighty, resembles nothing less than a dressed-up corpse. There is a touch of necrophilia in having potent young men lining up to see her. It seems that rigor mortis will set in at any moment. Had Myra Breckinridge been intended to be a horror film Miss West's performance might have been successful.

(Harry Medved & Randy Dreyfuss, The 50 Worst Films of All Time)

Most ghastly of all is the ancient Mae West, who was obviously encouraged to parody herself as a much younger movie star. With her hand still on her hip, West struts through scenes mentally undressing

those male secretaries and tossing off those double entendres. Considering that she looks like an escapee from the Hollywood Wax Museum, such verbal pelvic thrusting seems absolutely perverse. But in a movie that features Raquel Welch, in a star-spangled cutaway bathing suit, sodomizing a cowboy stud with a strap-on dildo, nothing Miss West does can come as any shock.

(Michael Sauter, The Worst Movies of All Time)

JOANNE WHALLEY-KILMER

Actress, Navy SEALs (1990)

Whalley-Kilmer looks ill-at-ease and wholesome throughout, like Olivia Newton-John duped into jamming with Motorhead.

(Christopher Tookey, Sunday Telegraph)

FOREST WHITAKER

Director, Hope Floats (1998)

Under the flaccid direction of actor-turned-director Forest Whitaker, the storyline lies inert and lifeless for long periods, padded out and weighed down by great wodges of middle-of-the-road rock music that made me feel as mutinous as Sid Vicious at a Mantovani concert.

(Christopher Tookey, Daily Mail)

BO WIDERBERG

Writer, Director, Elvira Madigan (1967)

The use of Mozart's Piano Concerto 21 on the soundtrack serves only to emphasise the appalling and unbridgeable artistic gulf between Mozart and Bo Widerberg.

(Christopher Tookey, Sunday Telegraph)

ESTHER WILLIAMS

Wet, she's a star; dry, she ain't.

(Joe Pasternak)

Actress, Jupiter's Darling (1954)

Esther Williams' pictures are generally just so much water over the dame. This one tries to be different. Esther even tries to act - a spectacle almost as alarming as that of the Burmese fish that climbs trees.

(Time)

ROBIN WILLIAMS

Robin Williams' technique is to say 500 things with a joke rhythm, and at least two of them might be funny.

(Paul Rudnick, aka Libby Gelman-Waxner, Premiere)

Actor, Jack (1996)

Williams can be funny (as in Mrs Doubtfire) or moving (as in Awakenings), but here he is simply obnoxious, constantly bending his features into an ingratiating smarmy grin, working so frenetically to act vulnerable and get in touch with his "inner child" that he should be had up for inner child abuse.

(Christopher Tookey, Daily Mail)

Williams, a once-funny comedian now suffering from Sally Field syndrome (i.e., he desperately wants to be loved), is the last actor in the world who should be encouraged to unleash his inner child, since nowadays he continually behaves like Shirley Temple trapped in the body of the Laughing Gnome.

(Anne Billson, Sunday Telegraph)

Actor, Bicentennial Man (1999)

He emanates a smirking smugness, a plastic piety. He's Uriah Heep with a tan, dripping with greetings-card sentiment and fake humility. He plays the whole movie as though expecting shortly to be canonised.

(Christopher Tookey, Daily Mail)

Actor, License to Wed (2007)

Robin Williams, whose stock-in-trade gurning has become almost creepy, should call it a day.

(Peter Whittle, Sunday Times)

For sheer hatefulness, there's no one to touch Robin Williams in Licence to Wed. He plays an over-zealous pastor who won't bless the union of his parishioner Sadie (Mandy Moore) and her fiancé Ben (John Krasinski) unless they pass his marriage preparation course. Even at the outset, Williams is unintentionally creepy, with numerous inappropriate references to extramarital sex, venereal disease and Viagra, some of them in front of small children. When he meets Ben, Williams ogles Sadie and asks the prospective groom "So what do you do — besides Little Sadie?" Do Hollywood film-makers really believe that modern priests behave like a witless, X-rated version of Groucho Marx? Williams' character turns from sleazy to psychotic as he puts his programme into operation. It involves bugging the young lovers' bedroom and listening to their amorous encounters. And Williams eavesdrops with a young acolyte who appears about 12 years old. What else do they do? Download pornography together?

(Christopher Tookey, Daily Mail)

TENNESSEE WILLIAMS

Writer, The Fugitive Kind (1960), based on his play Orpheus Descending

(Said to Tennessee Williams after a screening) Darling, they've absolutely ruined your perfectly dreadful play.

(Tallulah Bankhead)

BRUCE WILLIS

Actor, Writer, Hudson Hawk (1991)

It's not just the incoherent plot or the juvenile jokes, the senseless cartoon violence or the budget-busting demolition derbies. It's also the way Willis and Silver serve up these insults with such smug self-satisfaction. It's as if their movie was some sort of private Planet Hollywood party to which we'd been magnanimously invited. The trouble is, they're all drunk and we're still sober.

(Michael Sauter, The Worst Movies of All Time)

A miserable fiasco, and as horrible a commentary on the banality of Mr Willis's psyche, as Harlem Nights was on Eddie Murphy's… The good news is that the film should lose every cent of its 55 million dollar budget. Mr Willis and his team have discovered the 20th century equivalent of alchemy: how to turn gold into purest lead.

(Christopher Tookey, Sunday Telegraph)

Its utter failure can only be explained by some form of madness having overcome the people involved in its making.

(Philip French, Observer)

Actor, Color of Night (1994)

I can understand Willis wishing to extend his acting range, but as a psychiatrist he is slightly less convincing than Mickey Rourke might be playing the lead in The Marcel Proust Story.

(Christopher Tookey, Daily Mail)

Actor, Last Man Standing (1996)

Willis lacks the grandeur for this kind of role: he looks less like an assassin than someone who might slide out from under your car and try to overcharge you for an MOT.

(Christopher Tookey, Daily Mail)

OWEN WILSON

Actor, Wedding Crashers (2005)

Wilson is rather underused, mainly mooching around mooning after McAdams, and the producers' attempts to turn him into every girl's dream - feathering his hair, sticking him in tight T-shirts - have rather the opposite effect.

(Catherine Shoard, Sunday Telegraph)

MICHAEL WINNER

The first rule for a young director to follow is not to direct like Michael Winner. The second and third rules are the same.

(Anonymous)

Director, Death Wish (1974)

Poisonous incitement to do-it-yourself law enforcement is the vulgar exploitation hook on which Death Wish is awkwardly hung.

(Variety)

Objectionable vigilante trash from the objectionable Winner.

(Geoff Andrew, Time Out)

Director, The Sentinel (1976)

Winner, for some reason, decides the best way to show minions from Hell is to have a large group of real life handicapped and deformed people dressed in rags. Is this offensive, or is it just me?

(Ned Daigle, Bad Movie Night)

Director, Death Wish 2 (1981)

So ineptly directed and edited that it was an insult even to audiences that were looking for a bad movie.

(Roger Ebert, Chicago Sun-Times)

Director, The Wicked Lady (1983)

The hoary, the tedious and the disagreeable are married with an infelicity rare even in costume.

(Dilys Powell, Sunday Times)

Director, Appointment With Death (1988)

Providing even the meager pleasures of vicariously visiting exotic climes is beyond the ability of the director, Michael Winner. He does something here that you'd think was darn near impossible - he manages to make the Holy Land look dowdy.

(Hal Hinson, Washington Post)

The dead hand of director Winner falls on an already lifeless script.

(Christopher Tookey, Sunday Telegraph)

Director, Bullseye! (1990)

A masterpiece of its kind: impressively, magnificently, astonishingly lousy in an unprecedented multiplicity of ways. Ealing Comedy as reinterpreted by neolithic man.

(Christopher Tookey, Sunday Telegraph)

Director, Parting Shots (1999)

Michael Winner is the worst director of all time. Some would claim that the American auteur behind Plan 9 From Outer Space, Edward D. Wood, deserves that title, but Wood had to work with inadequate resources and deadbeat actors, and his work does betray a kindly nature. Over a quarter-century, Winner made films of unsurpassed nastiness. He repeatedly took first-rate actors and made them look incompetent.

(Christopher Tookey, Daily Mail)

Essentially the equivalent of vanity publishing: a film directed by Michael Winner, produced by Michael Winner, written by Michael Winner, edited by Michael Winner, and made for Michael Winner to watch, perhaps in company with Michael Winner's current girlfriend.

(Mark Steyn)

A ghastly pudding of ineptitude that the director would surely send back were it served at one of his dinners.

(Jason Solomons, Mail on Sunday)

This looks like little more than another case of the director slapping together a film with his celebrity friends. True friends, though, tell you when you're embarrassing yourself.

(Richard Falcon, Sight and Sound)

RAY WINSTONE

Actor, Tank Malling (1988)

Ray Winstone blunders about like an idiot.

(Kim Newman, Film Review)

Actor, King Arthur (2004)

Ray Winstone plays the aptly named Sir Bors as though he has just come out of an especially thuggish episode of EastEnders.

(Christopher Tookey, Daily Mail)

SHELLEY WINTERS

Actress, What's the Matter With Helen? (1971)

The short answer to Curtis Harrington's What's the Matter with Helen? is that she is overplayed by Shelley Winters.

(New Statesman)

Actress, The Poseidon Adventure (1972)

Overacting in a gray wig that makes her resemble Miss Piggy's grandmother, Winters performs the most crazed of the film's many madcap surprises. When Hackman is trapped underwater, Winters waddles forward to exclaim, "I was the underwater swimming champ of New York for three years running. Swimming through corridors, and up and down stairwells — I'm the only one here trained to do things like that!" (Honorable mention must be awarded to Stella Stevens, who snaps, "Will you shut up?"). Winters then dives in and saves Hackman, while doing an underwater ballet that is unparalleled

in Bad Movie madness; her dress floats up over her head, showing off Winters's mindbending pantyline and buns.

> (Edward Margulies & Stephen Rebello, Bad Movies We Love)

NORMAN WISDOM

Actor, Press For Time (1966)

Maybe the reason why Norman Wisdom can have such a melancholy effect on the people who don't respond to him is that he tugs desperately at strings of social pathos that aren't connected any longer to a context. Sometimes he seems to be begging sympathy on false terms for a folk hero of the Depression. A lot of the elements in his style and look are pure period; the underfed physique, the Brylcreem, the clothes that sadly try to ape a fashion patented by a remote boss class, the nervy upward squints with his face pressed against the chests of policemen and battle-axes, the scampers for safety and the leaps on to the tops of lamp-posts. It is all very much as it used to be, except that the hero's troubles seem fabricated now that he hasn't the backbone of a time.

> (Penelope Gilliatt)

Actor, Double X (1992)

One minor flaw in the movie is that Mr Wisdom is about as convincing a computer whizz as Russ Abbott would be, playing Indiana Jones.

> (Christopher Tookey, Sunday Telegraph)

JOHN WOO

Director, Hard Boiled (1992)

Mr Woo may well be as hard boiled as his heroes. But the ideas in his films are poached; his morality is over-easy; he leave most of his characters fried and his audiences' brains scrambled. Mr Woo isn't God, Michelangelo, Mozart or Hitchcock: he represents cinema at its most decadent and pernicious. He is the bore of gore.

(Christopher Tookey, Daily Mail)

EDWARD D. WOOD

Writer, Director, Plan 9 From Outer Space (1959)

Gives the appearance of having been slung together by drunk mortuary attendants.

(Philip Strick, Science Fiction Movies)

So very bad that it exerts a strange fascination. It appears to have been made in somebody's garage.

(John Brosnan)

How bad is it? Give a monkey a camera and it'll make a better picture.

(Danny Peary)

ELIJAH WOOD

Actor, Hooligans/ Green Street (2005)

Elijah Wood looks like a mild-mannered hobbit trying to impersonate an orc, which is okay early on but horribly unconvincing later, when he is supposed to have evolved into a hooligan himself. When he gets angry, he looks like Peter Mandelson having a hissy fit.

(Christopher Tookey, Daily Mail)

WILLIAM WYLER

Director, Ben-Hur (1959)

A Griffith can make a hundred into a crowd while a Wyler can reduce a thousand to a confused cocktail party.

(Dwight MacDonald, Esquire)

MICHAEL YORK

Actor, Something for Everyone (1970)

Michael York is a supremely monotonous actor and has, moreover, the head of a blond rat.

(John Simon, National Review)

SUSANNAH YORK

Actress, The Killing of Sister George (1968)

Susannah York is unconvincing at everything: lesbianism, childishness, acting.

(John Simon, National Review)

LORETTA YOUNG

Actress

Whatever it was that this actress never had, she still hasn't got it.

(Bosley Crowther, New York Times)

SEAN YOUNG

Actress, A Kiss Before Dying (1990)

Sean Young wanders through the film with a distant expression, as though simultaneously listening to the test match through an ear-piece.
(Christopher Tookey, Sunday Telegraph)

PIA ZADORA

Actress, The Lonely Lady (1982)

Miss Pia Zadora has a real life rich husband who wants to make her a star. Croesus would not have enough in his coffers to do the job.
(William Russell, Glasgow Herald)

BILLY ZANE

Actor, The Phantom (1996)

This superhero (Billy Zane) isn't super at all: just an unsatisfactory mixture of Tarzan, the Lone Ranger and Batman - a masked man marooned in a puce leotard. In moments of danger, Zane looks like a damson in distress.
(Christopher Tookey, Daily Mail)

Actor, Bloodrayne (2005)

As you might expect from any movie that begins with the promise of a "special appearance by Billy Zane"... Bloodrayne is ghastly-bad.
(Gregory Kirschling, Entertainment Weekly)

Actor, Three (2006)

It could be that Kelly Brook regarded acting as an unnecessary exertion, in view of the amount of over-acting, most of it hysterically ill-judged, by Billy Zane, who practically foams at the mouth as Kelly's jealous husband, even before he starts painting his body like a savage and behaving like Mike Tyson on acid. "He doesn't usually act like this!" wails Kelly, early on, but she obviously hasn't watched Zane performing as much as I have. He plays her hot-headed hubby in exactly the same way as he played Kate Winslet's jilted fiancé in Titanic: like an egomaniac who has decided he has insufficient dialogue and is determined to make each line-reading as portentous and preposterous as possible.

(Christopher Tookey, Daily Mail)

FRANCO ZEFFIRELLI

Director, Sparrow (1993)

Zeffirelli has often been guilty of casting for looks rather than talent, particularly with regard to young men; here, he plumbs new depths. The film's his worst ever, a prettified horror with atrocious dubbing, risible dialogue and a less lively cast than might be found on a broken leg.

(Christopher Tookey, Daily Mail)

RENEE ZELLWEGER

Actress, Leatherheads (2008)

Zellweger's just awful, scrunching her features into that pouting, squinty, unadorable mush face that's made her last three or four characters look as if they've just had root canal surgery.

(Tim Robey, Daily Telegraph)

Actress, Case 39 (2009)

Renee Zellweger is perfect for a horror film: her mad face scared me out of my wits in Bridget Jones 2.

(Robbie Collin, News of the World)

Actress, New In Town (2009)

It's a laugh-free fiasco starring a cruelly lit Renee Zellweger who, as she nears 40, nails the lid on the coffin of her once-flourishing career as a ditzy leading lady. Playing a hard-hearted executive from sunny Miami, intent on downsizing a failing food factory in ice-bound Minnesota while wearing absurdly high heels, she more and more resembles a gurning, tottering chipmunk.

(Christopher Tookey, Daily Mail)

This film has been described elsewhere as "Bridget Jones goes to Fargo." Which sadly isn't quite accurate, because at the end Renee Zellweger doesn't get fed face-first into a woodchipper.

(Robbie Collin, News of the World)

CATHERINE ZETA-JONES

Actress, Intolerable Cruelty (2003)

Zeta-Jones, as I'd feared, isn't quite up to it. There's a certain try-hard coldness about this performance: her eyes betray a mind that appears to be constantly trying not to forget something. While Clooney might be some kind of substitute for Cary Grant, Zeta-Jones is no Rosalind Russell.

(Jason Solomons, Mail on Sunday)

Increasingly, she resembles a drag queen's idea of glamour. And, even

after her Oscar for *Chicago*, there is the question of whether she actually has much talent. Her facial expressions are so limited they make Roger Moore's raised eyebrow and Joan Collins's pout look like comedic subtlety. Whether because of premature plastic surgery or too much make-up (she's turning orange with age), her face is starting to look like a triumph of the mortician's art.

(Christopher Tookey, Daily Mail)

Actress, The Terminal (2004)

Zeta-Jones is hardly convincing as someone who is supposed to have spent half a lifetime dumping reheated meals on economy-class laps. This is a girl who definitely turns left when she boards a plane.

(Matthew Bond, Mail on Sunday)

The romantic subplot between lumpish, middle-aged Viktor (Tom Hanks) and a gorgeous, sophisticated flight attendant (Catherine Zeta-Jones) rings utterly false... The only immigrant she'd be likely to go for is Conrad Black, in the days when he still had a corporate credit card.

(Christopher Tookey, Daily Mail)

Actress, The Legend of Zorro (2005)

Zeta-Jones doesn't act, so much as pose for her close-up. Yes, the camera loves her, but not as much as she loves herself. She stands there with that little smile of hers that says: I'm so beautiful, you should sit back and enjoy the view. That's possible, but only if you can stay awake.

(Cosmo Landesman, Sunday Times)

Zeta Jones looks trapped like a doe in the headlights by her epically silly character arc and an impressively absurd degree of decolletage. Not since Angelina Jolie in *Lara Croft: Tomb Raider* has an actress been so comprehensively upstaged by her own breasts.

(Tim Robey, Daily Telegraph)

Catherine speaks Spanish like a woman who wouldn't touch a burrito without rubber gloves and a surgical mask.

(Mark Ramsey, Moviejuice)

Actress, The Rebound (2010)

Catherine Zeta-Jones won a CBE this year "for services to the film industry". Yet she hasn't actually had one of her movies in UK cinemas since 2007. Mind you, on the strength of The Rebound, that's one of the best services to the film industry old cheetah-features could make.

(Robbie Collin, News of the World)

CHRISTOPHER TOOKEY

Christopher Tookey was educated at Tonbridge School and Exeter College, Oxford, where he was a History Scholar, President of the Union, Editor of Isis, President of the Etceteras and Musical Director of Oxford Theatre Group. He also directed the winning new play in the Sunday Times-NUS Drama Competition.

Since 1993, he has been the film critic for the Daily Mail, the UK's best-selling mid-market daily newspaper. Between 1994 and 1998, he was Chairman of the British Film Critics' Circle, producing and presenting their annual awards ceremony in aid of the NSPCC. He is author of the non-fiction book The Critics' Film Guide and www.movie-film-review.com, the biggest collection of film criticism in the world.

For several years before 1993, he was TV and Film Critic for the Sunday Telegraph and TV critic for the Daily Telegraph. He has also been theatre critic for the Mail on Sunday and written for Prospect, the Sunday Times, Observer, European, Books & Bookmen and (in the USA) National Review.

He is a prolific broadcaster, interviewer and interviewee on radio and TV, and has worked in the theatre and television, as a writer, composer, director and producer.

The hundreds of TV programmes he has directed include the award-winning rock series Revolver (ATV), the acclaimed Channel 4 series After Dark, the Emmy-winning Network 7, the ratings successes Showtime, Luna and Celebrity Squares (Central), and international chart-topping rock videos including Katrina and the Waves' Walking On Sunshine.

He has composed and arranged theme music for several long-running television series and composed 12 stage musicals, produced at the Theatre Royal, Windsor, Haymarket and Phoenix Theatres Leicester, Arts Cambridge, Belgrade Theatre Coventry, Bush and Gate Theatres on the London fringe, and Theatre Royal, Haymarket.

Also in the West End, he has produced and directed shows at the Theatre Royal Haymarket, May Fair, Piccadilly and Fortune Theatres.